# CHARACTER COMPASS

# CHARACTER COMPASS

*How Powerful School Culture Can
Point Students Toward Success*

Scott Seider

Harvard Education Press
Cambridge, Massachusetts

Library of Congress Control Number 2012937964

Paperback ISBN: 978-1-61250-486-5
Library Edition ISBN: 978-1-61250-487-2

Published by Harvard Education Press,
an imprint of the Harvard Education Publishing Group

Harvard Education Press
8 Story Street
Cambridge, MA 02138

Cover Design: Ciano Design
Cover Photo: Image Source/Getty Images

The typefaces used in this book are Adobe Garamond Pro and Futura.

# Contents

# Foreword

In today's media, it is hard to escape the impression that many of America's problems are due to our schools, and particularly to the schools that deal with our least advantaged children. Some pundits criticize the teachers, arguing that they are not securing adequate performance on standardized testing instruments; other pundits criticize students and families, suggesting that they are not prepared to benefit from public education. And, of course, some pundits direct equal fire at both camps. But just think for a moment about the major crises that the United States has faced over recent decades, ranging from financial meltdowns prompted by greed and dishonesty on the part of the already wealthy to wars waged without adequate preparation or a realistic assessment of what could and could not be achieved. In these and many other cases, the finger of responsibility does not point to those with few resources. Rather, responsibility rests primarily with, as author David Halberstam labeled them, "the best and the brightest," the very individuals who received the highest grades, attended the most elite schools, garnered prestigious academic and professional honors, and then descended upon the centers of power in the Capitol and on Wall Street.[1] How ironic, then, that policy makers in the United States insist today on an educational focus that has led repeatedly to disasters, rather than rethinking our educational priorities.

As we reflect on these events and consequences, one fact stands out. Except for mission statements, the character of young people—their behavioral, ethical, and moral facets—is not, and has not been, on the national educational radar screen. The *formation of good character* receives little more than lip service in the educational institutions our youth attend, the admissions tests and folders they present, the grades they receive in university or graduate school, and the hurdles they face as they ascend the institutional or corporate ladder. Indeed, if anything, it is often the young individuals who exaggerate their accomplishments, know how to "end run" their peers, and receive (and often pay for) special help in preparing for tests and admissions interviews who land in positions of power.

It is high time to direct our focus elsewhere—to an educational system that places at its center the development of good character. Such a focus is precisely the goal of Scott Seider's important and compelling book. Although the three schools portrayed in *Character Compass* serve students from low-income urban communities, the commitment to character development at all three schools has important ramifications for students and schools in a diverse range of settings. Indeed, all three schools explicitly seek to teach human virtue, to inspire young people to lead lives dedicated to serving others. It is crucial to illuminate these institutions—to discern what they are trying to achieve, and to ascertain where they succeed and where they could improve.

Understanding contemporary efforts in the United States to inculcate positive character traits is an overarching goal of Scott Seider's work. In his already notable career, this psychologist-educator has directed his scholarly attention to those individuals who are *not* interested chiefly in career advancement—such as students who work long hours in shelters for the homeless—and to those personal traits that lead to lives of service. No starry-eyed optimist, Seider recognizes the challenges that confront idealistic youth as well as the obstacles faced by educators who hope to inspire and nurture the better angels of our young populations. At the same time, Seider exhibits a quiet confidence that dedication and courage can be fostered under favorable circumstances.

In the present study, Seider describes three distinct efforts in the Boston area to help young people lead virtuous lives. He looks at Boston Preparatory Charter Public School, an institution that teaches ethical philosophy as a means of inculcating a moral sense; Roxbury Preparatory Charter School, which seeks to develop the personal traits that lead to work of excellent quality and a sense of personal responsibility; and the Academy of the Pacific Rim Charter Public School, which focuses on the development of civic character as a means of serving one's community. In carrying out his study, Seider employs an impressive blend of quantitative and qualitative measures. He examines improvements during the academic year on instruments that measure specific character traits, strengths, and values. At the same time, he conducts in-depth interviews of select students to convey the deep as well as the holistic facets that test scores alone cannot convey.

This book will not give comfort to those in search of the "silver bullet" of character education. If we do not take the analogy too far, we can compare this study to one that would seek to improve the health of elderly people. No single pill or exercise regimen will improve all indices of health; each has its privileged area of application. By the same token, each approach portrayed here self-consciously emphasizes one aspect of character, and that, indeed, is where its successes chiefly lie. At the same time, it is not essential to follow only one of the regimens. Just as an elderly person can benefit from a judicious combination of pills, physical exercise, and brain gymnastics, so, too, can the young person benefit from an educational regimen that includes formal philosophical study, activities in the community, and the inculcation of character traits of persistence and self-regulation. Still, one should not attempt to do too much; a key takeaway from *Character Compass* is that an identification and focus on a specific set of outcomes is preferable to a scattershot approach, which may lead to confusion rather than to success.

Looking at artistic representations, psychologists distinguish between the *central figure*, to which the eyes are powerfully drawn, and the *background*, which is designed to provide support for the dominant colors and shapes. In the educational domain in this country, and perhaps around the globe, we desperately require a shift of figure and ground. Recently, the academic performances of the best and the brightest have loomed so large that all other features are relegated to the background, if they are attended to at all. In the dispensation that I favor, we should place the character of our young people at the center of the educational firmament. Tests, grades, and extracurricular activities are very important, and it is notable that the schools portrayed here do well on such measures. But academic performance should be incorporated and nurtured in ways that support the central goal: the fashioning of individuals with strong and positive character traits. Recalling the lessons of Halberstam's landmark volume, we should acknowledge that the political and financial problems of the last decades were not caused by students who had learning problems or by teachers who did not exhibit "annual yearly progress." On the contrary, many of the debacles of recent times can be laid quite squarely at the feet of those who rose to the top of these systems and then proceeded to aggrandize themselves. A renewed focus on character would constitute a positive development throughout the world. In navigating such a powerful reversal of frames—character development as *the* central figure in our educational system—Scott Seider is an indispensable guide.

*Howard Gardner*
*John H. and Elisabeth A. Hobbs Professor of Cognition*
*and Education, Harvard Graduate School of Education*

# Introduction

Character development has been a goal of the American education system since its inception.[1] Thomas Jefferson cited the development of children's civic character as a key motivation for the establishment of public schools in the United States. John and Elizabeth Phillips founded New Hampshire's Phillips Exeter Academy in 1781 to promote both the "minds and morals of the youth under their charge." Horace Mann, one of the founding fathers of universal public education, argued that public schools could instill in unruly children the values, such as respect and self-discipline, necessary for a productive adulthood. More recent incarnations of character education have included Lawrence Kohlberg's just community schools and William Bennett's *Book of Virtues*.[2]

Over the past decade, however, the intensive focus upon high-stakes testing ushered in by the No Child Left Behind Act in 2001 has pushed character education to the back burner of many American schools.[3] With both students and educators facing significant pressure to demonstrate that students are achieving "adequate yearly progress" in core subject areas such as reading and mathematics, many school leaders have reluctantly given short shrift to character education as well as art, music, health education, and even history and science.

While the pressure from high-stakes testing has not abated, several key players in the education reform movement have begun to put their own mark on character education. Rather than viewing character development as a goal distinct from student achievement, these educators have come to see character education as a tool for facilitating students' pathways to and through college. Journalist Paul Tough's recent cover story in the *New York Times Magazine*—entitled "What if the Secret to Success Is Failure?"—

1

profiled two New York City schools on opposite ends of the socioeconomic spectrum that are both utilizing character education to promote student achievement.[4]

The century-old Riverdale Country Day School serves elite New York families who can afford the school's annual $38,000 tuition. Just a few miles away, 92 percent of the children attending the KIPP Infinity Middle School in Harlem qualify for free or reduced-price lunch. Yet both schools have come to believe that supporting their students' success in college and beyond entails bolstering students' self-discipline, optimism, curiosity, and a number of other character strengths. KIPP Infinity—one of 109 charter schools operated across the United States by the Knowledge Is Power Program—even issues to students a character report card designed to provide feedback to students and their families on eight different dimensions of students' character development that range from gratitude to grit to self-control.

Riverdale Country Day and KIPP Infinity are by no means the only stakeholders in the education reform movement utilizing character education to support student success.[5] Younger charter school networks such as Uncommon Schools and Achievement First have incorporated character development goals into their mission statements, mottoes, and teacher evaluation systems. Teacher training organizations such as the New Teacher Project are adding character education workshops to their professional development offerings. The Relay Graduate School of Education— the newest school of education in the United States—cites a mission of training teachers who can develop in students the academic skills and character strengths necessary to be successful in school and life. Teach For America explicitly seeks out corps members who demonstrate high levels of "grit."

This resurgence of interest in character education has focused primarily upon what is referred to as *performance character*. Performance character can be defined as the qualities necessary to achieve one's potential in endeavors ranging from art to academics to athletics.[6] Examples of performance character strengths include perseverance, ingenuity, and optimism. In his *New York Times Magazine* profile of Riverdale Country Day and

KIPP Infinity, Tough observed that the character strengths emphasized at both schools lean "heavily toward performance character: while they do have a moral component, strengths like zest, optimism, social intelligence, and curiosity aren't particularly heroic; they make you think of Steve Jobs or Bill Clinton more than the Rev. Martin Luther King Jr. or Gandhi."[7] In other words, the latest iteration of character education seeks to foster in students the qualities possessed by entrepreneurs and politicians rather than activists or moral exemplars.

There are several reasons for this focus on performance character development. First, an important series of research studies by University of Pennsylvania psychologists Angela Duckworth and Martin Seligman have found performance character strengths such as self-discipline to be stronger predictors than IQ of middle school students' academic grades, school attendance, hours spent doing homework, and acceptance into highly competitive high schools.[8] Self-discipline refers to a student's ability to persevere in the attainment of a higher goal rather than being distracted by opportunities for immediate gratification. For example, it requires self-discipline to prioritize doing one's homework over watching television or to persevere on a challenging long-term assignment despite boredom and frustration.

A related line of research by Duckworth and University of Michigan psychologist Christopher Peterson has focused on a character strength they refer to as "grit" and define as one's "perseverance and passion for long-term goals."[9] These scholars found that undergraduates at an elite university with high levels of grit earned better grade point averages than their peers, even when controlling for IQ scores. They also found that grit was the strongest predictor of West Point students' ability to persevere through Cadet Basic Training as well as the likelihood of adolescent participants in the Scripps National Spelling Bee advancing to the final rounds of the competition.

These findings by Duckworth, Seligman, and Peterson are only the latest in a long line of research that has found an individual's ability to engage in deliberate and sustained practice to be highly predictive of his or her success in a particular endeavor.[10] The current emphasis, then, within the education reform movement upon students' performance character development is supported by a robust body of scholarship demonstrating a strong relationship between student achievement and performance character strengths such as perseverance, self-discipline, and grit.

Of course, the current emphasis upon performance character development at schools such as Riverdale Country Day and KIPP Infinity is also reinforced by an American educational system that places a heavy emphasis upon students' test scores. For elite private schools such as Riverdale Country Day, increasing students' SAT scores, Advanced Placement results, and acceptance rates into prestigious universities raises the school's ranking within the independent school world and in the eyes of prospective students and parents. Likewise, urban public schools such as KIPP Infinity must demonstrate students' continued improvement on state standardized tests in order for their charters to be renewed by the city or state departments of education. Over the past decade, more than one hundred public schools in New York City alone have been closed due to poor performance on state tests, and the current chancellor of the New York City schools has signaled a willingness to shutter schools achieving even mediocre results.[11] In short, school leaders and other stakeholders interested in character education have strong incentives to favor curriculum and practices designed to bolster students' performance character strengths—qualities that have been shown to have a direct effect upon student achievement as measured by standardized tests.

The character education practices currently being implemented at KIPP Infinity and Riverdale Country Day are worthy of all the attention they have received. However, it would be a mistake for educators, parents, or policy makers to perceive performance character development as the sole "character foundation" upon which students' success can be built. *Character Compass* seeks to broaden the current dialogue about character education through portraits of three high performing schools in Boston, Massachusetts. All three schools have made character education central to their mission of supporting student achievement, yet they have done so in three very different ways. Namely, Boston Prep has focused its character education efforts on *moral* character development; Roxbury Prep emphasizes *performance* character development; and Pacific Rim privileges *civic* character development.

The three schools portrayed in *Character Compass* are charter schools—publicly funded primary and secondary schools supervised by the state board of education—but they were not selected *because* they are charter schools.[12] The three schools are also urban schools serving primarily low-income youth of color, but neither were they selected for their location or student demographics. Rather, the three schools featured in *Character Compass* are schools that have built powerful and productive cultures atop three very different character foundations. All three schools cite success in college as a primary goal for students, but their distinctive approaches to character development equip their respective student bodies with different sets of tools for achieving this goal. In highlighting these distinctive approaches, as well as their differential effects, *Character Compass* seeks to offer useful insights to educators, parents, and policy makers across a wide range of schools and communities about the *different* ways in which character education can form the foundation of students' success.

Can an investigation of character education practices at three urban charter schools be relevant to the work of educators at traditional public schools, suburban public schools, or independent schools? We believe the short answer is "yes," and in fact, one of our research team's newest projects involves an elite independent school in California whose stakeholders found the character education efforts of these three East Coast charter schools to be highly instructive to their own goals for students' character development. Of course, that does not mean there are no differences between different types of schools.

Certainly there are descriptions and findings in *Character Compass* that will ring particularly true to stakeholders affiliated with charter schools similar to the three profiled here. Moreover, the relative autonomy enjoyed by charter schools may facilitate these stakeholders' efforts to implement or refine character education programming in their own school contexts. That said, *Character Compass* may be of greatest value to precisely those stakeholders who face more significant hurdles in "making the case" for character education to a district superintendent, school committee, or state department of education. Through quantitative survey data, qualitative interview data, and field notes from school observations, *Character Compass* demonstrates the role of character development in promoting student success and offers a conceptual framework for stakeholders committed to refining character education practices in their own school contexts. In so doing, *Character Compass* provides robust support to parents, educators, and policy makers committed to making the case that character development is a sturdy foundation upon which a student's success can be built.

## THE THREE SCHOOLS

Boston Preparatory Charter Public School (Boston Prep) and Academy of the Pacific Rim Charter Public School (Pacific Rim) are located around the corner from each other in Boston's Hyde Park neighborhood. Roxbury Preparatory Charter School (Roxbury Prep) sits just a few miles away in nearby Roxbury. All three began as middle schools, though Boston Prep and Pacific Rim quickly expanded to offer grades nine through twelve, and Roxbury Prep recently decided to expand to the high school grades as well. All three schools are open to youth from any neighborhood in Boston, and places are awarded to students through a public lottery. Nearly 90 percent of the students attending the three schools identify as black or Latino, and two-thirds qualify for free or reduced-price lunch. This means that two-thirds of the students come from households supporting the equivalent of a family of four on less than $40,000 a year.[13]

What draws scores of visitors each year to Boston Prep, Roxbury Prep, and Pacific Rim is that their students' test scores are competitive with those of youth from some of the wealthiest communities in the state. The Massachusetts Comprehensive Assessment System (MCAS) is considered one of the most rigorous high-stakes testing systems in the country.[14] On the 2011 MCAS, only 60 percent of eighth graders in the city of Boston scored advanced or proficient on the English assessment, and only 34 percent of eighth graders scored likewise on the mathematics assessment. In contrast, 93 percent of Roxbury Prep eighth graders scored advanced or proficient on the 2011 English assessment, and 84 percent scored likewise on the mathematics assessment.[15] These scores placed Roxbury Prep—a school at which three-fourths of the student body qualifies for free or reduced-price lunch—in the company of the Wellesley Public Schools and Newton Public Schools, two of the wealthiest communities in Massachusetts, with median family incomes approaching $140,000 per year.[16]

The results were similar at Boston Prep and Pacific Rim. One hundred percent of Boston Prep tenth graders scored advanced or proficient on the 2011 Math MCAS, and 98 percent scored likewise on the English assessment. These scores rank Boston Prep—a school at which 73 percent of the student body qualifies for free or reduced-price lunch—as one of the highest-achieving high schools in the state. Directly *behind* Boston Prep was Dover-Sherborn High School—the public high school serving two Boston suburbs with median family incomes of approximately $170,000 per year.[17]

Tenth graders at Pacific Rim scored right on the heels of their Boston Prep counterparts. Specifically, on the 2011 MCAS, 97 percent of Pacific Rim tenth graders scored advanced or proficient on the English assessment, and 91 percent scored likewise on the mathematics assessment. These scores, as well, placed Pacific Rim in the company of well-heeled Massachusetts school districts such as Wellesley, Newton, and Dover-Sherborn.

Of course, success on high-stakes tests is not the ultimate objective of Boston Prep, Roxbury Prep, or Pacific Rim. Rather, all three schools make clear their unequivocal goal of preparing students to enter, succeed in, and graduate from college. Leaders at all three schools say that this intensive focus on college readiness informs nearly every one of their decisions about curriculum, culture, and school practices. Even the classrooms at all three schools are named after universities and decorated with that university's pennants, posters, colors, and mascot.

Boston Prep—which was founded in 2004—graduated its first senior class in June 2011. One hundred percent of the senior class received college acceptance letters from four-year universities that included Emerson College, Howard University, Providence College, and St. John's University.

Additionally, Boston Prep seniors earned nearly three-quarters of a million dollars in scholarship funding to support their college aspirations.

Pacific Rim graduated its ninth cohort of seniors in 2011, and 95 percent of the students in these graduating classes have matriculated to four-year universities (with 85 percent persisting beyond the first year of college). Graduates from the class of 2011 are now attending schools such as Brown University, Bryn Mawr, College of the Holy Cross, Johns Hopkins, and Syracuse University. And while Roxbury Prep only began the process in 2011 of expanding into the high school grades, its alumni are currently attending universities such as Bowdoin, Howard, Tufts, and Vanderbilt.

As a result of the success of their students, Boston Prep, Roxbury Prep, and Pacific Rim have all been recognized and celebrated as among the highest performing urban public schools in the United States.[18] Faculty, students, and parents at all three schools cite character development as the foundation upon which their students' success is built. Yet, the types of character education occurring at the three schools are actually quite distinct from one another.

*Character Compass* reports on a year spent exploring the distinctive character education practices—and their effects—at Boston Prep, Roxbury Prep, and Pacific Rim. My research team and I began the 2010–2011 school year by surveying the nearly one thousand students in grades six through twelve across the three schools. Our surveys contained measures of the various character strengths that one or more of the schools cited as critical to fulfilling their college preparatory missions. These qualities included integrity, perseverance, courage, compassion, social responsibility, community connectedness, and respect. Students completed this confidential survey in September 2010 and then completed a similar survey again during the final weeks of the academic year. By pairing students' responses on these pre- and post-intervention surveys, we were able to compare students' changes on the various character measures over the course of the school year, and across the three schools. These comparisons allowed us to determine whether students at one of the schools were demonstrating significantly different shifts in integrity, perseverance, or one of the other character measures than their peers at the other two schools.[19]

Our survey data offered insight into the nature of students' character development at each of the three schools, but quantitative surveys provide little sense of *why* or *how* this character development took place. For this reason, we spent the months in between our initial and follow-up surveys conducting interviews with ninety-three students, teachers, administrators, and parents across the three schools. The purpose of carrying out these interviews was to learn more about how students described and understood the impact of their respective schools upon their own character development as well as to gain the perspective of parents and teachers. We also conducted more than one hundred observations of community meetings, ethics classes, character education classes, advisory lessons, and enrichment activities across the three schools. Our detailed field notes from these observations deepened our understanding as well of the distinctive character education practices taking place across the three schools.

In the chapters that follow, we draw on our survey data, interview data, and field notes to portray the character development occurring at Boston Prep, Roxbury Prep, and Pacific Rim as well as the curricular and pedagogical strategies contributing to this development. The portraits of the three schools are bookended by a brief review of the research literature on character development and character education in chapter 1, and a discussion of the implications for the education reform movement in chapter 8. The literature review in chapter 1 establishes a theoretical framework for interpreting the portraits that follow, and the concluding discussion in chapter 8 guides parents, educators, and policy makers in reflection upon the relevance of these different models of character development for their own work with students. In so doing, *Character Compass* seeks to contribute to the current wave of interest in character education by expanding the dialogue about the *different* ways in which character education can contribute to student success.

# DIMENSIONS OF CHARACTER

## CHAPTER ONE

# Character and Community Meeting

Visitors to Boston Prep, Roxbury Prep, and Pacific Rim might initially perceive the schools to be nearly identical. Students at all three schools wear uniforms. At Boston Prep, middle school students wear a maroon polo shirt with the Boston Prep logo, khaki-colored pants, a black or brown belt, and black or brown shoes. Boston Prep high school students replace the polo shirt with a yellow button-down dress shirt and (for boys) a crimson and gold necktie. All three schools feature an extended school day and year, with the bulk of that time dedicated to the core subject areas. At Pacific Rim, the school year is 190 days long, and each school day begins at 7:45 a.m. and concludes at 5:00 p.m. Middle school students take two hours of English language arts and two hours of mathematics each day.

All three schools utilize a disciplinary system based upon merits and demerits. A student at Roxbury Prep might receive a demerit for a uniform violation, gum chewing, disruptive behavior, or inappropriate language. Eight demerits earn Roxbury Prep sixth-grade students an afterschool detention, while eighth-grade students are given detention after only three demerits. On the other hand, the middle school students at all three schools can earn merits (or, at Roxbury Prep, "creed deeds") for actions that exemplify the school's values. For example, a sixth-grade Pacific Rim student might receive a merit for helping a classmate clean up a messy locker, while a Roxbury Prep eighth grader might earn a creed deed for tutoring a younger student struggling with her math homework. At all three schools, merits are treated as currency that can be exchanged for prizes such as school supplies, books, or movie tickets.

In short, then, a visitor to Boston Prep, Roxbury Prep, and Pacific Rim—taking in the school uniforms and extended school days, similar mission statements, and outstanding test scores—might be excused for assuming that the success of these three schools is built upon similar foundations. Such an assumption is correct in that all three schools perceive character development to be the soil in which their students' learning takes root. However, Boston Prep, Roxbury Prep, and Pacific Rim work to cultivate their students' character in very different ways.

The first sentence of Boston Prep's mission statement focuses on preparing students for college, but the second sentence presents the following recipe for this preparation: "An environment structured around scholarship and personal growth cultivates students' virtues of courage, compassion, integrity, perseverance and respect."[1] Almost every aspect of the Boston Prep school day is centered on those five virtues, including a weekly ethics class in which students in grades six through twelve learn about how philosophers such as Plato, Aristotle, and Rousseau understood these virtues. In both class discussions and written reflections, students then draw upon these perspectives to consider their own roles and responsibilities as students at Boston Prep and members of their respective families and communities.

Roxbury Prep's mission is, very simply, to prepare students to enter, succeed in, and graduate from college; however, one of the school's core values is that the groundwork for success in college entails mastering not only academic skills but life skills as well.[2] Toward this end, Roxbury Prep engages students in a weekly advisory class in which students learn "how to be positive players in their own education."[3] Lessons in advisory class include how to study and prepare for exams, engage in a successful interview, participate in an academic debate, and deliver a speech or presentation.

Finally, Pacific Rim—a school founded with the goal of merging Eastern and Western educational practices—characterizes *kaizen* and *gam-*

*batte* as "two Japanese words that describe the essence of our culture . . . and drive all that we do."[4] *Kaizen* is a Japanese principle that means working for the continuous improvement of the community, and *gambatte* is a Japanese word meaning to persist or never give up. Middle school students at Pacific Rim conclude every lesson by standing to receive their kaizen and gambatte class scores. This ritual entails the teacher awarding the entire class a grade that indicates the extent to which students effectively worked together during the lesson for the improvement of all (kaizen) and showed perseverance in learning that particular lesson's content (gambatte).

In even these short descriptions of character development at Boston Prep, Roxbury Prep, and Pacific Rim, one can begin to see ways in which both *character* and *character education* mean something different at each school. Developmental psychologist Marvin Berkowitz defines character as a "set of psychological characteristics that motivate and enable individuals to function as competent moral agents" and character education as "intentional strategies within schools to foster children's capacities and motivations to act as moral agents."[5] As is evident in the preceding paragraphs, there are a number of similarities, but an equal number of distinctions, in the particular characteristics upon which each school has chosen to focus its curriculum, culture, and practices. And, as my research team and I learned over the course of a year studying character education at these three schools, the choices made by school leaders and faculty about which character strengths to emphasize have profound effects upon their students' beliefs, values, and actions.

To begin to paint a picture of the *differences* in character education across the three schools, we turn now to another of their common practices: the weekly community meeting. By drawing on our field notes from a single community meeting at each of the three schools, we start to illustrate the different conceptions of character upon which Boston Prep, Roxbury Prep, and Pacific Rim have grounded their efforts to support student success. In the chapters that follow, we then expand upon these illustrations through data drawn from surveys, interviews, field notes, and student achievement data.

Interspersed within these community meeting narratives is an overview of the existing scholarship on character development that draws primarily from research in education and psychology, but also from ethics, sociology, and neuroscience. This overview is intended both to illuminate the narratives within the chapter as well as to establish a theoretical framework upon which ensuing chapters draw. Our goal is to offer educators, parents, and policy makers a lens into the *different* ways in which character development contributes to the success of three high performing schools. Although there are significant differences in the focus and results of character education at each of the three schools, they are united in treating character development *not* as another item on the overflowing plate of learning goals for their students, but rather as the plate itself.[6]

## BOSTON PREP COMMUNITY MEETING

Community meetings at Boston Prep are held on Tuesday mornings at 9:30 a.m. in the large open space in the center of the school that doubles as the cafeteria and auditorium. Located on a busy street in Boston's Hyde Park neighborhood, Boston Prep occupies the two-story brick building of a now-defunct parochial school. However, the former school's name—Most Precious Blood School—remains a fixture in white capital letters across the second floor facing the street, and a large crucifix is still affixed to the front of the flat roof. Passersby on Hyde Park Avenue might easily miss the four-by-three-foot sign on the school's front lawn announcing the building's current occupant along with the Boston Prep logo—five classic Greek columns supporting a roof emblazoned with a rising sun. The columns are intended to represent Boston Prep's five virtues—courage, compassion, integrity, perseverance, and respect—as well as to signal the classical elements of a Boston Prep education.

Beginning in the ninth grade, all Boston Prep students take four years of Latin. Moreover, Boston Prep students in both the middle school and high school engage each year in an ethical philosophy course through which they gain exposure to ancient philosophers such as Plato and Aristotle. At the middle school level, ethics class is taught by the students' homeroom teacher, while the high school ethics classes are taught by the head of school and a founding faculty member responsible for the entire philosophy curriculum. In this way, Boston Prep follows in the tradition of America's earliest universities, at which the final requirement for graduating students was a capstone course in ethical philosophy taught by the university's president.[7]

The Boston Prep school building has a classical feel as well. The first floor is designed with an atrium, a large open space in the center of the school that extends all the way up to the roof. Doors leading into the sixth-grade classrooms are symmetrically spaced along the sidewalls of this center space, and the folding cafeteria tables that are brought out each day for breakfast and lunch are coiled in between them. At the far end of the atrium is a raised stage that hosts Boston Prep's annual talent show and other performances. A majestic grand piano sits to one side.

The second floor of Boston Prep is little more than a rectangular catwalk with a chest-high railing and the seventh- and eighth-grade classrooms spaced symmetrically along the longer sides of the rectangle. Draping down from the catwalk so as to be visible from the atrium are brightly colored banners proclaiming the names of universities attended by Boston Prep faculty. With Boston Prep's first senior class having graduated in June, those banners will no doubt be supplanted shortly with the names of universities attended by Boston Prep alumni.

A number of bulletin boards line both the first- and second-floor walls of Boston Prep. Particularly notable are the "Ethics in Action" bulletin boards that offer concrete examples of Boston Prep's five virtues. The Courage bulletin board features photographs, quotations, and narratives about the Little Rock Nine—the nine African American teenagers responsible for integrating Arkansas's Central High School in 1957. A quotation in the center reads, "Without courage, wisdom bears no fruit."

As 9:30 a.m. draws near, Boston Prep students begin to fill up the auditorium, entering from what appears to be all directions. Sixth-grade students simply emerge from their classrooms that open out into the auditorium and are guided by their teachers to the front of the room. The youngest students get the front-row seats. Seventh- and eighth-grade students are led in single-file lines down the stairs from the second-floor classrooms, and high school students—distinctive in their yellow dress shirts and ties—emerge in more amorphous bunches from the basement level of Boston Prep, where the high school students and faculty are currently relegated. Each middle school and high school homeroom has assigned spaces on the floor of the Boston Prep auditorium, and many teachers join their homerooms on the floor as well. Other faculty members choose to stand beside their students along the perimeter of the room with arms folded or clipboards clutched in their hands. When everyone is seated and silent, Head of School Scott McCue steps to the center of the room to begin.[8]

McCue is a tall, thin man in his late thirties clad each day in a suit and tie. He is not only Boston Prep's head of school but also its founder, having successfully written the charter application that allowed Boston Prep to open its doors in the fall of 2004. One of the key components of that application was a new approach to character education. According to McCue, "We felt like a lot of schools had done a good job teaching conduct to kids. To sit up straight and make good eye contact and be polite and say please and thank you. And there were also some examples of schools where there were some deliberate conversations about the most ethical ways to act, about what students' moral values were. But we felt that there was a real niche to do it sequentially, to promote a certain degree of rigor and authentic inquiry . . . just like we do in math instruction or history instruction or any other academic sequence."

"Good morning," Mr. McCue greets the Boston Prep community in a calm, even tone. The entire community responds in kind. "Today, members of our sophomore class will be building on our tradition of excellence with the MCAS. We have a lot to do today, so let's go to it!"

Mr. Johnson, a tall man in his late twenties with a short haircut and eyeglasses, steps forward. Music from the game show *Jeopardy!* blares from the auditorium's speakers. "Welcome to MCAS Legacy!" Mr. Johnson announces in an avuncular tone. "Last week, we saw Jesse and Tasha battle it out for the mantle of the MCAS Legacy. This week, we will see who is battling it out for the title of Most Improved. Remember, you can win free tuition to any public university in Massachusetts!" At this last line, a large number of students snap enthusiastically.

In Massachusetts, any high school students who score advanced on either the English or math MCAS (and proficient or higher on the other) are eligible for the Adams Scholarship, which provides free tuition to any state college or university in Massachusetts. More than 90 percent of Boston Prep's class of 2011 were Adams Scholarship recipients.

"Today's legacy," Mr. Johnson continues, "is Boston Prep senior Adam Taylor. Adam loves basketball, bad haircuts, walks on the beach, and Boston Prep! Most importantly, Adam scored proficient on his tenth-grade MCAS after years of 'needs improvement.'"

The student body snaps encouragingly as a lean young man comes forward to take his place beside Mr. Johnson. Simultaneously, two Boston Prep teachers bring forward a large, four- by-four-foot piece of cardboard painted silver and hold it up to create a barrier between Adam and two empty stools that have been positioned in the front of the auditorium as well. Boston Prep students may be too young to realize it, but MCAS Legacy has stolen its format from an old network television show called *The Dating Game*, in which a male or female contestant was physically separated from several potential suitors. The contestant was then given an opportunity to ask the suitors a series of questions before deciding whom to take out on a date.

Mr. Johnson thrusts a microphone under Adam's chin as if he is conducting an interview. "So, Adam, what do you expect of someone interested in taking over your legacy?"

Adam pauses. "I'm looking for someone who works hard, strives to be the best, and backs it up."

"Let's bring up our contestants!" Mr. Johnson gushes. "Our first contestant is Coco Crispy. She thinks improvement and success is something that will just happen. And she doesn't like walks on the beach." Out from a sixth-grade classroom comes a male teacher dressed in a frumpy blue dress. Giggles ripple through the audience as the teacher takes his place on one of the stools. "Our second contestant," Mr. Johnson continues, "loves talking to her friends, getting good grades, emulating her big sister, and being an eighth grader. Give it up for Tatyana!" The students, particularly her eighth-grade classmates, snap enthusiastically as Tatyana takes her place on the stool beside "Coco Crispy."

"I have a question for Tatyana," Mr. Johnson begins. "Why do you deserve the MCAS Legacy for most improved?"

"Because every year I have raised my scores," Tatyana explains confidently, "and this year I am on my way to 'proficient.' I represent my school, my family, and I'm on my way to mad money!"

"I have a question for the contestants," Adam interjects. "I want to know what you do when you get your scores back and you're not happy with how you did."

"I'm happy with any score, really," answers the cross-dressing teacher playing Coco Crispy. "Last year I got a 3 percent, and that was way better than the year before."

"Well, I go through the work I showed and look for mistakes," answers Tatyana. "Then I look for resources to help me learn from my mistakes."

"One last question," says contestant Adam. "What are the top five ways to improve your score?"

"Oh, I know this!" calls out Coco Crispy. "Phone a friend!" The audience laughs at this reference to another television game show.

"Use reference sheets," Tatyana answers seriously. "Show all your work. Never give up on any question."

"I think it's no contest," announces Adam. "The person who shows the most perseverance and courage on the test is on pace to inherit my score. It's Tatyana!"

"Tatyana," exclaims Mr. Johnson in a deep baritone, "You are the winner of a lot of money! Free money!" Two teachers appear beside Mr. Johnson holding one of the super-sized cardboard checks awarded to game show winners. The line indicating the amount of the check reads "FULL TUITION," and the check is signed by John and Abigail Adams. "Remember," Mr. Johnson concludes, "that we've been brought to you by the John and Abigail Adams Scholarship Fund of Free Money! Thank you for playing MCAS Legacy!"

As Adam, Tatyana, Coco Crispy, and Mr. Johnson exit, Mr. McCue steps forward again. "Announcements?" he asks.

One teacher waves her hand. "Over the break we reorganized the library, and I'd like to recognize the students who came in to school to help me out with virtue commendations for their compassion." She reads off the names of five students, as the student body snaps its approval.

"And now," Mr. McCue says, "This week's DuBois Award will be presented by Mrs. Hieser."

## A CONCEPTUAL MODEL OF CHARACTER

What precisely is *character*? One challenge the field of character education faces is that "character" is conceptualized in a variety of ways. Some conceive of character as the possession or refinement of particular qualities such as patience, humility, or respectfulness. Others conceive of character as situated in particular types of prosocial behaviors such as sharing or helping. Still others conceive of character as one's belief in and adherence to particular principles such as the golden rule or equality for all.

Each of these conceptions of character has merit. As noted earlier, we rely on a definition of character from leading character education scholar and developmental psychologist Marvin Berkowitz. In the 2011 *APA Educational Psychology Handbook*, Berkowitz defines character as "a set of psychological characteristics that motivate and enable individuals to function as competent moral agents."[9] Two aspects of this definition are particularly appealing. First, Berkowitz's use of the phrase "motivate and enable" suggests that character is not simply possessing the motivation to do the right thing, but also developing the requisite skills and competencies. Second, the phrase "a set of psychological characteristics" emphasizes that there are a variety of character strengths upon which an educator or school committed to character development might choose to focus.

Berkowitz further conceptualizes character as consisting of three distinct components: the cognitive, affective, and behavioral. In other words, an individual's character can be described as the sum of that individual's thoughts, feelings, and actions. Or, as some character educators like to say, effective character education needs to influence not only students' heads (the cognitive), but also their hearts (affective) and hands (behavioral).[10] This trichotomous conception of character is represented in figure 1.1 and pulls together several disparate strands of research on moral and character development.

## Character and Cognition

The cognitive component of character in Berkowitz's model incorporates decades of research on moral reasoning, knowledge of moral facts, interpersonal intelligence, and social perspective taking.[11] For example, Harvard psychologist Lawrence Kohlberg—often considered the father of moral psychology—asserted that the key lever for deepening an individual's moral identity was to strengthen his or her capacity for moral reasoning. Toward this end, Kohlberg founded several "just community" high

**FIGURE 1.1**    Trichotomous conception of character

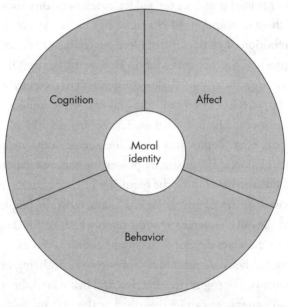

*Source:* Berkowitz (2011).

schools that sought to strengthen adolescents' capacity for moral reasoning by involving them in important decisions about school policy and practices. A number of Kohlberg's students have continued to focus on the role of moral reasoning in the production of moral action.[12]

Other character development scholars such as William Bennett, Kevin Ryan, and Karen Bohlin have proposed that the most effective character development entails introducing youth to time-honored virtues such as respect, patriotism, courage, honesty, and kindness.[13] According to Ryan and Bohlin, "It is necessary to help students wrestle with and understand the good—that is, what is true and worthwhile in life as well as what is right. To do this, we need to help them develop knowledge of the good . . . so that they learn to choose well among competing and attractive options in life."[14] Advocates of this approach to character development emphasize the development of "moral literacy" by introducing students to historical and contemporary figures who exemplify moral ideals as well as by offering students numerous opportunities to practice the habits of virtuous behavior.

Research by Howard Gardner on the personal intelligences and Robert Selman on perspective taking fall within the cognitive realm of character as well.[15] Psychology has traditionally defined intelligence as a general ability that can be measured by a single IQ score; however, Gardner's theory of multiple intelligences characterizes intelligence as composed of eight subintelligences that people use to solve problems and create products relevant to the societies in which they live. Within Gardner's taxonomy are *interpersonal intelligence*, an individual's ability to recognize and understand other people's moods, desires, motivations, and intentions, and *intrapersonal intelligence*, an individual's ability to recognize and assess these characteristics within him- or herself. The ability to reflect upon one's own moods and motivations and to consider these characteristics in others would seem to be critical to making ethical decisions and to treating others with respect. Because Gardner characterizes these abilities as intelligences with specifiable mental processes in the brain, they are best characterized as part of the cognitive component of character as well.

Finally, clinical psychologist Robert Selman has asserted that an individual's ability to navigate the social world and to resolve conflicts with others is highly dependent upon that individual's ability to engage in perspective taking—that is, walking around in another person's shoes.[16] Selman regards the conflicts and interactions embedded within literature as a valuable tool for helping school-age youth to strengthen their ability to consider the motivations, ambitions, and challenges of others. In this way, Selman's work combines Ryan, Bohlin, and Bennett's emphasis on moral literature with Gardner's focus upon interpersonal intelligence. Perspective taking, too, then, can be regarded as a cognitive strength critical to the development of one's character.

## Character and Emotion

The affective component of Berkowitz's model includes research on the development of emotions prioritizing the needs of others, such as empathy and altruism, as well as the ability to care for others.[17] Empathy can be defined as an emotional response to another person's situation or condition, and a robust body of research has demonstrated that feelings of empathy are a strong predictor of an individual's prosocial, cooperative, and altruistic interactions with others.[18]

Some of the most important work on the emotional roots of character can be found in sociologists Samuel and Pearl Oliner's studies of German citizens who served as rescuers of Jews during the Holocaust. The Oliners undertook this study with the goal of exploring the existence of what they termed the *altruistic personality*—"a predisposition to act selflessly on behalf of others which develops early in life."[19] The Oliners discovered that Germans who had served as rescuers or protectors during the Holocaust were less likely than their fellow German citizens to have heard their parents make racist comments about Jews when they were children, less likely to have been raised by parents who emphasized obedience, and more likely to describe their childhood families as supportive and loving. Perhaps as a result, these individuals scored higher than their fellow German citizens on psychological tests of emotional empathy for another's pain. Moreover, the Oliners reported that in rescuers' explanations of why they had risked their own lives on behalf of others, "the language of care dominated. Pity, compassion, concern [and] affection made up the vocabulary of 76% of rescuers."[20] All of these qualities can be characterized as pertaining to the affective component of character.

Perhaps the scholar most associated with the affective components of character education is Stanford philosopher Nel Noddings, who developed an approach to character education she labeled "care ethics." According to Noddings, teaching students about moral principles or moral facts does not provide sufficient motivation to act in moral ways. She asserts, instead, that "the educational task is to educate the passions, especially the moral sentiments. Faced with evil, we must feel revulsion. Faced with another's pain, we must feel the desire to remove or alleviate it. Faced with our own inclinations to cause harm, we must be both shocked and willing to face reality."[21] With the goal of instilling such passions in youth, Noddings advocates not for a particular curriculum focused on care, but rather on schools establishing a culture and ethos that offer students opportunities to engage in caring behavior. Community service learning represents one powerful venue for students to enact caring behavior; however, Noddings notes that opportunities for students to practice caring are also present in the classroom, lunchroom, and athletic fields. Cooperative learning, peer tutoring, and mentoring younger children are all mechanisms by which schools can work to instill in their students the ethic of care that Noddings perceives to be at the heart of one's character.

## Character and Behavior

Finally, scholarship on the behavioral components of character includes research into actions that range from engaging in community service to standing up to bullies to demonstrating perseverance or self-discipline. For example, in a national study of caring behavior, researcher Virginia Hodgkinson found that three out of four individuals whose parents engaged in community service when they were children now engage in community service themselves.[22] On the other hand, only one out of four individuals whose parents did not engage in community service during their childhoods engages in volunteerism as an adult. Other researchers have found that one of the strongest predictors of a commitment to volunteerism is a strong sense of personal efficacy.[23]

As noted in the introduction, a very different line of research into the behavioral components of character has focused on the relationship between perseverance and achievement across a wide range of endeavors. In addition to the recent work by Angela Duckworth and Martin Seligman with middle school students, a number of scholars have found that a key commonality among world-class artists, athletes, chess players, mathematicians, and neurologists is a willingness to engage in sustained and deliberate practice.[24] At the university level, Raymond Wolfe and Scott Johnson reported that self-discipline was the only one of thirty-two character traits that predicted college students' grade point averages more accurately than did their SAT scores, and Warren Willingham found that "follow-through" was a better predictor of college students' success in extracurricular activities than their IQ, SAT score, or high school rank.[25]

Certainly, the boundaries between the cognitive, affective, and behavioral components of character are not airtight. Nonetheless, Berkowitz's trichotomous character model provides a useful framework for integrating the scholarship on character development from a number of different strands of research that include moral development, character education, prosocial development, ethics, moral psychology, community service learning, and others.[26] At the same time, one might also reasonably argue that a conceptual model that combines volunteerism and perseverance under a single category is too broad to be of practical use to character educators. For this reason, we present later in this chapter an updated version of Berkowitz's conceptual model that maintains the cognitive-affective-behavior trichotomy but also subdivides the model into three concentric circles representing moral character, civic character, and performance character. This additional parsing provides a valuable theoretical framework through which to consider differences in character development of students attending Boston Prep, Roxbury Prep, and Pacific Rim.

## ROXBURY PREP COMMUNITY MEETING

Community meetings at Roxbury Prep are scheduled for Friday afternoons just prior to dismissal, which school director Will Austin describes as intentional: "It's the best way to ensure that our week ends well . . . for kids and staff to end their academic week and leave on a positive note."

Though Roxbury Prep enjoys an outsized reputation as one of the most effective schools in Massachusetts, the entire school fits onto the third floor of the Edgar P. Benjamin Healthcare Center in the Roxbury neighborhood of Boston. Students, faculty, and visitors climb up three flights of stairs to get to the school, and, as they climb, they can read the Roxbury Prep timeline painted along the walls of the stairwell. Roxbury Prep was founded in 1999 by two educators, Evan Rudall and John King. Rudall is now the chief executive officer of Uncommon Schools, an organization that manages more than twenty charter schools in New York, New Jersey, and Massachusetts. King currently serves as the education commissioner for the state of New York. He is the youngest commissioner in the state's history as well as New York's first African American and Puerto Rican commissioner.

Roxbury Prep's long single corridor is decorated with inspirational sayings from artists, academics, athletes, and statesmen. "Strength does not come from physical capacity," reads a quote from Mahatma Gandhi, "it comes from an indomitable will." A nearby quotation from basketball star Michael Jordan reads: "I've missed more than 9,000 shots in my career. I've lost almost 300 games. Twenty-six times, I've been trusted to take the game-winning shot, and missed. I've failed over and over and over again in my life. And that is why I succeed." Affixed to the classroom doors running up and down the corridor are posters announcing the name of each classroom: Suffolk, Regis, Georgetown, Howard. Each is named after the alma mater of a Roxbury Prep alumnus or faculty member.

At precisely 12:30 p.m., students proceed to Roxbury Prep's auditorium—where the community meeting is held—in silent, single-file lines. Student wear khaki pants and light blue dress shirts, and the boys wear neckties. No one speaks; few even whisper, not wanting to earn a demerit. This silence in the hallways is not simply the custom preceding Roxbury Prep's community meeting. Visitors to the school are often surprised to learn that students are expected to pass silently in the hallways en route to *all* of their classes. Teachers step into the hallway in between classes to enforce this silence.

Sixth-grade teacher Marleny Abrams explains, "We talk [to our students] about the fact that they're coming in a couple grade levels behind. It's not their fault, but we need to run faster so we can catch up and get to college. So how do we run faster? We don't waste time in the hall. And we don't waste time in class. And so we're in a hurry. We have a lot to do so we have to run faster."

Recognizing that some educators bristle at this level of comportment, school director Will Austin notes, "I think that the people who don't like it feel very uncomfortable with it for visceral reasons . . . I think that folks say, well, this largely white staff are making children of color walk silently between classes, and I always retort I think that all middle school hallways should be silent. I don't think it's specific to us. I'd love for Wellesley [Public Schools] to have silent hallways."

As the Roxbury Prep students move single-file toward the auditorium, a few stand out because of the bright T-shirts they are wearing over their uniforms or the stuffed animals tucked under their arms. The T-shirts are college T-shirts—Georgetown, Suffolk, Howard—representing the various colleges after which Roxbury Prep homerooms are named, and the stuffed animals represent those schools' mascots. A Suffolk ram, a Georgetown hoya, a Northeastern husky. Prior to the community meeting, the students in each homeroom had nominated the classmates whose actions over the past week merited one of the homeroom T-shirts or mascots. Visitors who think they understand early adolescents might be surprised to witness the exuberance with which Roxbury Prep students don the college T-shirts awarded to them or tuck the homeroom mascots under their arms.

Students stream into Roxbury Prep's brightly lit auditorium and take their places on the folding chairs assembled in neat rows. A lectern and microphone stand waiting at the front of the room, and a young faculty member wearing a dress shirt and tie stands behind the lectern waiting to begin the community meeting. "Good afternoon, Roxbury Prep," he begins when everyone is seated. "Please take a couple seconds to think about something positive that happened to you this week." After a pause, he continues, "Now I'll turn things over to last week's Spirit Stick winner,

Amina Eustace!" Students applaud enthusiastically as Amina, a tall eighth grader, comes to take her place at the lectern.

It is now Amina's job to serve as the master of ceremonies for the community meeting. She leans into the microphone, reading from a prepared script. "As you know, March 14th was Pi Day, a day to celebrate one of the most important mathematical numbers in the world. Today the math department would like to continue our tradition with a new set of competitors in our pi competition." She calls to the lectern a mathematics teacher, Mr. Lester—a tall, gangly man in his mid-twenties—who is wearing a T-shirt that reads "Pi Day 3/14" across the chest. The other members of the math department, scattered around the room with their respective advisories, have donned Pi Day T-shirts as well.

Mr. Lester calls up to the front of the auditorium the sixth-, seventh-, and eighth-grade students who won their respective grade-level contests earlier in the week. All three are girls. The other students, still seated, cheer wildly for their representative as each girl takes her place at the front of the auditorium. All three look nervous. Mr. Lester presents each student with a Pi Day T-shirt and then addresses the entire community. "Good afternoon, Roxbury Prep," he starts. "This is one of my favorite things we do, our pi recitation contest. Anybody who has tried to memorize anything knows it takes a lot of work. That becomes even harder in front of two hundred people, so I think everyone up here will appreciate your support through silent applause. They are going to recite as many digits as they can, and it will be amazing!"

At the previous week's community meeting, Mr. Lester had dramatically increased the excitement around this competition by announcing that the winner of the pi recitation contest would get to "pie" Mr. Austin. This announcement had caused the entire auditorium to devolve momentarily into a series of excited *oooooohhhs*. "Right now I believe the record is eighty digits," Mr. Lester had continued. "You can pick up a sheet with pi on it at the conclusion of today's meeting if you'd like to start studying this weekend."

The competition begins with the sixth-grade student. Mr. Lester projects several hundred digits of pi onto a screen set up in the front of the room, and directs the three contestants to face the audience. This way, the students in the audience can see the digits of pi projected onto the screen, but the three contestants cannot.

The sixth-grade contestant begins reciting digits of pi into the microphone in a quiet voice and gets to approximately fifty digits before running out of steam. The entire audience—but especially her sixth-grade classmates—applauds enthusiastically. The seventh-grade student goes next and recites nearly one hundred digits of pi. Finally, the eighth-grade contestant steps forward to take her turn. As she accepts the microphone, the entire student body calls out in unison, "positive leaders!" and then follows this chant with a rhythmic clap. Clap . . . clap . . . clap, clap, clap.

Roxbury Prep teacher Stephanie Davis explains the "positive leaders" chant this way: "Roxbury Prep is so difficult that once you are in the eighth grade, just making it to eighth grade is an accomplishment, and because of that, you are a leader and a positive influence on the kids that are struggling to get there in the sixth and seventh grades. And so whenever the positive leaders shine, they do the 'positive leader' cheer, and they're recognized because it's like, you have already fought this long battle to be here, and now you are just being a rock star!" Another Roxbury Prep teacher, Ana Briggs, adds: "I think the idea of stepping into this positive leadership role has just made being an eighth grader very, very special. All of a sudden, now they get the chant said for them, and before they were doing the chant for other kids. And I think they really step in with a sense of pride for that."

The Roxbury Prep eighth-grade pi contestant, Jenna, is a sturdy girl with a determined expression on her face. She faces the crowd and begins reciting the digits of pi. The tension in the room builds as she continues to rattle off numbers. She recites in quick bursts, firing off ten or fifteen numbers in rapid succession and then stopping to think before continuing. At one point, perhaps one hundred digits into pi, she pauses, uncertain. A few seconds pass. When she offers the next number in a hesitant tone, a sixth grader in the audience, unable to contain herself, yells out, "That's right!" Jenna makes her way haltingly, but accurately, for another thirty or so digits. When an error finally brings her run to an end, the entire student body erupts into thunderous applause. She is unquestionably the winner.

Suddenly, Mr. Tollinche—Roxbury Prep's burly school office manager, and the first face everyone sees upon entering the school—appears in the back of the auditorium carrying school director Mr. Austin over his shoulder. He walks purposefully down the center aisle as the entire student body virtually shrieks with excitement. Mr. Tollinche deposits the school director in the front of the auditorium, and Mr. Lester hands him a cardboard bull's-eye with a hole cut out in the center for Mr. Austin to position his face. In his early thirties, Mr. Austin is in his third year as one of Roxbury Prep's codirectors but his tenth year at Roxbury Prep overall, having served as a math teacher and dean prior to becoming a director. He grew up just a few miles from Roxbury Prep.

Another teacher hands Jenna a pie tin filled with whipped cream. The volume in the room begins to rise as Jenna moves closer to Mr. Austin and cocks back her arm, taking aim. Dozens of middle schoolers inadvertently rise up in their seats. The room reaches a fever pitch as Jenna thrusts the pie into the center of the bull's-eye and Mr. Austin's face.

A few seconds later, Roxbury Prep students are still collecting themselves as Mr. Austin—his face masked entirely by whipped cream—poses for a picture with Jenna and then makes his way back to his office to clean up. Jenna accepts high fives from sixth- and seventh-grade students on her way back to her own seat. Community meeting emcee Amina returns to the lectern, and the auditorium falls silent again. "It is now time for the awarding of the Spirit Stick," she announces.

## PERFORMANCE, MORAL, AND CIVIC CHARACTER

What about different *types* of character? Berkowitz's trichotomous character model does an excellent job of pulling together character development scholarship from a number of different disciplines by acknowledging the cognitive, affective, and behavioral components of character. As noted earlier in this chapter, however, one drawback to the model presented in figure 1.1 is that qualities representing vastly different facets of character are grouped together under a single category such as cognition. For this reason, Berkowitz and other scholars have drawn upon work by Thomas Lickona and Matthew Davidson that divides the broader construct of character into performance character and moral character.[27] More recently, David Shields has added a third character type—civic character—to this taxonomy.[28]

Lickona and Davidson define performance character as consisting of "the qualities such as effort, diligence, perseverance, a strong work ethic, a positive attitude, ingenuity, and self-discipline needed to realize one's potential for excellence in academics, co-curricular activities, the workplace, or any other area of endeavor."[29] These scholars are careful to note that performance character is not synonymous with performance. Whereas examples of performance might be a grade on a test, the execution of a Mozart concerto, or the completion of a ten-kilometer race, performance character consists of the character strengths necessary to achieve such outcomes. Put another way, performance character consists of "the skills that allow individuals to optimally regulate their thoughts and actions . . . [to] achieve levels of personal excellence in their conduct."[30]

If performance character can be conceptualized as a mastery orientation, then moral character is best conceptualized as a relational orientation. According to Lickona and Davidson, moral character "consists of the qualities—such as integrity, justice, caring, and respect—needed for successful interpersonal relationships and ethical behavior."[31] Berkowitz and William Puka have suggested that an important difference between performance character and moral character is that performance character strengths are neither intrinsically good nor bad but rather "derivative of the ends toward which they are applied."[32] For example, one can exhibit perseverance in pursuit of both ethical and unethical goals. In contrast, moral character strengths such as integrity or compassion can be understood as "interpersonal ethical imperatives"—in other words, as qualities that are intrinsically good in and of themselves.

As is evident in figure 1.2, we have also added to Berkowitz's model a concentric circle representing civic character. Civic character can be defined as "the knowledge, skills, virtues, and commitments necessary for

**FIGURE 1.2**  Taxonomy of character types

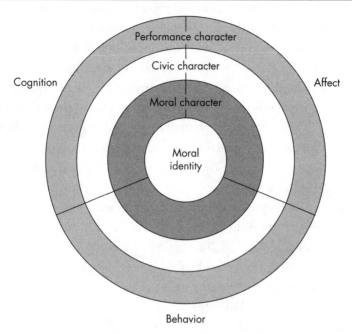

*Source:* Adapted from Berkowitz (2011).

engaged and responsible citizenship."[33] If moral character is situated in an individual's relationships and interactions with other individuals, then civic character is situated in an individual's role within local, national, and global communities. Examples of civic character strengths include civic and political knowledge, an ethic of participation and service, and the numerous social skills necessary to work productively with others for the common good.[34] The need for citizens with a strong sense of civic character was a key motivation for the establishment of public schools in the United States.[35]

In their own work, Lickona and Davidson conceptualize performance character and moral character as complementary and of equal status. They write, "Performance character must always be regulated by moral character to ensure that we do not do bad things in the pursuit of our goals, and moral character always needs performance character to enable us to be effective in carrying out our good intentions."[36] Shields makes a similar assertion about the relationship between civic character and the other character types, noting that "the disposition of becoming engaged civically loses its efficacy without dedication (a performance character strength) and loyalty (a moral character strength)."[37] These descriptions of the interconnections between the three types of character are useful ones. In figure 1.2, however, we follow Berkowitz's lead in portraying the three character types as three concentric circles with moral character positioned closest to (and performance character positioned farthest away from) an individual's moral identity.

Moral identity—positioned in the center of our conceptual model—has been defined by psychologist Larry Nucci as "the extent to which individuals integrate their morality into their subjective sense of personal identity."[38] Drawing on the work of Berkowitz, Bryan Sokol, and others, we conceptualize an individual's moral character as exerting the strongest influence upon an individual's moral identity, followed by that individual's civic character, and finally by that individual's performance character.[39] We establish this hierarchy within our model in large part because moral character and civic character concern themselves with "those qualities needed to be ethical—to develop just and caring relationships, contribute to community, and assume the responsibilities of democratic citizenship."[40] These qualities would seem to exert a greater influence upon an individual's moral identity than do the "qualities needed to realize one's potential for excellence" that constitute performance character.[41]

One final note is that the division of character into cognitive, affective, and behavioral domains is intended to remain fully present in the conceptual model presented in figure 1.2. For example, with regard to moral character, one might characterize moral reasoning as an example of the cognitive; emotions such as empathy or compassion as examples of the affective; and behaviors such as helping a friend in need or standing up to a bully as examples of the behavioral. With regard to civic character, one might characterize civic and political knowledge as examples of the cognitive; passion for the public good as situated in the affective domain; and service on a local school committee or efforts to defeat a controversial referendum as examples of the behavioral component of character. Finally, with regard to performance character, the ability to consider the perspectives or motivations of others is associated with the cognitive domain; qualities such as optimism and zest are associated with the affective domain; and the ability to persevere or practice self-discipline is associated with the behavioral domain. The distinctions across these categories are not airtight; however, we believe that the three-by-three design featured in figure 1.2—three concentric circles representing the types of character, and three wedges representing the components of character—serves as a valuable theoretical framework for our investigation of character development at the Boston Prep, Roxbury Prep, and Pacific Rim charter schools.

## PACIFIC RIM HIGH SCHOOL COMMUNITY MEETING

Academy of the Pacific Rim Public Charter School sits near the center of Boston's Hyde Park neighborhood just a few blocks away from Boston Prep, but a visitor to the school might nonetheless have trouble finding it. Nestled within an industrial park, Pacific Rim's nondescript three-story brick building is surrounded by businesses with names like Maverick Construction and Tramm Elevator Company. Only a small sign affixed to the side of the building announces the school's presence, with the school's name printed in thin, wispy Papyrus font across the school logo—two globes positioned side by side with the Eastern Hemisphere visible on one and the Western Hemisphere visible on the other.

Inside, Pacific Rim looks more like a traditional school building than either Boston Prep or Roxbury Prep. Each of the school's three floors is a long single corridor with lockers and classrooms lining the walls on both sides. The middle school occupies the second and third floors of the building, while the high school students are located on the ground level.

Pacific Rim opened its doors in 1997, having been awarded one of the first charters issued in Massachusetts. The school was founded by two retired members of the Boston School Committee who had become enamored with educational practices they had observed on trips to Taiwan and

Japan. The objective from the start was to combine the best of Eastern educational practices and values—high standards, discipline, and character education—with the best of Western educational practices and values—diversity, creativity, and individualism.

The school has evolved in many ways over its fifteen-year history, but the walls still evince its "East meets West" origins. Hanging throughout the building are beautiful framed prints of different Japanese characters with the definition of that character overlaid in English. To the side of each print is an illustration of a Japanese schoolboy reading a book and carrying a bundle of sticks on his back.

Each of the framed Japanese characters represents a character strength that Pacific Rim seeks to instill in its students. Perhaps most prominent are the Pacific Rim cultural touchstones—*kaizen* ("continual improvement of our community") and *gambatte* ("persist and never give up"). However, other characters exhort Pacific Rim students to be daring ("to muster the strength and will to do what we know we should do"), purposeful ("to have goals for each action and interaction throughout the day"), and respectful ("treat others with politeness, consideration, and appreciation"). Together, they form the Pacific Rim motto "KG-PRIDE," which stands for kaizen, gambatte, purpose, respect, integrity, daring, and excellence.

The long corridor on Pacific Rim's ground level opens at the far end into a large, sunny cafeteria, which is also the site of the high school community meeting. Unlike Boston Prep, Pacific Rim holds separate community meetings for its high school and middle school students, with the high school community meeting taking place on Wednesday mornings and the middle school community meeting on Monday afternoons.

Stepping into the Pacific Rim cafeteria a few minutes before the community meeting is set to begin, a visitor would find a handful of high schoolers and the dean of students, Jonathan Diamond, clustered around the lectern and microphone set up at the front of the room. The students are practicing speaking into the microphone, and Dean Diamond is offering feedback on whether or not they are effectively projecting. For several years now, the high school community meeting at Pacific Rim has been planned and executed by students. As social studies teacher Holly Anderson explains, "Each week a different advisory is in charge of running community meeting. That means they emcee it. They pick the theme for the day. They do some kind of presentation."

A few minutes later, Pacific Rim students start to pour into the cafeteria. They arrive in bunches, talking and laughing among themselves, and head toward the long tables reserved for their respective homerooms. While middle school students wear a uniform consisting of maroon polo shirts and khaki pants, the high school students observe a more flexible dress code. Students are expected to wear collared shirts tucked into khaki or black pants, and black or brown shoes.

The volume in the cafeteria, which had been approaching a good-natured but dull roar, falls silent when Dean Diamond—a man in his late thirties with a shaved head—steps up to the lectern and raises his hand. "Before I turn things over to Ms. Tran's advisory," he begins, "we have a couple announcements."

An athletic-looking male student steps to the front of the room. "The student government is sponsoring a clothing drive," he begins in an accent that suggests he was born outside the United States, "for students in orphanages who don't have warm clothes for the winter. Every advisory will have a garbage bag to put clothing in, and you have two weeks to collect the clothing. So it's a clothing drive, and the advisory that donates the most winter clothing will get a pizza party."

Next, a female teacher in her early forties steps to the lectern. "The Thespian Society is hosting a Halloween bake sale, and that will happen this Friday. Please help support our fundraising efforts this Friday. And, thespians, the cookie dough we ordered will be here tomorrow, and you should be able to pick it up anytime starting at 10 a.m."

Ms. Anderson—a woman in her late twenties with long hair and a nose ring—jumps up from her seat among her eleventh-grade advisory. "Don't forget we're accepting applications for the National Honor Society," she reminds students. "And you need volunteer hours to show you're committed to service. So I would recommend that anyone who is interested consider the volunteer opportunities just described." A number of students across the cafeteria nod their heads attentively, their interest piqued by this last suggestion.

Dean Diamond steps to the lectern once again. "One final thing before we turn it over to Ms. Tran's advisory. We used to have a 'no electronics' policy whatsoever. Thanks to your student government, we decided to let you use electronics such as headphones at certain points of the day. But, to clarify, during the school day, when you're walking from place to place, you cannot use headphones." A few students shift disapprovingly, but quietly, in their seats. Others nod their heads.

Dean Diamond gestures in the direction of Ms. Tran's advisory, and five students come up to join him at the lectern. Two are white, two are Latina, and one—the only male student in the group—is African American. A female student with streaks of pink in her hair approaches the microphone. "We're going to start with a definition of social justice," she begins, "which is that all persons irrespective of race, religion, age, or sexual orientation will be treated without prejudice. The idea that all men and women are created equal." When she steps back, a young woman with long dark hair takes her place.

"There are many examples of social injustice in our country," she explains. "Christianity is one of the largest religions in the world, and while there has been injustice against Christians, Christians have also committed injustices. The Crusades were Christians going to war against Muslims. Another example of injustice involves the situation around building a mosque at [September 11th site] Ground Zero. Because it's a mosque and not a church or temple, it's causing a great deal of controversy, which wouldn't happen if it were not a mosque. Our country has separation of church and state because our founders came here to escape religious persecution."

A third female student steps to the lectern. She reads off a series of names. Then she explains, "Those are the names of gay teens who killed themselves because today, in 2010, they weren't accepted for who they are. Social justice is equal rights for all. Gays have a very hard time, and in many states are not allowed to be married. Unfortunately, in this country, more states allow marriage between first cousins than between gay couples."

The male student takes over at the lectern. "There are blacks, whites, Asians, Hispanics, and Native Americans throughout history who have been persecuted for their race." He goes on to describe the harmful effects of racism and is followed by a female student who focuses on unhealthy portrayals of women in the media. When they finish, their classmates applaud cheerfully.

"Now Ms. Tran will present this week's Kaizen-Gambatte Award," Dean Diamond announces.

Ms. Tran moves to the front of the room. She faces the Pacific Rim high school students, who sit up straighter in their seats. "Have you ever heard that the squeaky wheel gets the grease?" starts Ms. Tran, a woman in her early thirties with wisps of gray hair. "It's usually used with a negative connotation, but I disagree with that. You can also think of it as the person who asks is more likely to get what they need. Or, you won't get what you need unless you ask for it. And I agree with that. As an advisor, I often encourage students to be squeaky wheels. It doesn't help to stew about a problem with a teacher or a bad grade, or even to complain about it, but it does help to go ask for help. And that will only be even more so the case in college when your classes will be a lot bigger, and professors will not know who you are unless you make them know you. Today, I want to recognize a student who is very good at being a squeaky wheel. She is also a good friend, a good student, an all-around good person, and someone who is very good at asking for help at the right times. As a result, her teachers are only too happy to help her out when we can, just as she is always happy to help other folks out. This week's winner of the Kaizen-Gambatte Award is Jackie Barlow!" The students break into genuinely enthusiastic applause as Jackie, a tall girl wearing an ecstatic expression, approaches Ms. Tran to accept her award and the congratulations of her classmates and teachers.

## FROM THEORY TO ACTION

In this chapter, we have sought to offer a theoretical framework for considering the distinct approaches to character development at the Boston Prep, Roxbury Prep, and Pacific Rim charter schools. Our theoretical framework recognizes "character" as possessing cognitive, affective, and behavioral components and as portioned into three different types: performance character, moral character, and civic character. In this chapter, we also offered narratives from a single community meeting at each of the three schools in our study. A single day in the life of a school is far too small a sample size from which to draw conclusions about that school's approach to character development; however, genuine differences in the ways the three schools approach character development *do* start to emerge in these narratives. The MCAS Legacy game show and other elements of Boston Prep's community meeting highlight the school's emphasis on moral character. High-stakes state assessments are typically characterized by educators in purely performance-oriented terms; however, Boston Prep's MCAS Legacy skit also emphasized the *moral* dimension of the exams by articulating the role that each Boston Prep student has to play in furthering the school's legacy as well as the extent to which students enter into these tests as representatives of their school and families. This emphasis on moral character was further underscored by the presentation of virtue commendations to students who had exhibited compassion. And, while mentioned only briefly in this chapter, even the school's DuBois Award—named after the first African American to earn a PhD from Harvard—seems intended to remind students that there are moral dimensions to one's accomplishments.

Likewise, the pi recitation contest at Roxbury Prep foreshadows the extent to which Roxbury Prep faculty and leaders emphasize the development of students' performance character strengths and qualities. Also mentioned only briefly in this chapter is the Spirit Stick—the weekly award at Roxbury Prep that is typically presented to a student who has exemplified the hard work and effort necessary to achieve success. As explained in greater detail in chapter 3 by Roxbury Prep faculty, students, and parents, the Spirit Stick not only honors a deserving student each week but also serves as a reminder to the entire school community of the sustained and deliberate practice necessary to deliver a powerful performance in endeavors ranging from academics to athletics to the arts.

Finally, Pacific Rim's emphasis on civic character is highlighted by a student-run (and student-planned) community meeting, numerous opportunities for community service, and the explicit role of student government in determining school policy. The promotion of civic character was further emphasized by the focus of the community meeting upon different groups of Americans contending with injustice as well as by Ms. Tran's presentation of the Kaizen-Gambatte Award to a student willing to be a strong advocate for herself and others. Even kaizen itself—the Japanese phrase meaning "commitment to the continuous improvement of the community"—points to the school's investment in fostering students' civic character development.

Certainly, all three schools aspire to have a positive effect upon their students' moral, performance, and civic character development, but there are also clear differences across the three schools in the particular character strengths they have chosen to emphasize through their curriculum, pedagogy, and practices. As noted, the narratives from the community meetings are not intended to serve as evidence of the schools' different character emphases, but rather as coming attractions for the more robust presentation of each school's character education practices and outcomes in succeeding chapters. In these presentations, we seek to offer valuable lessons to parents, educators, and policy makers about the *different* ways in which three high performing schools utilize character education as the foundation upon which to build their students' success.

# MORAL CHARACTER
# AT BOSTON PREP

# CHAPTER TWO

# Do the Right Thing

An early December high school community meeting at Boston Prep began with several announcements from students. "The yearbook is on sale now, and you can save ten dollars if you purchase it now rather than waiting until the end of the year." "The strength and conditioning club will be lifting weights this afternoon." "The service learning club is holding its meeting during lunch."

Then a teacher in her mid-twenties stood up. "We're now taking applications for the Honor Council," she announced. "The Honor Council proactively plans events and activities that build integrity for the entire high school community, and they work with people after incidents of violating the honor code." A few students nodded, the teacher returned to her seat, and the meeting segued into a community building game in which students answered trivia questions about their advisors and vice versa.

The section of the Boston Prep honor code on academic integrity begins with the sentence, "Cheating and plagiarism represent breaches of community integrity and trust," and then goes on to describe several types of behavior that constitute cheating or plagiarism. This portion of the code sparks little debate among teachers, students, or parents. More controversial, however, is the statement a few paragraphs down that reads: "We all share the responsibility for maintaining a safe, positive learning environment. Students who have knowledge about serious disciplinary infractions or potential serious disciplinary infractions must contact a teacher or administrator immediately." Boston Prep's founding principal, Amanda Gardner, explains, "It's called the Student Responsibility section [of the code]. We tell students that if they know something unsafe is going to happen and they don't tell us about it, they are just as liable as the kid who actually does the thing."

This explicit responsibility to inform on classmates doing the wrong thing is a violation of the moral code that many Boston Prep students have learned from their families and friends. According to eighth-grade teacher Kelsey Morales, "there are tons of students who come in, I would say it's 75 percent, saying that snitching is absolutely never okay to do . . . and that you should be a social outcast if you snitch." Seventh-grade teacher Eric Albans notes as well that his students offer significant resistance to the Boston Prep perspective on student responsibility: "I think it goes against a little bit of what they're already being brought up with, or just what they get from their neighborhoods, their peer cultures."

Among Boston Prep's high school students, this question of whose ethical code takes precedence came to a head over a pledge developed by the Boston Prep students and teachers serving on the 2010–2011 Honor Council. Specifically, the council members proposed a pledge that affirmed Boston Prep students' commitment to integrity by not engaging in behaviors such as cheating or plagiarism, and also not accepting such behavior from their classmates. When the council's student representatives presented the pledge to their classmates at a community meeting, half of the senior class refused to sign.

Twelfth-grade student Flavia explains that she decided not to sign the pledge because of "the part where if you saw a person cheating or not showing integrity, that you would speak up and tell a teacher . . . That would be a really hard part of the code for me to do because I always grew up learning that you shouldn't tell on other people, especially if it's not your business. So that's why I didn't sign the code this year . . . because I knew it would be something that I couldn't live by 100 percent." She adds, "I felt like getting teachers involved wouldn't necessarily even teach the [offending] student that that's not the right way to go. You know, I felt like if I had seen someone cheating, I could have pulled them aside and been like, 'This is not really helping your education,' but I think for me to just go to the teacher and be like, 'Oh, they're cheating,' and they get suspended doesn't mean they learned a lesson and saw how it hurt themselves and society."

Another twelfth-grade student, Lena, refused to sign the pledge as well, saying, "I wasn't comfortable telling on someone else or giving up someone else's thing. I'm in school to get my education, and this person is going to learn that like cheating is not the way to go, but I wasn't the person that was going to get them to get that lesson." Twelfth-grader Abner *did* sign the pledge, which he interpreted as a commitment to stop dishonest or unethical behavior, though not necessarily by informing a teacher. According to Abner, "If I know that somebody is cheating, I go up to that person and tell them, 'Oh, you know, it's really not helping you. It's not helping your education' . . . I just took it as [a pledge] I would solve the problem myself because, you know, I'm an upperclassman. I can help other people."

Faculty and administrators at Boston Prep weren't sure how to respond to the dissension in the senior class over the Honor Council's pledge. On one hand, half of Boston Prep's first senior class—the students who had been present since the school's opening in 2004—were refusing to sign a pledge that affirmed their commitment to engaging in honest and ethical action. On the other hand, a number of those students, like Flavia, justified this decision by explaining that the pledge compromised their personal integrity—their commitment to acting in accordance with their own beliefs.

Further complicating matters was the fact that Boston Prep seniors were in the midst of a yearlong thesis project focused on developing a personal code of ethics. High school ethics teacher Alex Leverett had defined a personal code of ethics for seniors in early September as "a statement of provisionally stable ethical beliefs according to which one commits to live," or, more informally, "the rules you live by." Students asked a number of questions on that first day of ethics class about the personal code of ethics they were expected to develop over the course of the academic year.

One prescient question was "How are you going to help us if you disagree with our personal code of ethics?"

"It's not my job to tell you what to think," Leverett had responded. "Then it's no longer your personal code of ethics. I will be honest, though. When I disagree with you, I will provide a rationale, but I am not here to convince you to agree with me or with our five key virtues." One could reasonably say, then, that the Boston Prep seniors who signed the Honor Council's pledge and also those who refused to sign it were *both* demonstrating a commitment to acting with integrity.

Boston Prep's Honor Council had been charged with planning events and activities that contributed to the culture of integrity within the school. While the council's members undoubtedly expected a warmer reception to their proposed pledge, the genuine debate it inspired was just one of a multitude of ways in which Boston Prep students engaged in earnest reflection on moral and ethical issues over the course of the academic year. Perhaps it comes as no surprise, then, that at the conclusion of the school year, Boston Prep students demonstrated a significantly higher commitment to two moral character strengths—integrity and empathy—than their peers at Roxbury Prep and Pacific Rim. Boston Prep students' commitment to integrity serves as the jumping-off point of this chapter, while their demonstration of empathy is the focus of chapter 3. Both chapters seek to highlight the pedagogical and curricular levers by which Boston Prep fosters the moral character development of its student body.

## MEASURING INTEGRITY

As mentioned in the introduction, students at Boston Prep, Roxbury Prep, and Pacific Rim all completed surveys at the start and conclusion of the academic year. Included in these surveys were five items adapted from the Academic Motivation and Integrity Survey.[1] These items included statements such as "I might cheat to get an 'A' if I knew I wouldn't be caught" and "I might cheat in a class where I had a bad teacher." Students responded to all of these items along a five-point Likert scale that characterized each statement on a continuum that ranged from "A lot like me" to

"Not like me at all." All together, these items formed a robust composite of the character strength of integrity.[2]

To analyze students' pre- and post-intervention survey data, we then fit a multilevel regression model in order to compare the shifts in integrity scores of students across the three schools from the beginning to the end of the academic year.[3] Perhaps not surprisingly, students at all three schools expressed great optimism about their commitment to integrity in the surveys completed during the opening weeks of the school year. On average, high school students at each school rated their commitment to integrity as greater than 4.0; middle school students' ratings averaged a whopping 4.5. As for the source of this optimism, keep in mind that in the opening days of the academic year tests had not yet been taken, essays not yet assigned, progress reports not yet issued, and thus, ethical crossroads not yet confronted. It appeared to be relatively easy for students at all three schools to earnestly characterize themselves as possessing high levels of integrity. However, our analyses revealed that students at Boston Prep—both in the middle school and in the high school—were significantly more likely ($p < .05$) to maintain this strong commitment to integrity over the course of the school year than their peers at Roxbury Prep or Pacific Rim.[4]

The mean integrity scores for students at Boston Prep, Roxbury Prep, and Pacific Rim at the beginning and end of the academic year are presented in figures 2.1 and 2.2. At the time of the study, Roxbury Prep offered only grades six through eight, though the school has subsequently sought and received approval from the Massachusetts Department of Elementary and Secondary Education to expand to the high school grades as well.

As is evident in figures 2.1 and 2.2, students at Boston Prep, on average, completed the academic year having maintained (or nearly maintained) the high commitment to integrity with which they began the year. In contrast, their peers at Roxbury Prep and Pacific Rim demonstrated significant declines in this commitment. The effect upon students' integrity of being a student at Boston Prep, rather than a student at one of the other two schools, was a relatively small one.[5] However, when considering this small effect size, one must bear in mind that this study was not com-

FIGURE 2.1    Mean pre- and post-intervention integrity scores for high school students at Boston Prep and Pacific Rim (n = 279)

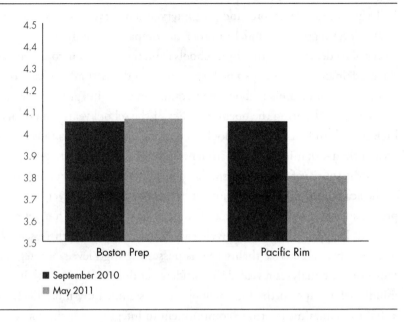

■ September 2010
■ May 2011

paring Boston Prep, Roxbury Prep, and Pacific Rim to other urban public schools, but rather to each other. In other words, the effect of attending Boston Prep upon students' integrity is in comparison to their peers at two other high achieving schools with an explicit commitment to students' character development, and who also cited integrity among their core values. With this comparison in mind, we find notable the significant difference in integrity scores between Boston Prep students and their peers at Roxbury Prep and Pacific Rim. Also worth bearing in mind is that a recent U.S. Department of Education study of seven nationally recognized character education programs found that none of the programs exerted any discernible effects at all upon more than six thousand participating students.[6] For both of these reasons, the strong commitment to integrity (and empathy) that Boston Prep students demonstrated over the course of the academic year is worthy of further investigation.

FIGURE 2.2  Mean pre- and post-intervention integrity scores for middle school students at Boston Prep, Roxbury Prep, and Pacific Rim (n = 541)

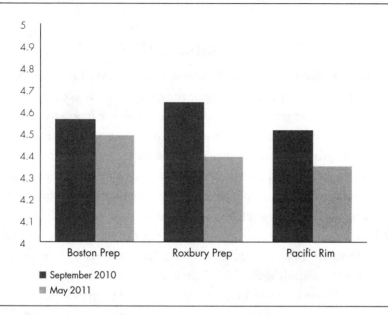

The key question, then, is how did Boston Prep do it? All three schools—Boston Prep, Roxbury Prep, and Pacific Rim—serve predominantly low-income students from the city of Boston. All three schools admit students via a randomized registration lottery that prevents the heads of school from picking and choosing among the families interested in sending their children there. Finally, the students at all three schools are earning scores on the Massachusetts state assessments that are competitive with peers from some of the toniest suburban communities in the state. What, then, is Boston Prep doing differently to support its students' moral character development? This chapter provides a window into Boston Prep's efforts to mold the moral character of its student body by drawing upon interviews with thirty Boston Prep students, teachers, and parents, as well as more than eighty observations of Boston Prep community meetings, ethics classes, and enrichment activities. In so doing, it seeks to provide useful insights to educators, parents, and policy makers committed to strengthening the moral character of their own youth.

## ESTABLISHING A MORAL CHARACTER FOUNDATION

As noted in chapter 1, Thomas Lickona and Matthew Davidson define *performance character* as consisting of the qualities, such as diligence and perseverance, that are necessary to achieve excellence in academics, athletics, and other endeavors, while *moral character* consists of the qualities, such as integrity and respect, that are necessary for engaging in successful and ethical relationships with others.[7] One might reasonably claim that the majority of American public schools—including Boston Prep—treat performance character strengths as central to their work with students, and their emphasis has only grown in the current era of high-stakes testing.[8] However, what distinguishes Boston Prep from many other American schools—including Roxbury Prep and Pacific Rim—is the intensity of its focus upon students' moral character development as well.

According to Boston Prep founder and Head of School Scott McCue, strengthening students' moral character has been central to the school's mission since its founding in 2004: "Young people are figuring out the kinds of adults they're going to be and the kind of ethical people they're going to become when they're in middle school or in high school. I think we just made a deliberate decision to insert ourselves into that conversation as a school. It's something that good teachers in good schools have always done to some degree. We were trying to do it in a way that was more deliberate and more structured, and that was central to our charter from the beginning." Toward this end, McCue and the other members of Boston Prep's founding team decided upon five key virtues that they believed could serve as a foundation for students' academic and character development: courage, compassion, integrity, perseverance, and respect. Notably, the majority of these virtues (e.g., compassion, integrity, respect) can be characterized as moral character strengths.

One indicator of the extent to which these five virtues permeate the culture and practices at Boston Prep is their central role in the orientation of incoming students. First, all incoming students receive a home visit prior to the start of the school year from a Boston Prep faculty member. According to middle school principal Amanda Gardner: "We go to the houses of all the students, and we sit down on the couch, and we talk about the school. And that's really the first conversation we have with students about the virtues."

This focus on the virtues is then amplified by a weeklong orientation session for new students in late August. Much of the focus of those orientation days is on introducing students to the policies and practices that govern life at Boston Prep—everything from the different components of the school uniform to the correct heading for students' homework assignments to how students can earn merits and demerits through their behavior. Over the course of this weeklong orientation, however, the only academic class that meets each day is ethics class. Gardner explains, "Ethics is the only class they take . . . and it's an overview, so they do quick lessons on each of the virtues, and then the rest of the year is sort of those virtues in focus." In other words, Boston Prep faculty and administrators believe it is crucial for incoming students to step into Boston Prep on the first day of school with a working definition of each of the five virtues, but then those definitions are fleshed out and investigated over students' succeeding years at Boston Prep.

Recalling these orientation sessions from the start of the academic year, sixth-grade student Re'Shon says, "At the orientation, they gave us a paper, and I think my advisor made me read aloud all of the five key virtues. But, like, I didn't even know what they meant before I came." Her classmate, Maria, adds that learning about the virtues during orientation set off a light bulb in her head: "The teacher was talking about the five virtues, and it was like, 'Whoa, okay, effort determines success.' And then, well, this orientation hit me because, when they said that, I was like, 'When I grow up, I want to be an actress. So I'm going to strive for it, and I'm going to be what I want to be.'" For Maria, Boston Prep's introduction to the five virtues felt like a road map for achieving her goals.

The emphasis upon moral character at Boston Prep was also evident in students' perceptions of their teachers' expectations for them. Ninth-grade student Alisha explains, "I think the school wants us to develop our work ethic in the academic classes, as well as our personal ethic. Because it's no use to have good academic skills and be successful when you're a stingy person, [or] you don't really have morals." Eddie, another ninth-grade student, adds, "I think they want us to be the best human being we could possibly be. They want us to be ethical. They want us to be intellectual. They want us to go to college. They want us to lead good lives."

Middle school students at Boston Prep recognize the school's aspirations for their moral character development as well. Seventh grader Stephon describes Boston Prep as encouraging students to "find a way to be better and learn to be a better person," and eighth grader Robert believes that Boston Prep aspires for him to become an "ethical, well-behaved, and intelligent student. One that strives for success and wants to go to college." Finally, eighth grader Jessenia references Boston Prep's weekly W. E. B. DuBois Award in her explanation of the school's aspirations for its students. According to Jessenia, the DuBois Award—which is presented each week to a student who has exemplified one of the five key virtues—is awarded to Boston Prep students who are "not the smartest, and they're not the best athlete. It's mostly for people who have character and will strive to do whatever they have to do to get a good education or do whatever they have to do to be compassionate and build up their character." The character emphases at Roxbury Prep and Pacific Rim are the focus of subsequent chapters, but neither the students at Roxbury Prep nor Pacific Rim describe their respective schools' aspirations for them in such moral terms.

Boston Prep's weekly DuBois Award serves as a useful indicator as well of the school's commitment to moral character development. At the first community meeting of the academic year, Head of School Scott McCue reminded students that W. E. B. DuBois was the first African American to earn a PhD from Harvard, and that the DuBois Award is presented each week to a student who epitomizes DuBois's scholarship and integrity. Speaking of the DuBois Award, tenth-grade student Brandi says, "I think it's a good way to continue the legacy of W. E. B. DuBois. When you're a student who is like him, that is why you get it. I think it's a good way to just kind of like [say] you have characteristics of a world leader. You are this much closer to getting there."

All three schools give out a weekly award to a deserving student: the Spirit Stick at Roxbury Prep, the Kaizen-Gambatte Award at Pacific Rim, and the DuBois Award at Boston Prep. Unlike the awards at the other schools, however, the DuBois Award carries with it the moral weight of a historical figure whose trajectory opened doors for subsequent generations of African Americans. At one Boston Prep community meeting, the guest speaker was Michael Curry, the incoming president of the Boston chapter of the National Association for the Advancement of Colored People (NAACP), an organization that DuBois helped to found. In addressing the student body, Curry—who grew up in a Boston public housing development—explained, "One of the first things I studied in college was about W. E. B. DuBois and his founding of the NAACP. I got fascinated with his writings and his work to mobilize his community, and to try to deal with what African Americans were faced with during that time, and continue to face today. So the challenge for me in college was to soak all that information in and figure out what I wanted to do about it."

Curry went on to talk about utilizing his college education to reduce gang violence in Boston and, more recently, to convince local news organizations to hire more reporters of color and to cover a greater diversity of news stories about urban life. He told Boston Prep students, "You can make a difference—you have an opportunity as a young person to make a difference in your community," and concluded his talk by presenting a copy of DuBois's *The Souls of Black Folk* to the weekly winner of the DuBois Award. In his speech, Curry emphasized the historical importance of W. E. B. DuBois in making America a more equitable nation for all citizens and simultaneously urged Boston Prep students to utilize the education they receive at Boston Prep and then in college toward moral ends. The presentation of the DuBois Award serves as a weekly reminder to the entire Boston Prep community of the scholarly *and* ethical aspirations underpinning their teaching and learning.

## TEACHING MORAL CHARACTER

The primary lever through which Boston Prep seeks to influence the moral character of its students is ethics class. Each week, students in grades six through twelve engage in a lesson on ethical philosophy aligned with one of the school's five key virtues. At the middle school level, ethics class is taught by students' advisors. Every Tuesday morning, Boston Prep's middle school homerooms divide into two or three advisory groups apiece, and groups of six to eight students join their faculty advisor in a tight circle to consider the weekly ethics lesson.

The ethics lessons themselves have been developed by Alex Leverett, one of the founding faculty members at Boston Prep. He began as a middle school writing teacher, but then transitioned to focusing on the ethics curriculum full-time. In this role, Leverett is responsible for developing a unique ethics curriculum for Boston Prep's sixth-, seventh-, and eighth-grade students. He prepares detailed lesson plans for teachers at each grade level, develops materials to accompany the lessons, and delivers the entire package to teachers ahead of the Tuesday morning ethics lesson.

Leverett also develops the ethics lessons for Boston Prep's high school grades, but he teaches the tenth-, eleventh-, and twelfth-grade ethics lessons himself, as the philosophical content embedded within these lessons requires an instructor with significant expertise in classics or philosophy. Leverett used to teach the ninth-grade ethics classes as well, but, for the past two years, those have been taught by Head of School Scott McCue. McCue explains that, for him, teaching ethics to the ninth graders offers an opportunity to build relationships with Boston Prep students as they enter the high school. Describing the ninth grade as an important transition year for Boston Prep students, McCue notes, "I needed a platform to talk to high school students . . . and not just at community meeting, not just reacting to something bad that's happened." By spending a year working with ninth-grade students to contemplate the role of ethics in their lives, McCue establishes a baseline relationship with high school students that allows him to better support them throughout their final three years at Boston Prep.

Boston Prep is by no means the first school to engage middle and secondary students in philosophical inquiry.[9] In the 1970s, Columbia University philosopher Matthew Lipman began advocating for the introduction of philosophy into K–12 classrooms and founded the Institute for the Advancement of Philosophy for Children at Montclair State University.[10] Likewise, University of Massachusetts philosopher Gareth Matthews wrote several books in the 1980s that advocate for introducing children to philosophy.[11] In their advocacy, however, these and other scholars have focused primarily on the role of philosophy in promoting children's critical thinking and academic skills. At Boston Prep, ethics class certainly aspires to strengthen students' critical thinking, but the primary focus is on the development of students' moral character.

So what precisely does ethics class look like? In the sixth and seventh grades, ethics classes focus intensively upon introducing students to the five virtues. For example, in one seventh-grade lesson Boston Prep students learned that integrity can be defined as "taking responsibility," and they read an excerpt from Mahatma Gandhi's memoir about stealing a bracelet from his brother and then making the decision to confess the theft to his father. After completing the reading, students discussed why Gandhi had made the decision to confess and why people are sometimes reluctant to admit their mistakes.

Eighth-grade teacher Kelsey Morales explains that, whereas the sixth- and seventh-grade ethics lessons emphasize understanding the five virtues, "in the eighth grade . . . it's much more philosophical. And it's about the way you see yourself and the way you see society, and what it means to be a good person and make hard choices." For example, in a lesson on the virtue of respect, Boston Prep eighth graders read an excerpt from a Platonic dialogue in which Thrasymachus argues that justice can be defined as that which benefits the most powerful. Students then discussed this conception of "might makes right" justice. "You don't necessarily get power because you earned it," one student offered. "Nowadays, anybody can get power. And, if you're a ruler, you should make rules for everybody." Another student—referencing his teacher—observed, "Some of your rules we have to follow, but if you say we have to sit on the floor, no, we don't."

The lesson concluded with an excerpt from Dr. Seuss's *Yertle the Turtle*—a children's story in which Yertle the Turtle, the king of Sala-ma-Sond, forces his fellow turtles to stand on each other so that he can perch atop them and enjoy the best view in the kingdom. Boston Prep students first discussed how Yertle's actions might align with Thrasymachus's conception of justice, and then segued into whether or not Yertle had acted virtuously. "No, [because] he put the other turtles through excruciating pain," one student offered. A second student chimed in, "I say no, because he wasn't showing compassion to the other turtles." The juxtaposition of a Platonic dialogue with Dr. Seuss managed to deeply engage eighth graders poised on the border between childhood and adolescence.

Boston Prep high school students are quick to distinguish between the ethics classes they encountered in middle school and those they engage in now at the high school. Ninth grade student Alisha explains, "Middle school ethics class was really basic. You get the foundation of ethics. Like, you don't really have deep group conversations. It's just, this is what courage is, this is what compassion is . . . I feel like, in high school, it gets to the point where [Mr. McCue will] give you a good concrete definition of courage or compassion, but it's up to you whether to debate back and disagree."

Likewise, tenth-grade student Jorge recalls, "Sixth-grade ethics class was more teacher organized. The teacher told you this, and you basically wrote things according to what the teacher said. But, in high school, things are more student-run and with that you can like . . . shape your own ethical values." This perspective is underscored by the introduction to the high school ethics course syllabus: "Ethics class is [now] a kitchen, not a restaurant. There is no more restaurant, no more waiter or waitress. There is only a kitchen, and you are the chef. You will 'cook up' your own ideas about the meaning and value of ethics and the five key virtues . . . The study of ethics is the creation of delicious and nutritious beliefs about what is right, wrong, good, and bad—beliefs that will in the long run keep you on the path to a good life." Again, this language makes clear that, at Boston Prep, character development is conceptualized in primarily moral—rather than performance or civic—terms.

Students in ninth-grade ethics class began the academic year by learning about Aristotle's Doctrine of the Mean—the idea that virtue involves feelings and actions that are neither excessive nor deficient. Mr. McCue noted that sometimes it can be difficult to determine what the intermediate course of action is, and, in a subsequent ethics class, students compared the different approaches of Martin Luther King Jr. and Malcolm X in their struggle for civil rights. "They're both ethical people," Mr. Mc-Cue noted at the outset of the discussion, "both courageous and responsible for the civil rights we have today. But they have different opinions on violence. Which approach was more ethical?" One student asserted that Malcolm X's approach was the intermediate response: "Be respectful to everyone. If the police hit you, that's when you fight back." Another student volunteered, "I'm in the middle. Martin Luther King is deficiency, and Malcolm X is excess." A week later, students had the opportunity to reflect in writing about the applicability of Aristotle's Doctrine of the Mean to their own interactions with teachers, parents, and friends.

Students in tenth-grade ethics class investigated the concept of a social contract by reading *Crito*, the Platonic dialogue in which Socrates explains why he will not flee Athens to escape his death sentence. Students then debated the most virtuous course of action for Socrates. One student argued, "He should run for his life so he can [continue to] spread his beliefs and philosophy." Another countered, "He should stay loyal to the Athenian social contract since he lives there and is a citizen."

In subsequent classes, students applied their understanding of the social contract to the cases of Pat Tillman and Muhammad Ali. Pat Tillman was a professional football player who chose to join the U.S. military after the September 11th attacks out of a feeling of obligation to defend his country. Boxer Muhammad Ali, on the other hand, refused to fight in the Vietnam War, arguing that his religious faith prohibited him from doing so and also that America had not yet fulfilled its end of the social contract to African Americans. In debating Ali's decision, one student noted, "Pat Tillman decided to let go of his career because he went to war. Muhammad

Ali should have partaken in the same social contract." However, another classmate countered, "[Ali] didn't have the full power of the social contract behind him. He didn't have every single right that white people did, and then they're telling him to go fight for his rights." In these discussions, Boston Prep students were thinking critically about the actions of historical figures, but, in so doing, they simultaneously explored what it meant to them personally to live with courage, compassion, integrity, perseverance, and respect—the character virtues prized by Boston Prep.

## SEQUENCING ETHICS

Head of School Scott McCue explains that the goal from the start was for the ethics lessons in each grade level to build upon each other: "We felt there was a real niche to do it sequentially, and that would promote a certain degree of rigor and authentic inquiry that couldn't be done with the same kind of lesson that comes up every year about respect or courage." What this means in practice is that Boston Prep students investigate the five virtues each year in ethics class, but the nature of these investigations, and even the definitions of the virtues themselves, grow deeper and more complex each year. For example, eighth grader Jessenia says that she learned as a sixth grader that courage meant to "be brave," whereas now, in the eighth grade, courage has come to mean "taking positive risks." She explains of each virtue: "Over the years, they elaborate it more and put it in more sophisticated terms. This year, it's take positive risks because being brave is really different from positive risks, but people don't know that. Like going through the dark woods on your bike. That's really brave, but that's not really courage because it's not taking a positive risk since it's dangerous. But taking a positive risk is like raising your hand during class to answer a question if you're not really sure you know the answer or asking a question and saying, 'Oh, I don't really understand.'"

Ninth-grade student Alisha believes that this gradual "complexifying" of the ethics curriculum allows the individual lessons to sink in more deeply. When she began at Boston Prep, she explains, she would have characterized a student who talked back to the teacher as demonstrating courage; however, "in Ethics 9, you think more about, like, how does this affect those around you? Like if I was to climb this mountain, how does it affect those around me? [Now] I think courage is bravery, but it's bravery that's not reckless. And in sixth grade, you don't know that."

The sequencing of Boston Prep's ethics curriculum is also evident in the lessons on integrity. In the sixth grade, students learn that integrity means to tell the truth, and the accompanying lessons focus on opportunities in students' everyday lives to be honest or deceptive. As eighth-grade teacher Kelsey Morales explains, "In the sixth grade, it's a lot about just trying to understand how you can be a person who practices these things on a daily basis in your life. And I think that we emphasize the small things you can do."

In the seventh grade, the definition of integrity shifts to taking responsibility for one's actions, and, as noted earlier in this chapter, one lesson involves students reading an excerpt from Gandhi's memoir in which he describes both stealing a bracelet from his brother and confessing the theft to his father. In this lesson, students and their advisor lingered particularly on Gandhi's peculiar explanation that "there could be no cleansing without a confession." When one seventh-grade teacher asked students what they thought Gandhi meant by a "cleansing," one student offered, "You can't be forgiven until you confess." Another suggested that "it cleans you by making your life easier," and a third added that "now his dad can trust him again." The group went on to share examples from their own lives in which they had failed to show integrity and described what they had then done to fix their respective mistakes.

Boston Prep twelfth-grade student Abner describes these middle school lessons on taking responsibility as having had a significant impact upon his own commitment to integrity: "I don't get sent out [of class] now, but like before when I used to, when you were younger, you would always say, 'Oh, I didn't do such and such.'" Abner explains that, for him, an important step in his character development occurred during the transition to high school. Although he was still getting sent out of class for poor behavior, he believes the turning point was finally admitting to the dean of students, "'Yeah, I did that' and having the integrity to tell [myself], 'Yeah, I did that,' and take that responsibility.'" For Abner, learning to take responsibility for his poor decisions was an important step in committing to do better.

Eighth-grade students at Boston Prep learn that integrity means to be authentic or true to oneself. Perhaps the most fascinating lesson within this unit focused on the biography of Harvey Milk, a San Francisco city councilor and gay rights activist who was one of the first politicians in the United States to publicly identify himself as a gay man. Students began the lesson by describing people in their lives around whom they felt most comfortable being themselves and then read an excerpt from Milk's biography. When they finished reading, their advisor, Jeffrey Granderson, asked, "What effect did Harvey Milk's authenticity have on other people?" One student volunteered, "Hopefully a lot of people saw an openly gay man, but half of the people hated him." A second student noted, "I think eventually people realized that they're prejudiced against gay people, and that gays can also be human and successful." A third added, "It's kind of like Muhammad in Islam. He had this idea for a new religion that he thought everyone should follow, and everyone boycotted him." Finally, a fourth observed, "Harvey Milk did the same thing as Martin Luther King for gay rights." For homework that evening, students were assigned to reflect in writing upon the question: "What can YOU do to help others feel comfortable about who they are?"

This conception of integrity as being true to oneself is referenced by eleventh-grade student Theresa in her description of contending with a low grade in her U.S. History class. According to Theresa, "I realized that my AP [Advanced Placement] U.S. History grade was not where it's supposed to be. So it's low. And for me to figure out what to do, I had to be true to myself. I had to use integrity. I had to say, 'Theresa, what are you doing?'" As was the case for Abner, the scaffolding of Boston Prep's ethics lessons—and the gradual "complexifying" of what it means to act virtuously—allowed Theresa to digest these lessons and genuinely use the virtues as a tool for living a better life. As tenth grader Nick observes of ethics class, "I know we only have it once a week, but I feel like you can't expect to build a good character overnight. And it takes a really long time through ethics class because we're continually rebuilding ourselves."

Boston Prep's efforts to offer students an increasingly complex understanding of the five virtues are supported by the work of developmental psychologist Jean Piaget and his successors on cognitive development. According to Piaget's model, students likely enter Boston Prep in the sixth grade with limited capacity for theoretical thinking.[12] As a result, ethics lessons that define the virtues in highly concrete terms—courage means to be brave, integrity means to tell the truth—are appealing and accessible to Boston Prep's youngest students. Piaget characterized early adolescence, however, as the period in which individuals develop their capacity for formal operational thinking. In other words, Boston Prep's seventh- and eighth-grade students begin to strengthen their capacity for reflective thought and for considering abstract systems of meaning. In accordance with this cognitive development, ethics class begins to offer students more theoretical perspectives on the virtues. At these grade levels, courage becomes defined as taking a positive risk, and integrity takes on the definition of being responsible for one's actions.

As adolescents move into their high school years, their cognitive development allows for increasing facility with what Sharon Daloz Parks terms "third-person perspective taking," the ability to consider simultaneously the perceptions of both oneself and others.[13] The high school ethics curriculum takes advantage of this increased capacity for perspective taking by asking students to step into the shoes and circumstances of historical figures at a moment in which these figures are confronting an ethical crossroads. For example, the tenth-grade ethics unit on the social contract, described earlier in this chapter, added further complexity to students' understanding of integrity when they considered Muhammad Ali's decision to go to prison rather than fight in the Vietnam War. In this lesson, students contemplated the difference between an individual's character and reputation, as Ali's decision to be true to himself and his principles greatly damaged his reputation with the American public. In so doing, students carried out two different discussions simultaneously: 1) whether or not Ali made the right ethical decision, and 2) which quality—character or reputation—mattered more in their own lives. Students in the earlier grades at Boston Prep would have been overwhelmed by such a complex discussion, just as high school students would have grown bored by the lessons on honesty and responsibility in which their younger peers were engaging.

Because ethics lessons align with students' capacity for reasoning and reflection, Boston Prep faculty are able to engage their students in discussions of moral matters that provide an optimal level of challenge, prompting learning in what Lev Vygotsky refers to as students' "zone of proximal development."[14] It is this goal of providing Boston Prep students with ethics lessons that grow each year in complexity—and, thus, meet students at their developmental level—that Head of School Scott McCue characterizes as unique to Boston Prep's approach to character development.

## SPEAKING THE SAME LANGUAGE

Character development can be defined as a relational or interpsychological process.[15] Stated more simply, an individual's character does not develop in isolation, but rather is influenced by the viewpoints and perspectives of those with whom he or she interacts. An additional and important result of ethics class, then, is that it creates a common vocabulary for Boston Prep students and faculty members to discuss the five virtues. This common vocabulary greatly increases the opportunities for members of the Boston Prep community to influence each other's identity and character development. Middle school principal Amanda Gardner notes, "If you're walking around Boston Prep during recess and you're really listening to what the kids are saying, you're going to hear a lot of kids using language about the virtues. And sometimes they're sort of ragging on each other, like, 'Oh, you weren't showing integrity there!' Or, you know, 'What kind of respect is that?' And it's funny, but it's unique and I think it's palpable." Tenth-grade student Jorge echoes Gardner's words: "Inside of school we joke around and say, 'Oh, you persevere' and 'You show courage,' and yeah, we're joking about it, but we actually mean what we're saying behind it."

Sixth-grade teacher Shauvon Ames expresses skepticism that ethics class *teaches* Boston Prep students how to be virtuous: "Kids are doing good things, families are doing good things long before they come to Boston Prep, before we start talking about ethics or virtues." However, Ames describes ethics class as valuable for "giving us some common language to use that we can make each experience, whether it's a positive experience or a challenging experience, we can make it a learning experience because there's common language used." On a similar note, Principal Gardner observes that ethics class is "just a shared experience, you know. I can run a community meeting where I talk about . . . 'Remember when we read about [Dr. Seuss's] Sneetches and respect in the sixth grade?' It's just a nice, shared experience."

How precisely does a common language around the virtues promote the development of students' moral character? When a seventh grader new to Boston Prep was slated to join the University of Guelph homeroom midyear, the homeroom teacher reminded his students of the way in which they had previously welcomed a new student: "I don't want to throw Jennifer out there too much, but she has been doing a wonderful job in this homeroom. But she hasn't been doing it by herself. She's gotten wonderful support from other people in this homeroom to make that transition smoothly. So this new person is going to need your compassion and support to be successful . . . And we'll be asking a few people to play a particularly important role in helping this new Guelph member to get adjusted, but we'll be asking you all to help out." In these words, the teacher drew upon the virtue of compassion to prepare his students to welcome a new member of the class. Importantly, every student in the class already had experience thinking, learning, and reflecting upon the language he was invoking.

There are numerous other ways in which the common language of the virtues presents opportunities for teaching and learning. Each afternoon, Boston Prep students participate in extracurricular activities that range from photography to chess to yoga. At a community meeting in April, awards were presented for students' exemplary performance in these various activities. Nearly every teacher presenting an award invoked one of the virtues in his or her remarks. For example, the teacher leading a service-learning enrichment activity noted that the student with whom she was most impressed "initially wanted to do a different project, but then was incredibly passionate about the project we chose to focus on. And she also raised the most money outside the school for the Walk for Hunger, showing courage and perseverance." Likewise, the yoga instructor explained, "It takes a lot of personal integrity to push yourself in yoga, and two students really pushed themselves every day, and showed a great desire to get better and better." Recall that Vygotsky labeled character development as a relational process. The fact that members of the Boston Prep community share a common language around the virtues deepens their ability to support each other's character development.

At a community meeting just prior to a junior class trip to Rome, Head of School Scott McCue explained to the entire student body, "There are students [going] on that trip who have never been on an airplane before, and . . . then they're going to walk around in a city where they don't know the language and the culture. And the reason we do that is because going to a foreign city gives students a chance to be courageous." Similarly, a few weeks later at the last community meeting before the Thanksgiving break, the high school principal reminded students that Thanksgiving represents an opportunity "to give thanks to those who showed us compassion throughout the year." In both of these examples, the community's common vocabulary served as the foundation upon which Boston Prep faculty sought to help their students learn from a particular teachable moment.

Another significant benefit to the common language established in ethics class is that Boston Prep students and faculty possess a terminology for offering each other praise. Each week at community meeting, any member of the community can stand up and publicly offer a virtue commendation to someone who has exemplified one of the key virtues. For example, at a community meeting in December, a high school student stood up and offered a virtue commendation for compassion to a teacher who "works with me all the time and shows a lot of patience." In March, after the boys' basketball team had beaten the faculty in the annual student-faculty basketball game, Coach Brown stood up at community meeting to acknowledge his players:

The virtue I want to talk about today is integrity. Often, we talk about integrity being "tell the truth." Another way integrity is practiced is being able to look within yourself and ask the question, "Am I doing everything I can?" . . . And when you have that integrity, success is going to come. The virtue commendation is going to the eighteen boys who defeated the men on Friday night. And the reason is because, with those eighteen boys, a process has happened. Because we had practice at 9 a.m. the next morning. Because when they asked themselves after being victorious Friday night, they said, "We're not giving enough. We can do more." Think about that in your own work.

Referencing virtue commendations like these, eleventh-grade student Wayne says, "I think my favorite part of community meeting would have to be the virtue commendations . . . because it's a chance for you to acknowledge people that are doing well, and especially people who weren't doing so well to begin with."

In terms of the effects of such praise, tenth-grade student Jorge says that one of the aspects of Boston Prep he most appreciates is that "you find yourself in the spotlight more and teachers acknowledge your accomplishments more." On a similar note, eleventh-grade student Theresa explains, "I don't realize what I do until somebody tells me that I actually do it," and offers this example: "I got a virtue commendation for giving Mr. Leverett a Get Well Soon letter . . . and I didn't know [until the commendation] that it really lit up his day." The research literature on praise has found that one of the key characteristics of effective praise is that it is highly specific.[16] By articulating precisely which virtue the recipients have exemplified, and tapping into the common vocabulary around these virtues, virtue commendations provide members of the Boston Prep community with highly effective reinforcement for moral actions.

Boston Prep's five virtues also offer a common vocabulary for discussing students' *mis*behavior. When middle school students are sent to the dean's office for misbehavior, they first complete a written report on which of the virtues they were not following in the classroom, and then engage in a discussion with the dean of students about how they can do a better job of exemplifying that virtue going forward. Similarly, middle school teacher Brian Mao explains that when he engages in a disciplinary conversation with one of his students, "I know I have a specific language to use with them to tell them exactly why and how things went wrong." Again, because character development can be conceptualized as a relational process, a common vocabulary facilitates communication between members of the Boston Prep community about the nature of their interactions with one another.

One important example of Boston Prep utilizing the language of the virtues to *pro-actively* address misbehavior relates to school bullying. As a result of several high-profile bullying incidents in Massachusetts schools, in 2010 the state legislature enacted a law requiring public schools to adopt antibullying curricula at every grade level.[17] While many schools have struggled to find a meaningful way to address this issue with their students, Boston Prep chose to embed antibullying lessons directly into its ethics curriculum and engaged students in reflection upon bullying through the lens of virtues such as courage, respect, and compassion. For example, a seventh-grade ethics lesson on respect engaged students in debate about whether spreading rumors about a classmate could constitute bullying, and then introduced the concept that individuals sometimes harm each other not physically, but emotionally. Brian Mao explains that he subsequently referenced this lesson several times when discussing actual conflicts with his students. Mao notes that students who get into altercations with other students will often respond with, "Well, you know, I wasn't pushing them. I wasn't hurting them," to which he replies, "Could you have been hurting them emotionally?" Mao believes "that [distinction] is really helpful for them." Again, a common vocabulary facilitated the relational processes involved in students' character development.

An eighth-grade ethics lesson on bullying offered students a case study of a teen, Carl, who was driven to suicide by bullying from his peers over his presumed homosexuality. After reading the case study, the teacher asked students, "How could Carl's teachers and peers have drawn on the five virtues to prevent the bullying from happening?" The following is an excerpt from the ensuing discussion:

STUDENT 1: The principal could have done something, like brought in the police.

TEACHER: Which virtue would that take?

STUDENT 2: Compassion, because it's helping someone succeed.

TEACHER: So, two people have said adults could have done something. What do you think?

STUDENT 3: Carl's friends should have stood up to the bullies instead of just letting that happen.

TEACHER: So Carl's friends could have shown courage?

STUDENT 2: I think they were scared because they didn't want to get hit by the bullies too.

TEACHER: How could they have shown courage? What else could they have done?

STUDENT 4: I would have gone up to him. It would have been hard for me.

STUDENT 1: I would have said, "Carl, ignore the other people, I'm on your side."

STUDENT 5: I'd pretend I'm the bullies' friend, and then I'd tell them Carl has a notorious uncle who will kill you.

The last suggestion aside, one can see here that the impact of a typical discussion about bullying is deepened by the common language with which the teacher and students can analyze the case study together.

This is not to say that the common vocabulary around the five virtues has no drawbacks. Eighth-grade teacher Kelsey Morales says of her students: "Sometimes I think they tune out because they hear it so much." As a result, Morales admits that she sometimes deliberately uses synonyms for the virtues in an effort to keep her students fully engaged. On the other hand, when her students invoke one of the virtues in conversation, Morales notes, "Sometimes I need to ask again, 'So what do you really mean by that? What do you mean you weren't respecting somebody else? Do you really know what you did wrong?'" She fears that, in some cases, the language of the virtues replaces genuine reflection rather than enhancing it. This concern is seconded by teacher Shauvon Ames, who notes, "There are some kids who are very, very thoughtful, and there are some kids who are like, 'okay, I know this language, let me use the language.' And we have to prompt them to make sure it's connected to them as opposed to just . . . using the language fluently." In short, then, a common vocabulary is no guarantee that every discussion of moral matters will be fruitful; however, at Boston Prep, the common language of the virtues plays an important role in helping students and faculty members to learn deeply from each other's praise, feedback, and perspectives.

## ENGAGING IN REFLECTION

The opportunities for conversation and interaction around a common vocabulary represent a powerful lever for students' character development. Another such lever is the reflective writing in which students engage at the conclusion of every ethics unit. As eighth grader Robert explains, "Every unit [of ethics class] is based on one virtue, and at the end of that unit we have an essay, which is called the treatise. And, basically, we give examples from our real lives about how we've shown this virtue or what we can do to help make the virtue more a part of our lives." A number of middle schoolers admitted that the virtue they struggle with the most is respect. Sixth-grade student Re'Shon says that, on a recent treatise, "what I wrote about was responding to my parents when they say something to me. Like trying not to respond too much about what they say. Sometimes they might aggravate me because sometimes parents say the same thing over and over again, and it kind of gets annoying." Seventh-grade student Cara adds, "I decided to write about respect because I need to be more respectful towards my teachers, my parents, and people around me in class." She believes that the treatises assigned in ethics class are useful "because when you reflect on your behavior, it gives you motivation to want to do better because you see what you've done."

Tenth-grade student Brandi voices agreement with Cara about the value of reflective writing. While not always appreciative of ethics class as a middle schooler, Brandi explains that "over the years now, looking back, I'm like, look at how it's been beneficial for me to write essays, you know, just kind of think more thoroughly about things." Like a number of high school students, Brandi cites courage as the virtue about which she is currently most reflective: "I wrote [recently] about my growth in courage. But it's funny because I think I've grown a little bit in courage, but at the same time I feel like I'm lacking in it. I feel like I'm taking leadership within classes and participating, but when it comes to it, I'm scared of people judging me, especially in school." Similarly, tenth-grade student Jorge explains that, in a recent reflection assignment, "what I said was that I needed to grow in courage. I have the traditional courage, you know, speaking up to people I don't know, representing the school as an ambassador and being that leader. But then courage according to Socrates, like I don't have that courage. Every time I have the chance to do something, I step back because I'm afraid of what people will think and what they're going to say, and all my life I've been like that."

Much of the contemporary research on adolescent identity development focuses on the ways in which new social media such as Facebook and MySpace encourage adolescents to articulate various aspects of their identities, including preferences in music, television, cinema, friends, quotations, and causes.[18] Likewise, online blogs have been shown to explicitly promote identity development by providing adolescents with opportunities to record and reflect upon their daily experiences, personal relationships, aspirations, challenges, and frustrations.[19] In so doing, these new social media provide adolescents with a virtual space to reflect and make decisions about who they are and what they value.

In a deliberately low-tech fashion, Boston Prep's ethics class offers students a similar opportunity for reflection upon their beliefs and values. As previously described, students complete each unit in ethics class by writing a treatise in which they link their newfound understanding of a particular virtue to actual circumstances in their own lives. The term *treatise* strives to connect students' reflective writing to the work of ancient philosophers rather than a modern digital society, but these assignments share similarities as well with the new social media in which students are also engaging. As with their social profiles on Facebook and MySpace, Boston Prep students are asked in their treatises to articulate who they are and what they believe in—to make decisions about the identity they present to the world. Similar to a blog that invites comments from an online audience, Boston Prep students receive feedback from advisors and classmates on the subject matter within their treatises. In her scholarship on adolescents and blogging, Katie Davis writes that blogging "supports the critical task of identity formation by making it possible for individuals to form a theory of themselves and their role in society."[20] While Davis's work focuses explicitly on online reflection, her description is perhaps even more apropos for the treatise assignments embedded in Boston Prep's ethics class, as these assignments directly engage students in reflection upon issues of moral character.

Of course, one significant difference between the treatise assignments in which students participate at Boston Prep and their online opportunities for identity exploration is that students regard their online spaces as free from the watchful eyes of parents, teachers, and other adults. The treatises, on the other hand, are explicitly written as part of a school assignment for a formal class. As a result, eighth-grade teacher Kelsey Morales admits that she worries one hindrance to students' reflection in ethics class is their desire to write what they believe their teachers want to read. According to Morales, "They know what a teacher wants to hear. Because they know what's considered a really good example of courage versus not a good example of courage. I think they want to do it quickly and get it out of the way. They want a good grade most of the time, and I think it's hard to be reflective at the age of twelve." Teacher Shauvon Ames expresses a similar concern and describes a recent conversation with one of her students in which she told him, "You're making this sound good, but this is not genuine. So, where's the genuine story? And the genuine story might not be so fantastic, but where is the real story?"

The challenge—at least for Boston Prep middle school students—of engaging in earnest reflection about their moral character is underscored by eighth-grade parent Karen Clements. Clements describes how she handles instances where her daughter feels uncertain about *how* to reflect on her relationship to one of the virtues: "So what we'll do is maybe go over the events of the day or throughout the week and see if she can pick something where she lived up to that virtue or wasn't able to live up to that virtue as an individual. Or what she's seen other people doing that weren't living up to the virtues." Despite her daughter's occasional difficulty, Clements notes, "I have to say over these three years, she has a larger vocabulary on these values. And she can pick them out and knows when something's not right." It would seem, then, that—though not entirely seamless—the writing in which Boston Prep students engage in ethics class provides a space for earnest reflection upon who they are and how they fit into the world around them, the two questions that psychologist Erik Erikson famously characterized as the central concerns of adolescence.[21]

## CHAPTER THREE

# Walk in Another's Shoes

In a February ethics class, Boston Prep ninth graders began a unit on compassion by delving into a passage from Aristotle's *Nicomachean Ethics* on true friendship, or what Aristotle refers to as *philia*.[1] Head of School and ninth-grade ethics teacher Scott McCue explained to his students, "Philia is a bond that connects two humans who have any significant relationship with one another. Philia involves one person desiring the good of another, for the sake of another. For example, if *A* and *B* are in a relationship with true philia, then *A* will wish the best for *B*, and not because *A* wants anything in return for his kindness. *A* wants what's best for *B* for the sake of *B* . . . We can learn a lot about the virtue of compassion by studying Aristotle's account of philia in *Nicomachean Ethics*."

In *Nicomachean Ethics*, Aristotle distinguishes true friendships from those of utility and pleasure. As a means of grasping these distinctions, Boston Prep ninth graders watched several short video clips and then discussed the type of friendship depicted in each. One clip portrayed a friendship of pleasure between NASCAR drivers Ricky Bobby and Cal Naughton Jr. in the 2006 film comedy *Talladega Nights*. A second clip depicted a friendship of utility between Woody the cowboy and Buzz Lightyear in the 1995 animated film *Toy Story*. This introduction to Aristotle's taxonomy of friendships allowed for a much deeper investigation of the concept of philia the following week in ethics class.

When Boston Prep ninth graders walked into ethics class the following week, a "Do Now" assignment was already waiting for them on the
whiteboard. The assignment read: "Ralph Waldo Emerson said, 'The only
way to have a friend is to be a friend.' In your journal, put this quote into
your own words and explain what Emerson means." Mr. McCue gave his
students five minutes to respond to the prompt in their journals and then
began class with a follow-up question: "This is a simple line with rich
meaning. What does it mean?"

"In order to be friends with someone," one student volunteered, "you
have to be a friend."

Another suggested, "You're friends with them because of how they are,
not because of what you think you should do."

"I agree," a third student said. "To have a good friend and know that
friend is real, genuine, you have to be a friend to that person as well. Like
the golden rule."

"What does this quote from Emerson have to do with what Aristotle
said about friendship?" Mr. McCue asked. "If I'm a fun person with a nice
car and I throw wonderful parties, what's wrong with me thinking that'll
give me friends?"

A student waved her hand emphatically. "That's not true friendship for
Aristotle. To Aristotle, friendship is shared character."

Mr. McCue nodded. "What do I need to do then if I really want friends?"

"Be yourself," one student suggested.

"Do what you normally do," added another.

"I think there's more to it," Mr. McCue prodded.

"If they do things for you, do things for them," volunteered a student.

Another student raised her hand to speak. "Aristotle said that in every
way each friend gets the same thing. In order to have a friend, give the
same caring to them."

The student beside her chimed in: "You know what you said about parties? If you party all the time, you have connections, but are those party
people who come to your house really your friends?"

After a few more comments, Mr. McCue handed out an additional excerpt from *Nicomachean Ethics* and then divided the class into groups to

delve into particular portions of the reading. After ten minutes of group work, the class reconvened to continue their discussion. A student raised her hand. "I didn't understand why Aristotle said bad people can't have philia," she said, referring to the reading. "Why couldn't a bad person just have philia with another bad person?"

"Good question," Mr. McCue told her. Then he addressed the entire class. "Everyone point to a friend in the room." The classroom quickly transformed into a sea of arms. Jasmine—the young woman who had asked the question—pointed to her friend Sheryl, sitting a few rows away. Mr. McCue turned back to Jasmine. "I heard Sheryl say she doesn't really like you," he said. "You must have been in the bathroom when Sheryl said, 'I don't like her. I'm tired of her.'" Mr. McCue paused for a moment as the rest of the class listened in fascination. "Jasmine, do you believe me?"

Jasmine shook her head. "I just don't."

"How do you know?" Mr. McCue prodded. "You weren't there."

"I know she's a good friend," Jasmine insisted.

Another young woman raised her hand to help Jasmine out. "Jasmine knows Sheryl has good character," she added.

Mr. McCue nodded emphatically. "That's the key," he said. "According to Aristotle, bad people have friendships based on utility, and so they are vulnerable to slander. Since Jasmine knows that Sheryl has integrity and respect, she knows that Sheryl's character is true, and that she wouldn't do that."

Another young woman raised her hand to ask a question. "What about saying something to someone's face?" she asked. "Couldn't that be true friendship?"

Mr. McCue opened up the question to the class. A young man piped up, "I have friends and associates. If I'm struggling in Latin, I'll use associates for utility. I'm still going to keep it real with them, but I'm not telling them my life story. But if it's a best friend, it's hard to say something because you don't want to hurt that person's feelings. There's a line between being fake and telling someone the truth."

"Remember from October what Aristotle said about the magnanimous person?" Mr. McCue asked the class. "If you are a magnanimous person, you wouldn't hesitate to tell the truth."

"What if your friend gets angry with you for telling the truth?" a student asked.

"If it's a true philia friendship," Mr. McCue answered, "then that person will appreciate the truth." He cleared his throat. "I have one last question for you to think about. What's wrong with friendships based upon pleasure or utility?" He took a moment to scan the classroom and then added, "Let's hear from some people we haven't heard from today."

A young man sitting in the back of the classroom raised his hand. "Once you run out of advantages, then you run out of friends, so you can't really rely on them."

"Fake friendships dissolve," volunteered another student. "What's the point of having a friendship like that?"

"I agree," said a third student. "Friendships based on utility won't last because you don't really like them for who they are. You just like them because they entertain you."

Mr. McCue took a few more comments and then brought the class to a close. "For homework," he explained, "you're going to read an excerpt from a book called *The Pact*. It describes three doctors who grew up in a difficult neighborhood in Newark, New Jersey, and developed a relationship that I think is a good example of philia. Read it, and we'll talk about it next week."

## MEASURING EMPATHY

In chapter 2, we sought to demonstrate that the emphasis at Boston Prep upon moral character development had a significant effect upon students' commitment to acting with integrity—a moral character strength. We turn our attention now to Boston Prep's impact upon students' empathy—another moral character strength.

Empathy can be defined as a tendency to react to another's experiences.[2] A growing body of research suggests that empathy is positively associated with prosocial behaviors and negatively associated with antisocial behaviors. For example, several scholars have found that empathy is an important ingredient in building and maintaining peer relationships in adolescence.[3]

Children with high levels of empathy are more likely to help a classmate being bullied and less likely to engage in bullying themselves.[4] Other scholars
have found that individuals with high levels of empathy are more likely to
engage in volunteer work, return incorrect change, give money to a homeless person, do a favor for a friend, and donate money to charity.[5]

While there was significant debate in the 1970s and 1980s about
whether empathy was a cognitive trait or an affective trait, there is growing consensus in the research literature that empathy is a multidimensional construct with both cognitive and affective components.[6] The
cognitive dimension of empathy is an individual's ability to engage in
*perspective taking*—to view situations from a third-person perspective by
taking account of one's own and others' subjective perspectives.[7] The affective component of empathy includes feelings of warmth, compassion,
and concern for others.[8]

The survey administered to students at Boston Prep, Roxbury Prep, and
Pacific Rim at the beginning and conclusion of the school year included
items adapted from the Children's Empathic Attitudes Questionnaire developed by Jeanne Funk et al.[9] These items solicited students' agreement
or disagreement along a five-point Likert scale with several statements describing the extent to which students experienced distress when witnessing
an upset classmate, a classmate without any friends, or a classmate who
has gotten into trouble. All together, these items formed a robust composite of the moral character strength of empathy.[10]

As noted in chapter 2, we analyzed students' pre- and post-intervention survey data by fitting a multilevel regression model that compared
the shifts in empathy of students across the three schools over the course
of the school year. While there were no significant differences in students
across the three schools at the middle school level, we found that Boston
Prep high school students demonstrated significantly ($p < .05$) larger shifts
in empathy over the course of the academic year than their peers at Pacific
Rim (Roxbury Prep does not yet extend to the high school grades).[11] Put
more simply, students at Boston Prep demonstrated, on average, larger increases in empathy over the course of the school year than their peers at
Pacific Rim.

The effect of attending Boston Prep upon participating students' empathy scores can be characterized as a small one.[12] As noted in chapter 2, however, it is important to bear in mind that the school to which Boston Prep is being compared is another high performing urban school with its own explicit commitment to character development. In other words, comparing the increases in empathy of Boston Prep students to their peers at *all* Boston high schools might well have demonstrated that the curriculum and practices at Boston Prep have an even more robust effect upon the empathy of participating students. In the remainder of this chapter, we seek to highlight the explicit curricular and pedagogical practices that contribute to Boston Prep's significant effect upon a second moral character strength of its student body.

## TEACHING COMPASSION

The affective dimension of empathy—compassion—is one of Boston Prep's five key virtues. As a result, Boston Prep students at every grade level engage in a unit of study in ethics class focused on this moral character virtue. As noted in chapter 2, Boston Prep deliberately structures these units so that they move from highly concrete in the middle school grades to more abstract in the high school grades. The goal is to expose students at every grade to ethical content that aligns with their cognitive development.[13]

In the sixth-grade ethics classes, Boston Prep students learn that compassion means being kind to other people and helping them out. Teacher Kelsey Morales explains, "We emphasize the small things you can do in the sixth grade such as, like when you go home and your mother is having to work late, and you know the dishwasher needs to be emptied, you just do it, not because you're going to get allowance money for it, but because you know you've got to help your family." Lessons involving such concrete examples of compassionate behavior are the type most likely to be instructive for youth in what Jean Piaget refers to as the "concrete operational" stage of cognitive development. In this developmental stage, youth are gaining the ability to view a situation from another's perspective; however, they do not yet possess the ability to grapple with the abstract or theoretical.[14]

Boston Prep eighth grader Robert explains that in the seventh and eighth grades—a period in which youth are transitioning from concrete operational to formal operational thinking—students learn a new definition of compassion focused on "helping people in a way that they can be successful." In the seventh grade, this development in students' understanding of compassion occurs through a series of lessons distinguishing compassion from pandering. As seventh-grade teacher Mr. Jonas explained to his students in one ethics class, "Pandering is when you give something to someone that is not in their best interests. It's something they want, but don't need." As part of this lesson, students went on to read the Langston Hughes short story "Thank You, Ma'am," in which an older woman shows compassion to a young boy who has tried to steal her purse by bringing him home for a hot shower and home-cooked meal. The following week in ethics class, students discussed whether a series of short vignettes constituted examples of compassion or pandering. One of the vignettes involved a student named Daniel who was struggling in his science class. His teacher decided to give him an A because she felt sorry for him. "How is this pandering?" Mr. Jonas asked his seventh graders.

One student explained, "The teacher is only trying to make Daniel happy because she pities him, but she is not helping him."

"She feels sorry for him," volunteered another student. "When you feel sorry for someone, you do what you have to do."

"Even give him the grade if he doesn't deserve it?" Mr. Jonas prodded.

"Yeah," the student responded.

Mr. Jonas shook his head. "Really? What happens when that student goes to college and hasn't learned what he is supposed to know already?" Sensing that his seventh graders were still shaky on the distinction between compassion and pandering, Mr. Jonas diverged from the lesson plan and asked students to brainstorm additional examples of pandering. The idea of privileging what would be best for a person in the long term, at the expense of his or her short-term happiness, was a challenging concept for students just beginning to develop their abstract thinking skills.

Students' continued cognitive development between the seventh and eighth grades is evident in the ways the eighth-grade ethics curriculum seeks to connect the virtue of compassion to the highly abstract concept of altruism. In one lesson, Boston Prep eighth graders learned about Martin Niemöller, a Protestant pastor living in Germany in the 1930s. A member of the Nazi party, Niemöller did not initially protest Hitler's persecution of the Jews and other minority groups until the Nazis assumed state control over German churches. Niemöller was ultimately arrested and sent to a concentration camp himself, about which he later famously wrote, "Then they came for me. And there was no one left to speak out for me."[15]

After they read about Martin Niemöller, Ms. Morales asked her eighth-grade students, "What's the most difficult kind of altruism?"

"Helping someone you don't know," a student volunteered.

"Did Martin Niemöller practice altruism toward non-Christians?" Ms. Morales followed up.

"I said, no," volunteered one student.

Another added, "He wanted to help, but not until he was in the concentration camps."

"I think it was too late," agreed another. Several more students expressed their opinions, and then Ms. Morales pushed her students to reflect upon the extent to which they personally behaved altruistically toward individuals, like sixth graders, whom they might not know very well. A number of boys in Ms. Morales's class pushed back against this idea that they should come to the aid of students they did not even know.

"We study it, but we don't really do it," one young man explained. "Because if you see two people fighting outside, you're not going to be altruistic and ask them to stop fighting."

Over the next several weeks, the ethics lessons continued to push up against the eighth graders' beliefs about the appropriate recipients of altruism. For example, in one lesson students read an excerpt from Senator John McCain's book, *Character Is Destiny*, which discusses Mahatma Gandhi's commitment to showing compassion to his enemies as a young man living in apartheid South Africa.[16] The majority of Boston Prep eighth graders balked at the idea of acting similarly toward their own enemies.

One student explained, "In elementary school, there were two girls who I tried to show compassion to, and they thought I was weak and started picking on me more."

"I couldn't show respect to someone who didn't respect me," volunteered another.

When a third student described her willingness to stand up for a friend being teased about her hair, Ms. Morales responded, "I think it's great you can stand up for friends. I think it's even harder to stand up for someone who isn't your friend, and we're going to try and work on the concept of compassion even for people who are not *your* people."

A week later, students considered Plato's assertion that justice is favoring the interests of the weaker. In this lesson, students read a short vignette in which a shy student named Gabriella was reluctant to join Marla and a larger group of girls during recess. After identifying Marla as the "stronger" and Gabriella as the "weaker" within the vignette, Ms. Morales asked her class, "What could the stronger do to show compassion for the weaker?"

"Marla could invite her into the conversation," volunteered one young man.

"A little thing like that could change someone's day or even their whole year," Ms. Morales agreed. "What if Gabriella becomes great friends with someone in that group? It's like a compassion chain reaction."

"But that's like the littlest thing in the world," interjected a young lady. "There are always circles of people, and you just walk right up to them."

"I think you have a lot more confidence than most people," Ms. Morales reminded her. "For me, that would be hard. And especially me as a middle schooler."

As is evident in these discussions, a number of Boston Prep middle schoolers expressed uncertainty about the lessons on compassion to which they were exposed in ethics class. Especially for those students who are only just beginning to think beyond the self, the idea of showing compassion to strangers, and even enemies, can be genuinely perplexing. Perhaps as a result of this uncertainty—despite the explicit lessons in ethics class—Boston Prep middle schoolers showed no significant differences in their empathy scores than their peers at Roxbury Prep or Pacific Rim.

However, these initial conversations about compassion in Boston Prep's ethics classes are important stepping-stones to the more complex philosophical discussions awaiting Boston Prep students in high school.

One such philosophical discussion was presented at the outset of this chapter, and a number of Boston Prep high school students characterized the ethics lessons on philia as having had a significant impact upon their worldviews. Ninth grader Colleston explains, "I think we really [already] know, 'Oh, this person may not be a true friend,' but we don't really know what to call it or how to categorize it, and I think that [ethics] unit and the reflection also helped me realize, well, according to Aristotle's standards, this person isn't really my true friend. They're just here for fun." Likewise, ninth grader Eddie says that ethics class has "definitely helped me pick out who my real friends are, and who are the people I need to cut off."

On the other hand, ninth grader Fletcher notes that the ethics lessons on compassion and philia taught him that *he* needed to make changes in his approach to friendships: "The whole friendship philia thing gave me a better understanding of what a true friendship is because . . . before, for me, it was based on utility and all that other stuff. But now I know how to fix my friendships, and it's been going great since I have an idea of what true friendship is." According to these students, learning about Aristotle's taxonomy of the different types of friendships exerted a genuine influence upon their attitudes and actions within their own relationships.

How precisely did these lessons on philia link to the virtue of compassion? After ethics lessons that helped Boston Prep ninth graders to distinguish between true friendships and those of utility and pleasure, students read an excerpt from *The Pact*, a nonfiction account published in 2003 by three African American men from Newark, New Jersey, who had delivered on a pact they made as teenagers to support each other in their joint goal of becoming medical doctors.[17] All three men had grown up in single-family households in neighborhoods filled with drugs and violence, and two had served time in jail as teenagers. In an interview with the *New York Times*, one of the men, Dr. Rameck Hunt, explains, "It's not like we had the support from home or a whole lot of mentors. We leaned on each other."[18] The philia evident in these men's relationships with one another is particularly notable given the research findings that exposure to violence is associated with lower levels of empathy.[19] Studies showing that 70–80 percent of urban teens have witnessed violent acts themselves only increase the importance of lessons like this one, which seek to strengthen Boston Prep students' own commitment to empathic, caring friendships.[20]

In the discussion in ethics class about *The Pact*, one student asked Mr. McCue, "What if you have a true friendship with someone, but that person gets very high honors, and you get high honors? Shouldn't you be just a little jealous so you can try to do better if it's a true friendship?"

"Aristotle would say no," Mr. McCue explained matter-of-factly. "He would say, 'Don't be jealous.'"

"I don't think there is any type of friendship without a little bit of jealousy," another student interjected. As the discussion moved forward, one could see and hear Boston Prep students grappling with precisely what it means to be a true friend and source of support to someone else. Psychologists Michael Nakkula and Eric Toshalis have observed that "empathy and compassion develop alongside the adolescent's ability to recognize and incorporate the needs of others."[21] Whether or not Boston Prep ninth graders agreed entirely with Aristotle's conception of philia, their investigation into the nature of true friendships contributed to significant increases over the course of the school year in their commitment to acting empathically.

## MAKING SENSE OF THE WORLD

Psychologist Erik Erikson famously characterized adolescence as the developmental period in which individuals move beyond a blind adherence to the beliefs and values of their nuclear family, and begin seeking out additional ways of understanding the world around them.[22] In so doing, adolescents confront for the first time the questions "Who am I?" and "How do I fit into the world around me?" Erikson suggested that, in order to address these questions, youth require exposure to "values and ideologies that transcend the immediate concerns of family and self and have historical continuity."[23] Sources of such ideas include "religion and politics, the arts and sciences, the stage and fiction."[24]

Erikson did not cite ethical philosophy as a source of exposure for adolescents to new values and ideologies, but the Boston Prep ethics class unequivocally exposes students to the frameworks through which a variety of philosophers and thinkers sought to make sense of the world. One could reasonably argue, then, that ethics class offers participating students a variety of lenses for examining the world around them at the very moment that these adolescents are beginning to seek out new perspectives and points of view.

At the high school level, one clear example of the way in which ethics class offers Boston Prep students a framework for reflecting upon both their actions and the world around them is Aristotle's taxonomy of friendships. As noted in the preceding section, a number of Boston Prep students characterize this taxonomy as offering them a framework and a language for evaluating the quality of friendships in their own lives. A second example can be found in the tenth-grade students' investigation in ethics class of Stoicism. As the students learned, the Stoic philosophers—and most famously, Epictetus—believed that negative emotions such as fear or sadness were caused by people's incorrect interpretations of the world around them.[25] In other words, individuals possess the ability to experience every situation in their lives as either an opportunity for growth and learning *or* anxiety and difficulty.

As part of their study of Stoicism, Boston Prep tenth graders learned about the experiences of Admiral James Stockdale, a decorated soldier and 1992 vice presidential candidate, who credited Stoicism with allowing him to survive seven years as a prisoner of war during the Vietnam War. Students also studied the writings of Tookie Williams, a founder of the Los Angeles Crips street gang, who chose to turn his years on California's death row into a positive experience for the world by becoming an advocate against gang violence. Perhaps most interestingly, Boston Prep tenth graders read and discussed a 1960 speech by Martin Luther King Jr. in which King revealed, "My personal trials have taught me the value of unmerited suffering. As my sufferings mounted, I soon realized that there were two ways I could respond to my situation: either to react with bitterness or seek to transform the suffering into a creative force." Drawing upon their ability to practice third-person perspective taking, Boston Prep high school students discussed the extent to which Stoic philosophy aligned with King's commitment to nonviolent protest as well as the potential for Stoic thinking within their own lives.[26]

A number of Boston Prep students describe as profound the impact of Stoicism upon their own worldviews. Tenth-grade student Jorge explains, "At first I disagreed with it, but now actually I agree with it. I feel like suffering in life . . . causes you to grow up, ponder the situation, and just use the suffering to become a better person and know how to handle the situation next time." Likewise, his classmate Brandi says that studying Stoicism increased her commitment to "taking responsibility for your own actions and, like, even if you fail, kind of learning [you're] just going to accept this and move on." She offers the example of doing poorly on a test for which she had put in significant time studying. In the past, Brandi characterized herself as someone who would have placed the blame on the teacher or the difficulty of the exam, but now she tries to tell herself, "It's time to grow up and just do better on the next test. And don't let it bring you down again."

Perhaps the Boston Prep student most enamored with Stoicism is tenth grader Nick, who characterizes Stoicism as "taking responsibility for your actions and not blaming anyone else" and notes, "I feel like that's played a really big part in my success now. I have honors [grades] now, and my behavior is better. Ethics class changes people and changes their perspective on things." Nick confesses that he recently went to the bookstore on his own volition to purchase a book on Epictetus: "If you had told me three years ago that I would be going to buy a book, period, then I probably wouldn't believe you. But I bought a couple philosophy books because I feel like it's playing a really big influence in my life." For each of these students, ethics class offers a new framework for making sense of the world and their role in it—the work that Erikson and his successors characterize as the central tasks of adolescence.

The ability of ethics class to provide Boston Prep students with a framework for reflecting upon the world around them is not limited to high school students. At the middle school level, one clear example of the way in which ethics class provides such a framework was evident in a seventh-grade ethics lesson that focused on differentiating between revenge and self-defense. The advisor, Eric Albans, began the class by asking students what they would do if someone hit them on the playground. "I would hit them back," one student volunteered, "and the consequences would be I would get suspended." A second student agreed: "If someone hit me, I would hit them back to defend myself. But you don't have the right to hit someone first."

As a means of exploring these concepts of revenge and self-defense, the students read a case study in which a fictional student named Ra-Isa hit another student, Kim, at recess for insulting her mother. Students then discussed this case within the context of an ethical framework they had already studied: Mahatma Gandhi's assertion that "an eye for an eye leaves the whole world blind." The following is an excerpt from this class discussion:

MR. ALBANS: What did Gandhi mean about "an eye for an eye leaves the whole world blind"?

STUDENT 1: More violence leads to more disrespect and doesn't solve anything.

STUDENT 2: If somebody is trying to attack you and you attack them back violently, then there is just more bloodshed.

MR. ALBANS: We talked about how violence can lead to a cycle where things just spin out of control. If Ra-Isa hits Kim, how would that make the situation worse?

STUDENT 3: If she punches Kim in the face, Kim will probably hit her back.

STUDENT 4: Ra-Isa hits Kim out of revenge but she thought she was defending herself.

MR. ALBANS: Why is it so difficult to solve conflicts nonviolently? Why do you think Ra-Isa confused self-defense and revenge?

STUDENT 3: Because you *want* revenge.

MR. ALBANS: Yes, why do you want revenge?

STUDENT 2: Because it's like human nature to want to hit someone when they say something to you.

MR. ALBANS: Yes, I like that reference to science. There are chemicals involved that make us want to hit someone back.

STUDENT 5: I have a little sister who gets on my nerves, and sometimes she does things that get me in trouble. And I started yelling at her, and my mom was like, "Don't do that, she's just a little kid." And I thought it was self-defense, but it was really revenge. I just wanted to hurt her because she got my phone taken away.

In this discussion, Mr. Albans helped students to distinguish between revenge and self-defense, and, later in the discussion, to consider ways in which violence can spin out of control when one seeks revenge. In response to this lesson, seventh-grade student Stephon notes, "If somebody hurts you, it does not mean you need to hurt them. 'Cause if you hurt them, you're not just hurting them, you're hurting everybody and yourself [as well]." Likewise, seventh grader Cara explains, "I learned that, it's like you don't have to always use violence to solve all your problems. Especially, like, if somebody's being violent towards you, there's other ways to handle it."

Such a framework for understanding conflict represents a sharp contrast to the ethical code that many Boston Prep students have learned from parents and peers. Eric Albans notes that when students at Boston Prep find themselves in trouble as a result of a peer conflict, "I'd say seventy to eighty percent of the cases, they're saying, 'Well, my parents say if I'm hit, I should hit back.'" Likewise, eighth-grade teacher Kelsey Morales says that one of the challenges in these types of discussions is that "as a school, I think we say that violence is not an answer, and they (the students) are saying, 'Well, you know, my mom said that's totally fine. And my family doesn't believe that, and so you can't really tell me to believe something that's different than my family.'"

The point in this example is *not* to assert that Boston Prep students must choose between the ethical codes offered by their school and their families. Rather, what Boston Prep's ethics class offers in this and other lessons is an additional framework for understanding the world and one's role in it. Just as standing up for oneself may be the most adaptive response to some situations, there is great value in students recognizing that there are other options in such circumstances. Building upon Erikson's work on adolescent identity development, Nakkula and Toshalis note that some of the existential questions that often become a part of the adolescent identity development process include: "How should I be in school relative to at home or with my friends? How do these different ways in which I am go together to create the complete me? How do I, or should I, do things differently in different places, different contexts?"[27] Ethics class gives Boston Prep students an opportunity to reflect upon questions that are already very much on their minds.

## TEACHING PERSPECTIVE TAKING

If compassion represents the affective dimension of empathy, recall that a student's ability to engage in perspective taking—to view situations from others' subjective perspectives—constitutes the cognitive dimension of empathy.[28] Perspective taking has been described colloquially as the ability to walk in another person's shoes, and the study of ethical philosophy affords Boston Prep students numerous opportunities for doing so. For example, in one ninth-grade ethics class, students learned about philosopher John Rawls's veil of ignorance as part of a lesson on cheating and integrity. As Scott McCue explained to his students, the veil of ignorance entails "imagining yourself in a different situation [in which] you don't know whether you'll be rich or poor, don't know if you will be powerful or weak. What conclusion does that lead you to? What should society do?" Students then drew upon this concept of the veil of ignorance to consider the consequences of cheating on a test from the perspective of other members of the class. In other words, how would students feel about the act of cheating if they didn't know whether they would be the cheater or simply another member of the class? Framed this way, perspective taking actually serves as the lever for applying Rawlsian principles to situations and decisions. In this example, one can see how the "cognitive awakening" in adolescence that allows individuals to engage in such perspective taking permits much deeper investigations of "core concerns such as existential meaning, purpose, truth, and identity."[29]

The role of perspective taking in considering such core concerns was also evident in the tenth-grade ethics unit on Stoicism described in the preceding section. For example, in one ethics lesson, Boston Prep students compared Stoic philosopher Epictetus's claim that all situations and circumstances are subject to interpretation to the philosophy espoused by former Los Angeles Crips gang member and death row inmate Tookie Williams. While on death row, Williams began to write letters and books for youth caught up in drugs, crime, and gang violence. In "My Letter to Incarcerated Youth, No. 1" he writes, "You or I can complain 24x7 about the problems of poverty, drugs, violence, racism and other injustices, but unless we choose to initiate a personal change, we will remain puppets of unjust conditions. Unless *we* change, we will be incapable of changing the circumstances around us." After reading this letter, Alex Leverett asked Boston Prep tenth graders, "Epictetus believed anything external was beyond our control, but Tookie Williams doesn't believe that. What does he believe?"

One student raised his hand. "In order to make changes to these problems, you must first change yourself and lead by example."

Another student added, "In order to change externals, you must change your internals."

"That's right," Mr. Leverett told them. "Tookie Williams says that his internal choices can affect the external. Epictetus says not really." Students debated the validity of these different perspectives until Mr. Leverett suggested, "Let's bring this home a little bit." He asked students to imagine being sent to Boston Prep's office for an offense that they may or may not have committed. "As you leave the classroom and enter Dean Melvin's office," Mr. Leverett asked, "what *don't* you have a choice about? What *do* you have a choice about?" Students brainstormed a list of externals that included Dean Melvin's perception of the situation, the accuracy of the teacher's account of the situation, stereotypical perceptions of teenagers, and the consequences handed down to them. Students next considered the internal factors over which they *did* have control—the attitude they took in Dean Melvin's office, the clarity with which they explained their perspective on what had happened, their ability to consider the perspective of the teacher who had sent them out of class, and the equanimity with which they responded to the consequences. As class wound down, Mr. Leverett noted: "I think that it is worthwhile to think deeply about why things happen the way they do in Mr. Melvin's office in terms of disagreements between teachers and students. Push past the thought that teachers are just trying to beat down on students. Think about what are the differences. Where do they come from? Then you can start to influence the opinions of teachers and Mr. Melvin. This is where I agree with Tookie Williams and disagree with Epictetus. You can influence the perceptions of others around you, and it is important to do so."

As made evident in Mr. Leverett's closing remarks, this ethics lesson engaged students in several different types of perspective taking. First, they considered the competing perspectives of Epictetus and Tookie Williams, and then moved on to the role of perspective taking in adjudicating a conflict between a teacher and themselves. In this latter case, Mr. Leverett sought to nurture in his students a "reciprocal" understanding of their interactions with faculty and administrators rather than a "unilateral" understanding. According to psychologist Robert Selman, reciprocal understanding is marked by the recognition that, in a given interaction, there are two or more individuals, each with his or her own wants and needs, whereas a unilateral perspective strongly emphasizes a single perspective.[30] Mr. Leverett recognized that his students' interactions with authority figures (and peers) would be significantly enhanced by their ability to consider the perspective of those with whom they were interacting.

Several Boston Prep students cite this practice in perspective taking to be the most important dimension of ethics class. Twelfth grader Flavia explains, "I think that the point of ethics class is to get to know who you really are and kind of like understand other people's views . . . I think it's kind of like getting you to explore how other people see life." Tenth grader Jorge notes, "Ethics class allows you to see different perspectives. Like you could be in a situation and you have your initial reaction, but being in ethics class you have this scenario and you have all these different perspectives of how to handle the situation." Finally, ninth grader Fletcher adds, "Everyone had a lot to say about ethics . . . and it's kind of interesting to see how other people think." As is evident in these students' comments, the process of adolescent identity development is greatly facilitated by adolescents' burgeoning ability to consider the perspectives of others and then to decide whether or not to assimilate those perspectives into their own emerging worldviews.[31]

Finally, a tenth-grade ethics lesson on the topic of one's reputation explicitly sought to tie the act of perspective taking to the virtue of compassion. For homework, students had read an excerpt from Epictetus's *Discourses* in which Epictetus noted that someone who slanders you is actually the wronged party, since he or she is a victim of misjudgment: "Setting out, then, from these principles, you will [be] gentle and forgiving to a person who reviles you, for you will say upon every occasion, 'It seemed so to him.'" When Mr. Leverett asked for students' opinions of this passage, a dozen indignant hands shot in the air.

"But sometimes people don't have a reason," one young man complained. "They say something just to be a jerk. There's no reason behind it."

"You don't have to agree with the reasons," Mr. Leverett reminded the class. "Epictetus would say to be kind and forgiving and not to act according to what you think is right, but what that other person thinks is right."

"Some people say things because it makes them feel better," another student noted.

"I don't think they should do that," Mr. Leverett agreed, "but I can try to see where they're coming from."

Another young woman waved her hand to speak. "I can think of someone who is constantly talking about me behind my back. She's insecure, trying to make herself feel better."

Mr. Leverett nodded. "Say another teacher was talking about me behind my back. In my mind, say he's doing that because he's insecure. He's threatened or intimidated by my prowess. What Epictetus is saying is that that teacher is suffering, and the response to the suffering of others is compassion. So if he's saying bad things about me out of insecurity, I need to be gentle, forgiving, and have compassion about his insecurity."

"But there's not a reason for everything!" another student protested. "Not everything you do always has a purpose!"

This tenth-grade ethics lesson explicitly sought to act as a lever for strengthening students' skill at perspective taking—the cognitive dimension of empathy—as well as students' commitment to treating others with compassion—the affective dimension of empathy. Such an explicit focus upon students' moral character development offers an explanation for the significant increases in empathy of Boston Prep high school students in comparison to their peers at Pacific Rim. Certainly, faculty and administrators at both schools seek to model empathy for their students and publicly reward examples of empathy among the student body. Boston Prep is unique, however, in explicitly engaging students in reflection upon the role of empathy in their interactions with others.

## ENCOURAGING STUDENT VOICE AND RESISTANCE

In the discussion of perspective taking in the tenth-grade ethics class just described, several students vehemently resisted both Alex Leverett's and Epictetus's claims about treating one's enemies with compassion and gentleness. Far from being evidence of the ineffectiveness of ethics class, this back-and-forth between Mr. Leverett and his tenth graders provides a valuable outlet for student voice and critical thinking in an otherwise tightly structured school day.

Boston Prep, Roxbury Prep, and Pacific Rim can all be characterized as emerging from the "no excuses" approach to teaching and learning. "No excuses" is a phrase originally coined by Samuel Casey Carter to describe high-poverty public schools featuring a strict disciplinary environment, extended time in school, and an intensive focus on traditional reading and mathematics skills.[32] The majority of "no excuses" schools could also be characterized as relying heavily upon teacher-led direct instruction as the most efficient means of delivering academic content to students. Aware that their students have a lot of ground to cover to narrow the achievement gap, teachers at such schools focus the bulk of their lessons on building academic skills, and the questions that they pose to students within these lessons typically have right and wrong answers. This is certainly the case at Boston Prep. However, both teachers and students at Boston Prep agreed that ethics class provides a much-needed opportunity for student voice and discussion. As teacher Kelsey Morales notes, the typical class at Boston Prep "is so skills-focused that [students are] not really debating things . . . So they really love [in ethics class] being able to have something where their personal opinion can always be there."

Boston Prep students at both the middle school and high school offer a similar perspective on the opportunities for student voice in ethics class. Eighth grader Robert characterizes ethics class as "a very outgoing class where you get to speak up, you get to share your opinions with everyone in your group . . . So for shy kids it's pretty easy to tell everyone what they have on their mind." Tenth-grade student Brandi adds that ethics class "is important because I feel like it's just another time for you to kind of express yourself and learn more from others." This sentiment is echoed by twelfth grader Abner: "I like that you can just go in [to ethics class] and speak your mind the way you feel about life and how people behave and all that stuff. You express yourself."

More than just providing an opportunity for student voice, ethics class also offers Boston Prep students a legitimate forum for questioning or pushing back against the ethical code championed by the school. Middle school principal Amanda Gardner characterizes Boston Prep as "highly structured" and an "efficient school" and notes that "it [is] great to have this safe, small space where you [can] teach students about why the virtue [is] really important for our community, and they [have] this space to push back." For example, in one of the antibullying lessons described in chapter 2, a seventh-grade student expressed his opinion that the student in the case study lacking virtue was actually the student *being bullied*: "He didn't try to get respect. He just let everyone do it, he let it happen."

Perhaps the most intriguing example of resistance was an eighth-grade ethics lesson just days before the Christmas break, in which students read a newspaper article about a homeless man who had delivered to police a wallet he found on the street, despite his own destitute condition and his inability to support two children from whom he was now estranged. The lesson positioned the homeless man as an exemplar of someone acting with integrity, but a number of students disagreed:

STUDENT 1: If you're homeless and are trying to survive, and you have nothing, how you can you survive if you're doing the right thing? You never know if that person will reward you for doing the right thing. You should probably take that chance of survival rather than doing the right thing at that point.

TEACHER: Is there any benefit to doing the right thing without getting a reward?

STUDENT 2: In this case, it's known that you did the right thing, but you're going to have a guilty conscience that you didn't provide for yourself or your own kids. He did the right thing, and he doesn't have a guilty conscience on that act. But he also has on his conscience that his kids are far away from him, and he can't buy for them what they need.

TEACHER: Does the amount of money matter? Is $170 going to make a big difference for his kids? Is it enough money to make a difference in the problems he is facing?

STUDENT 3: Yeah, the money is good because at McDonald's you could buy fast food for like two weeks. He could take a bus or a cheap flight on Southwest to see his kids. And he could just stay there.

STUDENT 4: Because you need to provide for your kids, right? I think he should help his kids as much as he can, and I think the thought counts. So giving the money to them is good.

In this excerpt, a number of students pushed back vigorously—and intellectually—against the conception of integrity implicit in their ethics lesson. Particularly fascinating about this example is the way it contradicts a point made by Boston Prep's head of school, Scott McCue: "I think a flaw sometimes in character education is people will talk about scenarios or ethical dilemmas which really aren't ethical dilemmas. You know, if you find a wallet sitting on the ground, what should you do with it? And that's not really a genuinely ethical dilemma. It's pretty clear what the moral mandate is in that case." Yet, in the preceding example, a number of Boston Prep students offered a passionate and well-reasoned argument against McCue's "clear moral mandate."

Ethics class also presents an opportunity for Boston Prep students to debate and push back against each other. For example, the discussion of the homeless man and the lost wallet really heated up when several other students countered that the homeless man *had* done the right thing by returning the wallet. Another eighth-grade ethics lesson focused on issues of equity by introducing students to Zimbabwean President Robert Mugabe's policy of redistributing farmland from wealthy white landowners to poorer black workers. In the ensuing discussion, one student volunteered, "I think it's fair but it's not just because [Mugabe] had to take it from the white people who worked for it to give to the poor people." Another student responded, "I disagree because black farmers work hard too. It's just that they weren't in the government at first. Basically it is fair now because both black people and white people have land." Similarly, in an eleventh-grade ethics class on libertarianism, students debated whether a basketball star earning more than $20 million a year, such as Kobe Bryant, should be obligated to give some of his income to individuals in need. Voicing the libertarian perspective, one student asserted, "Kobe is working hard, and he earned all the money he's getting, so no one should force him [to give away money]. It would be nice, but no one should force him." A smaller group of students objected. In one's words: "Look at the amount of people supporting him, buying his product, and the status he holds because he's a basketball player. We help him get the money he earns."

Boston Prep students describe these opportunities for debate as one of the most engaging aspects of studying ethics. Eleventh-grade student Wayne explains, "I like how sometimes we're able to debate about things because some kids in the class have completely different views about one topic and then others have a different opinion. And it's not like we're yelling at each other or anything. It's a time for us to feel where each other is really coming from." Ninth grader Alisha concurs: "Ethics class is a space where you're open to disagree or agree with somebody. You're not looked down upon when you disagree with somebody's idea or philosophy. You can debate, like go back and forth."

Adolescent development scholars characterize the opportunities for debate and resistance as crucial to students' development of a mature adult identity.[33] Recall Erikson's claim that adolescence is the developmental period in which individuals move beyond a blind adherence to the beliefs and values of their family members and teachers and, instead, begin to seek out new and different understandings of the world. Building on Erikson's framework, Nakkula and Toshalis add that "the very testing behaviors that historically have been either pathologized or dismissed as mere 'adolescent rebelliousness' are, rather, integral to an ongoing construction and interpretation of the developing self-in-the-world."[34] In other words, the resistance that Boston Prep students put forth in ethics class through "unpopular opinions, revolutionary ideas, [and] antiestablishment positions" can be regarded as a healthy and developmentally appropriate "trying on [of] possible selves."[35] Because Boston Prep is such a highly structured environment with strict guidelines for everything from students' dress to comportment, ethics class provides a crucial safety valve for student resistance.

Fortunately, many Boston Prep teachers recognize that student resistance in ethics class presents valuable opportunities for both character development and deep learning. As sixth-grade teacher Shauvon Ames notes, "I think probably the best classes are when I'm able to remove myself from the conversation, and the kids are kind of pushing back on each other. I think that's where the most learning happens." Another middle school teacher, Brian Mao, agrees that the best discussions in ethics class "are usually based on, okay, now we have these definitions that we agree on, that we want you to have. But what are those blurry boundaries that are confusing?" Likewise, eighth-grade advisor Jeffrey Granderson notes, "When kids are challenging the point of the lesson, I think those are the best discussions. Those are the moments when it becomes the most real . . . And I want ethics and advisory to be a safe space where kids can say, 'I didn't like this lesson. I don't agree with this point. I'm struggling with this. Kids in my neighborhood are doing this, and it goes totally against what we're learning here,' and like trying to help them make sense of that." In an otherwise highly structured school day, ethics class serves as a cauldron for students' identity and character development precisely *because of* the opportunities within the class for students to push back against their teachers, the Boston Prep code of conduct, and each other.

## TRANSFERRING CHARACTER

In *Nicomachean Ethics,* Aristotle wrote that the purpose of studying ethics is not "as it is in other inquiries, the attainment of theoretical knowledge: we are not conducting this inquiry in order to know what virtue is, but in order to become good, else there is no advantage to studying it."[36] Although Boston Prep students receive a letter grade each term for their work in ethics class that appears on their report cards alongside their other coursework, the effectiveness of ethics class ultimately rests in what students *do* with their newfound knowledge of a variety of philosophical perspectives.

This question of the *transferability* of the lessons in ethics class is one upon which Boston Prep faculty and administrators are constantly reflecting. Eighth-grade teacher Kelsey Morales says of her students, "We have the conversation a lot about how sometimes it seems like they're really making good ethical choices here, but the moment they walk out the door, there's somehow that separation." She adds that one of the primary objectives for the continued development of the ethics curriculum "is trying to figure out how to make that [curriculum] go with them and become a bigger part of who they are as a person, not just as a student here." Head of School Scott McCue spoke directly to students about this goal after a convenience store and restaurant near Boston Prep had complained about student behavior after school hours. As McCue noted to the entire student body, "There are all sorts of things happening [at Boston Prep] that can burnish or compromise our reputation . . . We had a difficult week last week outside the walls of Boston Prep, particularly in the neighborhood of Boston Prep." Reflecting on this talk, administrator Jeffrey Granderson notes, "What Mr. McCue was talking about . . . I think, is, how does the culture of the school get extended outside the walls of the school, past the hours of 8:00 a.m. and 4:15 p.m.? And our kids are asked to do so much within the walls of the school and, in many cases, to live an identity very different to that from the neighborhoods they're coming from. And so how to make those things line up is a big struggle."

Both chapters 2 and 3 began with a description of the ways in which Boston Prep students maintained higher levels of integrity and empathy over the course of the academic year than their peers at two other high performing schools, as measured by pre- and post-intervention surveys. Certainly these data provide valuable information about the ways in which Boston Prep is influencing the moral character of its student body. The chapter closes, however, with qualitative accounts by Boston Prep students and parents of how they understand the school's ethics program to have influenced the students' moral character development.

It should be noted that none of these students or parents cite Boston Prep's focus on moral character as part of their original motivation to enter the registration lottery to attend the school. Nearly without exception, parents and students attribute their initial interest in Boston Prep to its reputation as a safe school within the city of Boston and, additionally, as one that offers a rigorous academic program capable of preparing students for college. Nonetheless, the majority of students and parents who participated in qualitative interviews cite ethics class—and Boston Prep's broader focus on moral character—as having had a profound effect upon the students' development.

Perhaps the most compelling explanations by Boston Prep students of the impact of ethics class upon their beliefs and actions are those in which students can articulate precisely *how* the class has impacted them. For example, tenth-grade student Brandi says of the ethics lessons on integrity: "We're not saying we're complete saints or anything, but if you're going to go with the decision of cheating or not, that comes into your head. You're thinking 'Oh my God, what is this going to affect?' You kind of think of everything instead of just doing it and thinking 'I don't care.' Everyone gets that feeling, and I think it comes from ethics class." On a similar note, twelfth-grade student Lena explains how ethics class helped her to recognize the moral dimensions of everyday decisions and behaviors: "I think everybody sees ethics around them all the time, but they don't know it because they're not knowledgeable about it. And I think when you take ethics class, it kind of just opens your mind to how like the small little thought you had about picking up that pencil [for someone] was compassion."

Ninth-grade student Alisha credits ethics class with improving her ability to make ethical decisions. She explains that the point of ethics class is not to teach students the difference between right and wrong but, rather, "to enhance those senses, to make them stronger, and allow us to make better decisions." Eighth grader Jessenia believes that "if we didn't have courage, we probably wouldn't be as productive in class, and if we didn't have compassion, we wouldn't really connect with our friends. So having ethics class kind of reminds people every week about what we're here to do and how we should treat other people." Offering evidence for Jessenia's claim is her classmate, Robert, who adds, "Since sixth grade, I've actually seen people become better people . . . because ethics class has helped people understand how we should act and how we should treat other people." Likewise, sixth grader Re'Shon cites herself as an example, saying, "Something funny happened at [the last] community meeting that someone did, and like everyone started laughing, but I tried not to laugh because that might have made the person feel embarrassed about themselves. Since it was in front of the whole school, they might have felt disrespected." In this explanation, Re'Shon offers a concrete example of the way in which ethics class has influenced not only her knowledge of the five virtues, but her day-to-day efforts to exemplify them as well.

Boston Prep middle school students tend to describe the effects of ethics class upon their behavior within the walls of Boston Prep; however, a number of high school students characterize their knowledge of the virtues to be particularly helpful outside of school. Tenth grader Nick explains that lessons about the virtues "come up more outside of Boston Prep than inside of Boston Prep because when you're in Boston Prep, you don't need to think about the virtues because you're surrounded by everyone else that's trying to be virtuous. Outside the school, you have to think more about—is this a good idea or a bad idea? Is this ethical or is it not ethical?" His classmate Jorge adds, "Outside of school, the virtues play even more of a role because when you're outside of school, you have the freedom to either do what's virtuous and ethical or do what you're accustomed to, what your initial reaction is." According to Jorge, "Being in ethics class, you have all these different perspectives of how to handle the situation. You know, [like] hitting someone that hit you first, you're going to do something else instead of doing the obvious thing." In these comments, both Nick and Jorge suggest that ethics class plays a role in helping them to stop and think about the ethical implications of different types of behaviors in which they might otherwise engage.

Several Boston Prep parents also describe ways in which they see Boston Prep's focus on moral character impacting their children's actions. Eighth-grade parent Karen Clements says, "I think having ethics class is meaningful, and I think that it has absolutely helped Alicia in her understanding of what these values mean and how she can identify them in her everyday life." Lesley Wilson—the mother of a sixth grader and a ninth grader at Boston Prep—elaborates: "My oldest daughter thinks that it helps build a person . . . If she's hanging out with her friends, she'll say, 'Hmmm, you are not showing compassion. Hmmm, that is not respect.' You know, she's using them in her everyday language and her everyday life." These explanations by Boston Prep parents are perhaps the most powerful testament of all to Boston Prep's success in fostering the moral character of its students. As we'll discuss in succeeding chapters that focus on Roxbury Prep and Pacific Rim, there are numerous ways for schools to nurture the character development of their students. However, for those educators, parents, and policy makers committed to promoting moral character strengths such as integrity and compassion, there is much to learn from the ways in which Boston Prep has integrated the direct teaching of virtues with deep inquiry into moral matters.

# PERFORMANCE CHARACTER
## AT ROXBURY PREP

CHAPTER FOUR

# Prepare to Perform

Roxbury Prep faculty and administrators went all out for the last community meeting before the February vacation. Colorful streamers and balloons dangled from the ceiling. An enormous orange banner that stretched across the front of the auditorium read "Express Yourself!" in big blue letters. A plastic "red carpet" ran the length of the auditorium's wide center aisle. Poster board affixed to the walls reminded students to be mindful of their volume, eye contact, expression, and pacing.

As students streamed silently into the auditorium and took their seats, an eighth-grade teacher, Ms. Ferrara, said loudly to her students, "I know you're all nervous, but I respect the maturity I'm seeing." Two eighth-grade students—a boy and a girl—stood at the lectern in the front of the auditorium, waiting for everyone to be seated. A few minutes later, with a nod from School Codirector Will Austin, they got things going.

"Good afternoon, Roxbury Prep!" the girl spoke enthusiastically into the microphone. "Welcome to the fifth annual Roxbury Prep Powerful Speaking Extravaganza! My name is Jaivona, and I'm thrilled to be cohosting the event with my fellow positive leader, Nelson. We all chose a piece from a genre we liked—song, poem, part of a play, piece of fiction. Students spent weeks practicing, and now we're ready to go!"

Nelson leaned into the microphone. "Raise your hand if you're nervous," he asked. Nearly every student raised a hand upward. "It's really good we're here then," Nelson told the audience, "to overcome that fear. Today's event is not about speaking perfectly but about trying your best and getting better. Congratulations to everyone for being willing to try." The entire student body applauded thunderously.

When the noise subsided, Jaivona added, "Let's give a warm welcome to each of our distinguished judges." Two young women in their early twenties and an older gentleman in his forties or fifties stepped forward to introduce themselves. The two young ladies had graduated from Roxbury Prep in 2002 and were now in college. The older gentleman was an attorney in Boston who also served as a mentor in Roxbury Prep's "Real Men Read" program. After introducing himself, he added, "Public speaking is a part of my job every day. At some point, you will need to convince a group of people that you are correct, and you will need the skill to do that. So I applaud all of you."

Then Jaivona explained how the Powerful Speaking Extravaganza worked. "In these bags, we have the names of every Roxbury Prep student. If your name is called, you are a winner, and you will come on down and read your piece powerfully to the community. Judges will be giving you feedback and, later, awarding prizes."

And then they were under way. The first winner of the Extravaganza was an eighth grader, who recited Dylan Thomas's "Do Not Go Gentle Into That Good Night." The audience—particularly her eighth-grade peers—cheered wildly when she finished. "You did an amazing job," one of the female judges told her. "Your volume was perfect. One suggestion would be to slow down a bit."

Over the next half hour, twelve more students were chosen out of the hat to come forward, recite their pieces, and receive accolades from the audience and feedback from the judges. The pieces ranged from the prologue of *Romeo and Juliet* to song lyrics from Ben E. King's "Stand by Me" and the Flobots' "Handlebars." Other students performed monologues from August Wilson's *Fences* and Lorraine Hansberry's *A Raisin in the Sun*.

A few students spoke too softly or too quickly for the audience to follow them, but the majority performed admirably. A tall eighth-grade girl named Angelina offered a fierce rendition of Sojourner Truth's monologue "Ain't I a Woman" that had the students in the audience exclaiming in appreciation when Angelina declared in a powerful voice: "That man over there says that women need to be helped into carriages, and lifted over ditches, and to have the best place everywhere. Nobody ever helps me into carriages, or over mud puddles, or gives me any best place! And ain't I a woman?"

A seventh-grade boy with crutches and a bright blue cast on one leg won appreciative laughter from his classmates when he paused dramatically in his rendition of Shel Silverstein's poem "I Cannot Go to School Today" after the lines, "I cough and sneeze and gasp and choke, I'm sure that my left leg is broke."

When there were just a few minutes remaining in the community meeting, emcee Jaivona took the microphone again. "Everyone did a phenomenal job," she reported. "Just for presenting, our presenters each won a gift certificate to Borders Books. And our winner will receive a gift certificate, a book of speeches that changed the world, and a gourmet dinner with a friend and teacher." Meanwhile, the three judges had been conferring together in a tight huddle. Then one of the female judges stood up and whispered in Jaivona's ear. "The judges have made a decision," Jaivona reported, before announcing that this year's Most Powerful Speaker was Angelina, the young lady who had so effectively channeled the power and dignity of Sojourner Truth. The students applauded feverishly as Angelina returned to the front of the room to collect her prizes. The cheering only increased when a teacher placed an ostentatious purple crown on Angelina's head.

After Angelina had returned to her seat, Roxbury Prep Codirector Will Austin took over for Jaivona at the podium. "A few things before we leave for vacation," Mr. Austin told the now-silent Roxbury Prep student body. "Let me say that adults and kids know the last eight weeks of school have been challenging for lots of reasons. Hold on to the success you felt today because we'll need it when you get back from vacation. We have a lot to do. We need eighth graders getting ready for high school, sixth graders getting ready for their first MCAS exam, and seventh graders getting ready to be positive leaders. President Barack Obama once said, 'If success were easy, everyone would do it.' You need to work hard to be successful. Have a restful February break."

## MEASURING PERSEVERANCE

As described in the introduction, students at Roxbury Prep, Boston Prep, and Pacific Rim all completed surveys at the start and conclusion of the academic year that included a number of different character measures. The measure of perseverance consisted of four survey items adapted from Nansook Park and Christopher Peterson's Values in Action Inventory of Character Strengths for Youth.[1] These items solicited students' agreement or disagreement with several statements regarding the extent to which they followed through on homework assignments, paid attention in class when bored, and characterized themselves as hard workers. All together, these items formed a robust composite of the character strength of perseverance.[2]

Similar to the methodology described in chapter 2, we fit a series of multilevel regression models in order to compare the shift in perseverance scores of students across the three schools from the beginning to the end of the academic year. As was the case with the integrity measure, the middle school students at all three schools exhibited high levels of optimism in the opening weeks of the school year about their ability to persevere on their academic assignments. Specifically, students at all three schools reported mean levels of perseverance just under 4.0 along a five-point Likert scale. As for the source of this optimism, one might again speculate that surveys completed by students in the opening weeks of the academic year capture students at their most idealistic regarding their own levels of self-discipline and perseverance in carrying out their academic responsibilities. At the outset of the school year, students have not yet confronted decisions about completing their homework versus watching television, or studying for a test versus socializing with friends. However, our analyses revealed that students at Roxbury Prep were significantly more likely to maintain a high level of perseverance over the course of the academic year than their middle school peers at Boston Prep or Pacific Rim.[3] The effect size upon students' perseverance of attending Roxbury Prep in comparison to Boston Prep or Pacific Rim was a relatively small one.[4]

The mean perseverance scores for students at Roxbury Prep, Boston Prep, and Pacific Rim at the beginning and end of the academic year are presented in figure 4.1. As is evident in figure 4.1, Roxbury Prep students began the academic year with perseverance scores that were incrementally higher than their peers at Boston Prep and Pacific Rim. Over the next nine months, the quantity and rigor of the academic work confronting students at these three high performing schools led the mean perseverance scores of all three student bodies to decline. However, at the conclusion of

FIGURE 4.1   Mean pre- and post-intervention perseverance scores for middle school students at Boston Prep, Roxbury Prep, and Pacific Rim (n = 541)

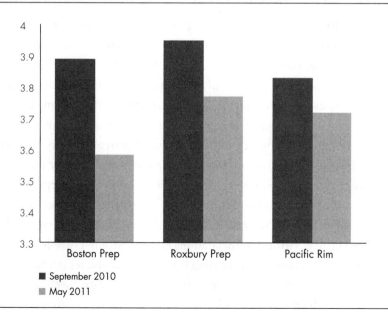

the academic year, Roxbury Prep students continued to demonstrate significantly ($p < .05$) higher levels of perseverance than their peers at Boston Prep and Pacific Rim. Boston Prep middle schoolers, in particular, demonstrated declines in their mean levels of perseverance that were nearly twice that of Roxbury Prep students.

In this comparison, one can see how Boston Prep's focus on moral character development and Roxbury Prep's focus on performance character development resulted in genuinely divergent character outcomes for their respective student bodies. In chapters 2 and 3, we focused on the particular levers through which Boston Prep teachers and administrators seek to deepen the moral character of their students. Now, we turn our attention to the mechanisms by which Roxbury Prep achieves similar results in the performance character realm. In so doing, we draw upon interviews with twenty Roxbury Prep students, teachers, and parents, as well as more than twenty-five observations of Roxbury Prep community meetings, advisory periods, and academic classes.

## PRIVILEGING PERFORMANCE

As noted in chapter 1, *performance character* is defined as "the qualities such as effort, diligence, perseverance, a strong work ethic, a positive attitude, ingenuity, and self-discipline needed to realize one's potential for excellence in academics, co-curricular activities, the workplace, or any other area of endeavor."[5] In chapter 1, we also sought to offer a glimpse of the intensive focus upon performance character development at Roxbury Prep by describing a community meeting in which three Roxbury Prep students showed off their ability to memorize and recite digits of pi. This pi recitation contest—and its explicit celebration of both performance and perseverance—distinguished the Roxbury Prep community meeting from those held at Boston Prep or Pacific Rim. As described in chapter 2, Boston Prep utilizes virtue commendations and the weekly DuBois Award to focus its weekly community meeting upon moral character strengths such as compassion, integrity, and respect. The community meetings at Pacific Rim—which receive a fuller treatment in chapter 7—focus on civic character development by entrusting rotating groups of students with the planning, content, and execution of the meeting's content and agenda.

The brief glimpse of Roxbury Prep's community meeting in chapter 1 cannot, on its own, serve as evidence of the school's explicit privileging of performance character development. However, our field notes from eleven weeks of community meetings at Roxbury Prep provide a fuller picture of the extent to which Roxbury Prep faculty and administrators use this weekly assembly to position performance and achievement at the center of the school's identity. By *performance*, we mean any type of learning experience that results in either a project or presentation. Another strong example of this privileging of performance is the "Powerful Speaking Extravaganza" described earlier in the chapter.

In his book *On Purpose: How Great School Cultures Form Strong Character*, Samuel Casey Carter writes of the importance of developing a powerful school culture through "slogans, rites, rituals, and other traditions that embody the school's principles."[6] Likewise, in *Smart & Good High Schools,* Thomas Lickona and Matthew Davidson recommend strengthening students' perseverance "through a high-challenge rite of passage."[7] Roxbury Prep's Powerful Speaking Extravaganza is both a tradition and rite of passage that emphasizes the school's commitment to exemplary performance as well as the hard work and perseverance that precedes such performances.

In her work on early adolescents' beliefs about intelligence, researcher Carol Dweck has found that students typically conceptualize intelligence through either an entity (fixed) framework or an incremental (growth) framework.[8] Students who conceptualize intelligence through an entity framework tend to regard themselves as having little control over their ability to be successful in school. In these students' minds, academic success is based almost entirely upon how "smart" a particular individual is or is not. In contrast, students who conceptualize intelligence through an incremental or growth framework regard their ability to be successful in school as directly related to their own efforts. As a result of these findings, Dweck has called for educators to actively engage students with entity mind-sets in *attribution retraining*—that is, teaching them to conceptualize intelligence, and therefore academic success, as a quality one acquires through hard work and perseverance.[9] The focus on performance at Roxbury Prep, coupled with the constant reminders from faculty and administrators about the hard work preceding those performances, serves as a frequent and important lesson for Roxbury Prep students on the idea that "effort determines success."

Both the pi recitation contest and Powerful Speaking Extravaganza are robust examples of Roxbury Prep's emphasis upon performance and performance character; however, Roxbury Prep faculty and administrators take advantage of nearly every one of the school's community meetings to highlight both performance and the hard work underlying that performance. In a September community meeting, the Roxbury Prep Science Team led an "Element Bee" in front of the entire student body in which three students and a teacher competed to demonstrate their knowledge of the periodic table during a recent chemistry unit. At a community meeting the following month, sixth-grade students participating in the Young Authors' Society shared excerpts from the novels on which they were working every day during their enrichment period. A week later, eighth-grade students demonstrated the estimation skills they were currently honing in math class by participating in a contest modeled after the television game show *The Price Is Right*. Other community meetings included students reading original haikus, limericks, and cinquains and performing choreographed step-dancing routines. Finally, in a community meeting prior to the December break, Roxbury Prep English teacher Caroline Travers challenged students to participate in a "So You Think You Can Read" competition—Roxbury Prep's adaptation of the popular television show *So You Think You Can Dance*. Travers explained to the students, "Two weeks from today, you guys will go home for a sixteen-day vacation. On that sixteen-day break, you'll have homework, family parties, sleeping, eating. But you'll also have a lot of time left over, and raise your hand if you like to read in your free time. We are looking for teams from each advisory who will get together and read a book over break, and then face off against other advisories to see who read and understood the book the best . . . If you have time to be in this comprehension battle, you'll need to take one of these forms and fill it out, and Roxbury Prep will order the books for you." Samuel Casey Carter writes that "great school cultures state what virtues or habits they expect to see on display at all times from members of their community."[10] In asking students to use their school vacation time to prepare for an upcoming "comprehension battle" with their classmates, Ms. Travers's challenge carried the implicit message that, even over vacation, Roxbury Prep students are expected to exhibit the focus and self-discipline necessary to use their time well and continue to learn.

In terms of the purpose underlying these performances, Roxbury Prep teacher Stephanie Davis explains that the community meeting gives students a chance to "share what they've learned, [and] it gives them a sense of accomplishment and a sense of purpose." Another teacher, Marleny Abrams, adds that the presentations also have a powerful effect upon the students in the audience: "It's incredible what it does to the [students'] aspirations. It changes what it means to be cool . . . I think the academic presentations make it cool to be a reader of the week. It is cool to be up there and present math." Roxbury Prep seventh grader Desmond seconds Abrams's perspective in his explanation that the performances at community meeting "represent all the good stuff we've done . . . [so that] kids in different grades will know what we're doing and see how, when they go to the next grade, they will have to be prepared for what we're doing." His classmate Kyla agrees that community meeting allows Roxbury Prep students "to show off our abilities . . . and maybe get people interested in some of the stuff that they think they wouldn't be." In short, then, a number of Roxbury Prep faculty and students characterize the emphasis on performance at the school's weekly community meetings as a significant lever through which Roxbury Prep establishes and reinforces a culture of achievement.

## EMBRACING A PERFORMANCE-BASED MISSION AND CREED

The focus on performance at every Roxbury Prep community meeting represents a lever through which the school reinforces a culture of achievement; however, the foundation of this culture lies in the school's mission, creeds, and guiding principles. As noted in the introduction, Boston Prep, Roxbury Prep, and Pacific Rim are all focused intensely on college readiness. However, there are notable differences in the ways that the three schools articulate their respective missions. In its two-sentence mission statement, Boston Prep first declares its intent to prepare all students for college, but then goes on to describe its mission of cultivating students' moral character virtues as well. Likewise, Pacific Rim includes in its mission statement a goal of empowering students to achieve their full intellectual and social potential. The Roxbury Prep mission statement, on the other hand, is focused succinctly and unequivocally on performance: "The mission of Roxbury Preparatory Charter School is to prepare its students to enter, succeed in, and graduate from college." Full stop.

This intensive focus on a particular performance goal—college acceptance and graduation—is underscored by Roxbury Prep codirector Will Austin: "We often say we want our kids to be good students but also good people . . . And I would say that if push came to shove, we emphasize the first over the second." He adds that, at Roxbury Prep, "I wouldn't say that character in and of itself is seen as a good. It's seen as a support to kids' academic progress." In other words, the character strengths that Roxbury Prep faculty and administrators are most invested in fostering in their students are the strengths most likely to promote achievement in students' academic and professional endeavors.

While Boston Prep's focus on moral character development was written into its founding charter, the intensive focus at Roxbury Prep upon performance character evolved more organically. Specifically, when Roxbury Prep first opened its doors in 1999, faculty and administrators developed a set of ten creeds that they characterized as essential to the Roxbury Prep community: scholarship, integrity, dignity, responsibility, perseverance, community, leadership, peace, social justice, and investment. While most of these qualities are performance character strengths, it is notable that this set of creeds also includes moral character strengths (e.g., integrity) and civic character strengths (e.g., social justice). Almost fifteen years later, these ten creeds remain a vibrant dimension of the Roxbury Prep culture. As eighth-grade student Byron explains, "Most of the students in the school, they want to base their actions off those creeds." However, what also became clear in interviews and observations at Roxbury Prep is that it is the performance character strengths among the ten creeds that play a leading role in the everyday language of Roxbury Prep students and teachers. For teacher Stephanie Davis, "the ones that come to mind the most and I see being rewarded the most are scholarship, perseverance, and responsibility." Teacher Chris Grover adds, "I think a lot of what is done at the school formally and informally is centered around those creeds. But I think we do a better job on some than others. There's things like peace and social justice which I feel like people believe in, but don't really do a lot of education on."

Moreover, it is notable that a creed such as dignity—which might be characterized as possessing both moral and performance qualities—is treated unequivocally as a performance character strength at Roxbury Prep. For example, community meetings at Roxbury Prep conclude with the emcee reminding Roxbury Prep students to exit the auditorium "with dignity." Likewise, Will Austin explains of the dignity creed: "You're likely to hear it in reference to uniforms . . . [and] to how kids are carrying themselves either in the hallway or in class." Finally, in an advisory lesson focused on how to carry out an academic debate, students began by answering a warm-up question: "How can you show dignity when you are one of the people in the discussion?" With Roxbury Prep's intensive focus upon performance character development, a creed such as dignity becomes an opportunity to offer students feedback on matters of comportment in their dress, demeanor, and class participation.

Roxbury Prep's focus upon performance character development as a lever for promoting academic achievement finds support in a robust body of educational research. Studies of gifted children by Lewis Terman, Melita Oden, and Ellen Winner revealed perseverance to be a stronger predictor than intelligence of success in adulthood.[11] Likewise, Benjamin Bloom's study of world-class artists, athletes, mathematicians, and neurologists revealed that one of the key commonalities across these high achievers was a "willingness to put in great amounts of time and effort," and Michael Howe's historical research on Darwin, Einstein, and other geniuses led him to conclude that "perseverance is at least as crucial [to their accomplishments] as intelligence."[12] Finally, Angela Duckworth and Martin Seligman have reported that self-discipline is a stronger predictor than IQ of middle school students' academic grades, school attendance, hours spent doing homework, and acceptance into highly competitive high schools.[13] These findings led them to conclude that "many of America's children have trouble making choices that require them to sacrifice short-term pleasure for long-term gain, and that programs that build self-discipline may be the royal road to building academic achievement."[14]

Perhaps not surprisingly for a school so focused on performance character, Will Austin notes, "I think the most important thing that we teach kids that can be applied to different aspects of the creed . . . is that there's an emphasis on individual accountability." Austin characterizes the idea that students (and teachers) are accountable for their actions, nonactions, and decisions as the "fundamental character thing we pass on to kids." This point is underscored by teacher Stephanie Davis: "I feel like we continuously expect the best from our students in terms of maturity and responsibility for their behavior. So it's an expectation that's set up really early on, which is helpful because we kind of take no excuses [from students]." Likewise, Roxbury Prep eighth grader Alanna describes this sense of responsibility as a quality that she and her peers have developed over the course of their three years at Roxbury Prep: "Now in eighth grade, you can't say like, 'I don't know' or 'It's not my fault' because you've learned how to improve a lot by the time you're in the eighth grade." Finally, teacher Caroline Travers notes, "We have our alums come back and speak to parents and students and say, 'I learned discipline while I was here, and I went to high school and I didn't have to learn that.'" According to these members of the Roxbury Prep community, perhaps the central performance character strength that Roxbury Prep seeks to instill in its students is an ability to take responsibility for the ways in which they do and do not meet their potential for excellence.

## FOCUSING ON THE FUTURE

The combination of Roxbury Prep's college-focused mission and emphasis on individual accountability means that faculty and administrators are continually pushing students to consider their behaviors and actions through the lens of preparing for high school, college, and beyond. As Roxbury Prep teacher Ana Briggs explains, "We just push them so hard. This idea, you're going to college, you have to go to the best high school you can, and where does all that [success] come from? It's how you're doing as a student." Likewise, teacher Marleny Abrams says that "every interaction we have with students is so mission-driven in our language. Even now when I discipline students, it's always like, 'Why would you do that? How is that going to help you? You have to hand in your homework because what are you going to do when you get to high school?' Sort of always connecting the action now to developing skills for the future." This strategy was even invoked during the Powerful Speaking Extravaganza by the attorney serving as a guest judge, who explicitly noted the ways in which exemplary public speaking skills would be useful to Roxbury Prep students as future professionals.

Several Roxbury Prep parents and students expressed their belief that this intensive focus on the future was crucial to the school's ability to elicit high levels of achievement from its students. According to eighth grader Alanna, "Roxbury Prep gets you ready early, so you can be prepared. Because, like, once you get out of school, it's life and it's tough, and you have to learn certain things that they teach you here." Roxbury Prep parent Eldredge Williams agrees: "The reality is that in order for the children to grow in today's world, they have to be prepared to deal with some of the best and brightest who have resources that are not allocated or available to them. And so preparing them at this stage of life will just make things a little bit smoother for them as they proceed in endeavors and grow." In this explanation, Williams offers a perspective that helps to explain the sense of urgency that marks nearly every moment of the Roxbury Prep school day. Namely, Roxbury Prep faculty, parents, and students know that, in order to matriculate to college, students will need to work twice as hard now and in high school to compete with their peers from more affluent communities. As Roxbury Prep teacher Marleny Abrams observed in chapter 1, "We [all] need to run faster so we can catch up and get to college."

Even Roxbury Prep's youngest students have internalized the notion that they must persevere now in order to prepare themselves for the future. When asked about the type of people teachers want their students to become, Roxbury Prep sixth grader Jerome replies, "I think that they're trying to make you a responsible student because in college there's nobody to look after you." Likewise, his classmate Loury answers, "A positive student, because when you're in high school, you'll have to do more stuff than you do in middle school." These responses are distinct from those offered by Boston Prep middle schoolers about their school's aspirations for them as students and individuals. As noted in chapter 2, Boston Prep students describe their school's dual objective of developing young adults who could be both scholarly and ethical. Even Roxbury Prep sixth graders, on the other hand, have adopted the more concrete language and goals of performance that typify the culture of Roxbury Prep. In both the subsequent sections of this chapter and also in chapter 5, we work to illustrate and unpack the particular levers through which Roxbury Prep instills in its student body such a powerful ethic of performance.

## TARGETING PERFORMANCE

In chapter 1, we described the "MCAS Legacy" game show that took place as part of a Boston Prep community meeting. In this humorous skit, teacher Mr. Johnson assisted an upperclassman in identifying middle schoolers worthy of carrying on the legacy of success that Boston Prep's older students had established on the high-stakes state assessments. As we noted in chapter 1, what was remarkable about this game show was that, despite the fact that high-stakes testing is typically characterized by educators in purely performance-oriented terms, Boston Prep—with its intensive focus upon moral character development—sought to emphasize instead its *moral* dimensions. In short, one might characterize Boston Prep as taking a performance-oriented experience—a high-stakes test—and "moralizing" it.

Just the opposite occurred in several Roxbury Prep advisory lessons. Roxbury Prep faculty took a lesson with moral dimensions and "performancized" it. The role of Roxbury Prep's advisory programming will be considered in greater detail in chapter 5, but here we'll offer as an example two seventh-grade advisory lessons that introduced students to the art of academic discussions. As the Suffolk advisory teacher, Mr. Haddock, explained to his class, "We'll be working on a skill you will use all the time in college and in high school, and that is having student-led discussions—where it's not the responsibility of the teacher to draw information out of you, but it's totally led by you guys." Mr. Haddock then arranged the classroom into two concentric circles with approximately ten students seated around the inner circle and ten students seated around the outer circle. After the classroom had been repositioned, Mr. Haddock explained that he would give the students in the inner circle a question to discuss for five minutes while students in the outer circle observed and took notes on specific dimensions of that discussion. Then the students in the inner and outer circles would switch places.

Over the two advisory lessons in which students engaged in this "fishbowl" activity, the majority of the questions that Mr. Haddock posed to students had moral connotations: "Would you cheat on a math final exam if you couldn't remember how to do the final problem? What would you do if someone were leaving vicious posts on a friend's Facebook account? What would you do if a friend became dangerously intoxicated at a party? What would you do if you saw a friend's boyfriend cheating with another girl?" Following students' discussions of each of these questions, Mr. Haddock facilitated a discussion that focused on performance character strengths rather than moral character strengths. Take, for example, the following excerpt from the discussion about contending with an intoxicated friend, which one might describe as having the highest of ethical stakes:

STUDENT 1: I think that you should call the police because being hated isn't as worse as you threatening someone else's life.

STUDENT 2: I disagree with you because, like in [the television show] *Skins*, there is this girl who was drunk or took a whole bunch of pills; she was fine when Stanley took her to the hospital. So you can wait and probably things are going to get better.

STUDENT 3: I disagree with [Student 2] because if she dies, everyone will blame you for it. And if someone calls 911, not everyone is going to get caught anyway.

STUDENT 4: If you call 911, everyone who is underage is going to get caught. I think she needs to go to the hospital. They won't ask you for her ID.

STUDENT 5: I was watching this movie, *Speak*, and she ended up being hated because she called the police and ruined the party, but I'm not sure if it's really a calling-the-police situation. Throwing up when you're intoxicated is pretty natural. I don't think it's a dying situation. You could always lie or pretend you were walking by and found them on the street.

STUDENT 1: I disagree with [Student 5] because you know you're not supposed to be doing this, and what if the party gets out of hand and someone in the neighborhood calls the police anyway? You might get caught anyways. I think you should take that person to the hospital because that person could die. And even if everyone is mad at you, they know they're not supposed to be there anyway.

A few minutes later, Mr. Haddock brought the discussion to a halt and called for comments from the students observing the discussion from the outer circle. "They all had well-constructed opinions, and they all spoke," volunteered one student. "There was no interrupting in the discussion."

"Their volume was good," another student chimed in from the outer circle.

"One suggestion is, Edgar kind of went off topic," offered a third, "and Nany had really good eye contact."

"I thought people did a good job of tracking the speaker," observed another student.

Mr. Haddock solicited several more comments, then brought this segment of the class to an end with the observation, "Ready for college! I love it!" Each of the aforementioned discussion topics followed a similar pattern in which both Mr. Haddock and the students in the outer circle offered feedback only on the *performance characteristics* of the discussion that had occurred among the students in the inner circle. The ability of these students to analyze the quality of their classmates' discussion was highly impressive, but it was fascinating to observe the extent to which the moral content of the discussions were not taken up. While faculty members at Boston Prep seek out every opportunity to explore with their students the moral dimensions of a particular lesson, Roxbury Prep faculty remain tightly focused on honing students' performance character strengths.

Roxbury Prep faculty took a similar approach to moral content in an eighth-grade advisory lesson. This lesson also focused on strengthening students' ability to engage in academic debate through a "four-corners discussion." In this lesson, students first watched a short video clip about the devastation to the city of New Orleans caused by Hurricane Katrina. The video concluded with comments by Georgetown sociologist Michael Eric Dyson that the U.S. government would not have allowed that devastation to occur if New Orleans was a majority white city.

At the conclusion of the video clip, Roxbury Prep teacher Ms. Briggs explained to her eighth graders that she was going to read a statement about the aftermath of Hurricane Katrina and that students who strongly agreed with the statement should move to the far-left corner of the room; students who strongly disagreed should move to the far-right corner of the room; and students who somewhat agreed or somewhat disagreed should move to the remaining corners of the room. She then offered the statement: "I believe the lack of help to New Orleans was racially motivated." The majority of students moved toward the "strongly agree" or "somewhat agree" corners. Only two students moved to the "strongly disagree" corner. Ms. Briggs gave the four corners of the room a few moments to speak among themselves and then called for opinions. A dozen hands from all four corners of the room shot into the air. Ms. Briggs called on students one by one to speak:

STUDENT 1: Even New Orleans now isn't fully recovered. If they did all they could, there would be major changes right now.

STUDENT 2: The government tried to give Louisiana what they thought was enough, but it wasn't really. Even though it was a big problem, they still have to care about the rest of America and put money towards that.

STUDENT 3: They can't just focus on New Orleans, even though they had a big hurricane.

STUDENT 4: I think if Obama were president, it would have gone differently for the people in New Orleans.

STUDENT 2: Hurricanes don't care what race you are.

Ms. Briggs paused the discussion. "Does anyone want to switch corners based on one of the arguments they heard?" Approximately six students moved toward the "disagree" corners of the room, apparently convinced by the arbitrariness of hurricanes.

Later in the period, students repeated this four-corners exercise on the issue of free speech. They watched a short video clip about an antigay religious group that expressed its views by protesting at the funerals of military veterans. When the video clip concluded, Ms. Briggs asked her students to respond to the statement: "I believe that the right to free speech is applied everywhere, even if it hurts people's feelings." Again, students scattered to the four corners of the room, and a spirited debate ensued. Similar to Mr. Haddock's fishbowl activity, Ms. Briggs offered feedback to students only about the performance characteristics of their debate—volume, civility, use of evidence, persuasive techniques, etc. She did not interject her own thoughts or respond to any comments by students about the actual content of the two discussions. Once again, while Boston Prep faculty actively seek to uncover the moral dimensions of academic content, Roxbury Prep faculty home in on the performance characteristics of content with even an explicitly moral dimension.

## GRAPPLING WITH MORAL CONTENT

In the previous section, we offered several examples of Roxbury Prep faculty choosing to prioritize a lesson's performance elements over its moral elements. Such pedagogical decisions align with Will Austin's explanation that "when push comes to shove" Roxbury Prep prioritizes performance character development over moral or civic character development. That said, there are certainly occasions in which Roxbury Prep faculty *do* raise with their students the moral, civic, or ethical implications of a particular lesson. Even in these moral moments, however, one can see the extent to which the common vocabulary shared by faculty and students at Roxbury Prep has been developed for grappling with performance, rather than moral, matters.

For example, one eighth-grade advisory lesson solicited students' reaction to a famous "trolley problem" that has long been a staple of ethical philosophy courses. In this moral dilemma, a runaway train (or trolley) is moving quickly down a track, headed directly toward a group of five innocent bystanders standing blithely on the train tracks. You, the reader of the moral dilemma, can pull a switch that will divert the train onto an auxiliary track, but the train will then strike and kill another innocent and unaware bystander.[15] The question, then, posed to countless university undergraduates over the past several decades, is *what is the right thing to do*? Ms. Ferrara posed this same question to her Roxbury Prep eighth graders. "I want you to know," she added, "there is no right answer, and there should be no judgment for anyone's answer. Who wants to share?"

STUDENT 1: I said the right thing to do would be to spare the five people, and that's what I would do.

STUDENT 2: If you kill five people, five families are suffering. Losing anybody is painful, but losing one is less bad than losing five.

STUDENT 3: I would kill the one person and then send my condolences to the person and explain what happened.

STUDENT 4: It's up to God, not me, to decide who gets to live.

STUDENT 5: I would kill one person because it's better, less painful to have one family grieve than five families. And I'd rather have one death on my conscience than five.

"This is awesome participation," Ms. Ferrara congratulated her students. She then showed the class a video clip from an introductory ethics class at Harvard University in which an auditorium full of college students grappled with this same question. The Roxbury Prep students watched in fascination as the Harvard students made similar points to their own, and then their professor began to complicate the problem. When the video ended, the Roxbury Prep students resumed their discussion:

STUDENT 3: The five people [on the tracks] should be smart enough to know there's a train coming.

STUDENT 6: It's easier for the one person to get out of the way. But that dude on the film brought up a good point. He said, if you kill the one, then you made a decision to kill a person instead of just letting things happen.

STUDENT 2: I want to switch my answer. I would kill the five because it's like [Student 4] says. You shouldn't play God and decide who lives or dies.

STUDENT 7: I also agree [with Student 4] about not playing God. If you veer to the right and kill the one person, the five people who saw what happened could probably come over and help.

STUDENT 8: I think you guys are only seeing the part where you're making the decision to kill that one person, but if you think about it, you have two choices. You staying straight, even though it's fate, you're making a decision. So either way you still have two choices.

The discussion continued on for several more minutes and, as the period came to a close, Ms. Ferrara took a poll of students' opinions. Fifteen students voted to direct the train toward the single victim; five students voted to let the train crash into the five bystanders; and four students characterized themselves as uncertain. "I've never seen the whole class so involved and respectful," Ms. Ferrara complimented the class. "I'm very impressed."

If the larger objective of this lesson was to engage students in academic debate or to give them a glimpse of what a university course looks like, then the lesson was absolutely a success. The students were highly engaged in the discussion and listened carefully to each other's perspectives. It was also notable—and perhaps useful for Roxbury Prep students to observe—that their perspectives did not differ dramatically in sophistication or logic from those of the Harvard students grappling with this same ethical dilemma in the video.

However, if the students had continued to watch the video of this ethics course at Harvard, entitled "Justice" and taught by political philosopher Michael Sandel, they would have seen that Sandel utilized this trolley problem to introduce students to several different ethical perspectives. For example, a utilitarian might approach this dilemma with the goal of causing the least pain to the fewest number of people, while a Rawlsian philosopher might determine the most ethical response by imagining the perspective of the most vulnerable participant in the scenario.

Psychology professors often utilize this same trolley problem to help their students interrogate inconsistencies in their ethical beliefs.[16] For example, why do so many students argue that it is ethical to flip the switch that will result in one bystander dying rather than five, but virtually none would be willing to *push* an innocent bystander onto the tracks in order to save those same five bystanders? None of these lessons emerged from this advisory lesson, nor did Ms. Ferrara comment directly on her own beliefs about the most ethical course of action in this scenario. At the top of the handout on which the trolley problem had been printed was a definition for Roxbury Prep students of ethics as "a system of moral principles and values . . . that one uses to guide his/her actions and decisions in life." However, at the end of this lesson, Ms. Ferrara had not pushed her students to consider the principles or values underlying their reactions to the trolley problem. Similar to her colleagues, Mr. Haddock and Ms. Briggs, in their respective advisory lessons, she instead focused her feedback to students on the performance characteristics of the discussion—the character "language" in which Roxbury Prep faculty and staff are more fluent.

A similar approach to moral matters occurred in a Roxbury Prep advisory lesson focused on the topic of bullying. As noted in chapter 2, the Massachusetts state legislature enacted a law in 2010 requiring all public schools to incorporate antibullying curriculum into their work with students at every grade level. In a seventh-grade advisory lesson, Mr. Rivera divided his class into small groups of three or four students and gave each a question about bullying to discuss. For example, one group discussed "What should you do if a bully confronts you?" while another tackled the question, "Why do bullies pick on people?"

Mr. Rivera gave each group a few moments to discuss their respective questions and then asked them to share. A young man raised his hand,

"Our question was, 'why do bullies bother other people?' and I said they want people to think they're cool."

Another boy in his group added, "I said a bully is someone who isn't getting enough attention at home, and they want to feel big."

The next group—which seemed intent on incorporating as many of their weekly vocabulary words as possible—explained in unison that "bullies are juvenile, vile, disgusting, violent, not friendly, insane. They're unfrank."

"So you're giving some opinions about bullies," Mr. Rivera commented. "Those are strong words, but they seem to fit in a lot of ways." After the rest of the groups had taken their turn, he explained, "Okay, now I want you to take out a piece of paper. You may know of someone in this school—we're not going to use names—someone in Roxbury Prep or outside of Roxbury Prep who is being bullied." A number of students nodded in agreement. "Without using any names," Mr. Rivera continued, "I want you to write that person a letter about what they should do. You'll address the letter as 'Dear friend,' and your goal is to address what it is they're being bullied about, and how they should respond."

While the majority of the students began working on their letters, one cluster of students sat stone-faced. When Mr. Rivera came over to the cluster to inquire about their progress, several claimed not to know anyone being bullied. Mr. Rivera started to explain the assignment again, but one of the boys in the group interrupted him, "I know what the assignment is, but I don't know anyone getting bullied."

When Mr. Rivera prodded another boy in the group about whether that was really the case, the young man responded, "No one comes to mind." Mr. Rivera assigned these students to instead address their letters to a "theoretical bully."

As class was winding down, Mr. Rivera asked a number of students to share their letters to a friend being bullied. One student advised the victim to stand up for himself. "Don't argue," he advised, "but talk nicely. In the bravest way possible, stand up for yourself."

"That was well written, man," Mr. Rivera told him.

A second student offered to read his letter. "Dear friend," he started, "I know that sometimes you get bullied, but you should not fight back. You should just tell someone. This does not mean you are a snitch. If they try to take something away from you, just run to security and tell them. Like the last time . . ." The student trailed off. "That's all I want to read of my letter," he said. It seemed clear that his letter had diverged into his own experience contending with bullies.

"I like your point that telling someone does not make you a snitch," Mr. Rivera remarked.

The lesson concluded with several more students sharing their letters. As was the case with the advisory lesson on the trolley problem, Roxbury Prep students and faculty seemed a bit uncertain about how to explore together a moral, rather than a performance, matter. In responding to the students' letters, Mr. Rivera's instinct was to comment on the quality of the writing ("That was well written, man"). Likewise, although a second student's letter seemed to allude to his own challenges with bullies, Mr. Rivera chose to respond, instead, to an intellectual point the students had raised ("I like your point that telling someone does not make you a snitch"). Perhaps this advisory lesson had been developed only to comply with Massachusetts's new law requiring schools to adopt antibullying curriculum, but it nonetheless revealed the extent to which the common vocabulary established at Roxbury Prep is designed for performance rather than moral matters.

Several Roxbury Prep faculty members have observed this dynamic themselves. For example, sixth-grade teacher Chris Grover feels that advisory lessons focused on perseverance and performance have a positive impact on Roxbury Prep students but that "the real kind of integrity character education, in my opinion . . . I think we're still figuring out how to do those lessons well." Likewise, eighth-grade teacher Ana Briggs notes, "We tried to do a social justice project [in advisory] a couple years ago. And we had the kids pick a topic in terms of social justice that they really liked or wanted to work on . . . And I don't think there was enough investment [from] both the teachers and the students to pull it off. So it kind of became this half-done kind of thing." Our interviews with Roxbury Prep teachers and administrators revealed a faculty deeply committed to social justice and who see their work at Roxbury Prep as a mechanism for making the world a more equitable one. Perhaps, then, the challenge underlying the project Briggs recalls was that Roxbury's Prep mission is so unequivocally focused on performance that a framework was not really in place to support a lengthy project with moral or civic, rather than performance, goals.

## COMBINING MORAL AND PERFORMANCE CHARACTER

Recall from chapter 1 that Lickona and Davidson characterize moral character and performance character as intertwined: "Performance character must always be regulated by moral character to ensure that we do not do bad things in the pursuit of our goals, and moral character always needs performance character to enable us to be effective in carrying out our good intentions."[17] Accordingly, at Roxbury Prep, the most effective consideration of moral matters occurred through the medium of performance. For example, in the final months of the school year, half a dozen Roxbury Prep students were expelled for bringing drugs to school and then distributing the drugs to classmates. According to Will Austin: "This was so many kids and so public that we just had to address it head-on . . . It affected too many kids and it was too pervasive for us not to."

Addressing these expulsions head-on included three performances by eighth graders at a community meeting about the behaviors of the expelled students. As Ms. Ferrara explained at the outset of this community meeting to the silent student body, "These three positive leaders are concerned about some of their friends and are up here to share some of their own reflections. Joshua is going to share a speech he wrote, and the techniques are based on Bill Cosby's 'pound cake' speech. Selina wrote a poem based on Sojourner Truth's 'Ain't I a Woman' rhetorical strategy, and Marvin wrote an original rap. As you can imagine, they are incredibly nervous, so we are going to support them."

The students got up one by one to share their original compositions. Like an older academic giving a presentation, Joshua warned, "As men, we need to be leaders. If a boy is a follower in school, he'll end up doing anything his friends are doing, and they'll use him until he is wasted."

In a rap entitled "Collaborative Effort," Marvin advised, "It takes a lot of heart to take a stand / but that is how you show you're a man. We definitely need motivation to succeed / Follow your dreams / don't be a crack fiend." And, finally, Selina admonished in a spoken-word poem: "Don't you think the world has enough crackheads? Staying in school has never meant so much. Three words that kids never seem to follow . . . Alcohol and drugs are death in disguise. Which road will you take?"

The Roxbury Prep student body applauded loudly and enthusiastically after each of these performances and, sitting in the audience, one could almost feel the school community beginning to unclench its tightly wound muscles from the drama of the past few weeks. All three students' performances were authentic and real, and they engaged head-on with the challenges that had led their peers and friends to be expelled. As Lickona and Davidson noted, grappling with moral matters often requires performance character strengths to effectively carry out one's good intentions.[18] Joshua, Marvin, and Selina all wanted to respond to the pain caused by the expulsions of their peers, and they relied on their powerful oratorical and writing skills to voice this response. In a school culture so intensively focused on performance character development, perhaps it is no surprise that Roxbury Prep students and faculty were most effective in taking on moral matters through the medium of performance.

This engagement with moral matters through performance was also evident in a Roxbury Prep community meeting following the 8.9 magnitude earthquake off the coast of Japan in March 2011. Three students addressed the Roxbury Prep student body to describe the death and devastation in Japan caused by both the earthquake and resulting tsunami. One student explained, "At Roxbury Prep, we have learned about the history of Japan, read *Sadako and the Thousand Paper Cranes*, and we would like to fold one thousand paper cranes to represent our wish to help Japan." A Roxbury Prep teacher then joined the students to explain that an organization called Students Rebuild had pledged to donate $2 to earthquake relief in Japan for every paper crane folded by primary and secondary school students. The teacher and students called for a volunteer in each advisory to coordinate the paper-crane-folding effort by learning how to make a paper crane and then teaching the rest of the advisory how to do so. A week later, a giant poster in the Roxbury Prep hallway showed tallies of the paper cranes folded in each Roxbury Prep advisory, and revealed that the Roxbury Prep community was already several hundred paper cranes toward their goal.

Similar to the student speeches just described, this response to the devastation in Japan felt authentic. Students heard a chilling, but accurate, account of the tragedy caused by the earthquake and were then presented with a task—a type of performance—through which they could play a role in alleviating the victims' pain. This was a framework familiar to Roxbury Prep faculty and students, and they responded with gusto. In both of these examples, then, one can see the Roxbury Prep community engaging effectively with moral matters in the language and framework the school had already established: performance. In chapter 5, we focus on precisely *how* Roxbury Prep seeks to use performance to strengthen students' commitments to perseverance, self-discipline, and achievement.

## CHAPTER FIVE

# Effort Determines Success

Per the custom at Roxbury Prep, the seventh graders silently entered their Vanderbilt homeroom in a single-file line before fanning out to their assigned seats. On each desk waited a "Do Now" for students to complete. In academic classes, the Do Now is typically a math problem or short-answer question that draws upon a skill the students learned in class the previous day. The Do Now question for Friday advisory lessons, however, is always the same for Vanderbilt seventh graders: whom will you nominate for the Vanderbilt Commodore of the Week award?

The classroom, painted an appealing sky blue, was dotted with a number of inspirational quotations. "Fall seven times, stand up eight," read a Japanese proverb. "I haven't failed," read a quotation attributed to inventor Thomas Edison, "I've identified 10,000 ways this doesn't work." In their seats, students wore frowns of concentration as they considered which classmate deserved to be recognized as the Commodore of the Week. As this was only the fourth Friday of the school year, few students had yet been recognized.

"Good morning, Vanderbilt!" exclaimed Mr. Haddock. "While Ms. Gooding collects your nominations, let me congratulate all of you on a successful trip to Blue Hills last Friday! Being absolutely focused on the goals and staying positive, refusing to give up, and showing character along the way, we showed we can take the Blue Hills . . . We made it to the summit. We can definitely make it out of seventh grade." A number of students nodded their heads in agreement. "Right now," Mr. Haddock continued, "we're going to do an activity that involves the blue chip and the red chip that Ms. Gooding has placed on your desk. What you will need to do is take one chip and balance it on its side. And once you have it balanced, your task is to take the other chip and balance it on top." He gestured at the whiteboard behind him, on which there was an illustration of one coin balanced on top of the other.

For the next five minutes, the Vanderbilt homeroom was filled with the sound of poker chips scraping and rattling against students' desks, followed by excited and then dismayed exclamations. "Okay," Mr. Haddock declared, when the hubbub began to subside. "Raise your hand if you have given up." Half of the students raised their hands. "Put the chips on the side of your desk," Mr. Haddock instructed, "and let's look at the packet Ms. Gooding is handing out. About half of you were enthusiastic to keep trying while the other half kind of gave up."

The students turned their attention to the handout labeled "Experiencing Struggle." The first two questions on the front page asked: "What are some reasons either you gave up or someone might have given up on this? What is another time where you gave up on something?" Mr. Haddock gave the students a few moments to write silently. Then he interjected, "Let's hear some ideas."

"It was aggravating that it kept falling," one student offered.

"It was impossible," volunteered another.

"A lot of people got frustrated," noted a third.

"What's a time you gave up on something else?" asked Mr. Haddock.

A boy in the front row raised his hand. "I can't beat my brother in this video game, so we don't play anymore."

"I tried to run the mile," added a young lady sitting behind him, "but then I started walking."

"My grade is so bad in science that I just give up," volunteered a third.

"Sometimes I get so many demerits I don't even care," agreed his classmate.

Today we are talking about resilience," explained Mr. Haddock. He pointed to the whiteboard. "Kadeem, please read the definition."

"Bouncing back after failure," Kadeem read loudly. "Or toughing it out."

"Thank you," Mr. Haddock told him. "Resilience relates to perseverance, which is one of our creeds, so not giving up. Now we are going to watch a very short commercial, but it features a quote you might have noticed out in the hallway. And then we'll think about how this connects to resilience." He moved over to his desk and tapped on his laptop. The whiteboard in the front of the room transformed into a screen projecting a YouTube video of a Nike commercial entitled "Failure." In the clip, basketball star Michael Jordan explained, "I've missed more than nine thousand shots in my career. I've lost almost three hundred games. Twenty-six times, I've been trusted to take the game-winning shot, and missed. I've failed over and over and over again in my life, and that is why I succeed."

"Okay," Mr. Haddock asked, after the commercial faded to black, "What does Michael Jordan mean there at the end, and how does that relate to our definition of resilience?"

A student waved his hand. "He keeps failing, but he learns from his mistakes."

"What he means," explained another, "is that if you make a mistake, you learn from it if you demonstrate resilience and keep trying."

"He means he has overcome all of the times he has failed to move forward," said a third student.

Mr. Haddock nodded his head at each of these responses but then added one of his own. "I think it's not just about learning from your mistakes, but also the only way you can be successful is if you keep trying to be successful. The only way you can make game-winning shots is if you keep trying to do it. That's really what we talk about when we talk about resilience. So it's about not letting failure get you down." He paused. "Let's do a one-minute quick write. I want you to identify times when you *want* to give up." He took a packet of blank index cards from his desk and began to move around the room, placing one index card on each student's desk. "I want you to write one of those examples you come up with down on this index card." The room grew quiet as students scribbled examples onto their respective index cards.

After a minute had passed, Mr. Haddock instructed his students to pass up their index cards, then waited until all of the cards were in his possession. "Now we're going to do two things with these cards," he told his students. "First, we're going to symbolically destroy them, and then we're going to strategically combat them." He ripped the stack of twenty-five cards in two. A number of students muttered unhappily as the examples they had spent the last minute developing disappeared into the trash can. "These aren't going to hold us back in the future," Mr. Haddock told the class. "So the last thing we're going to do today is think of things we can do and tell ourselves to help ourselves during these challenging times, to show resilience." He gave students thirty seconds to jot down ideas on the final page of their handout and then started soliciting volunteers.

"I identify what is going wrong and what I need to do right to make the situation better," explained one student.

"When I want to give up on my homework, I take some breaks," volunteered another student.

"Work harder," said a third.

"Think of the outcome," advised a quiet student seated in the front row.

"Do what you have to do so you can do what you want to do," said another boy.

"Don't say you can't do it," added another.

The intercom crackled, and the voice of Mr. Austin, the school codirector, came over the loudspeaker to announce the start of community meeting. "Good work today," Mr. Haddock told the class. "Now the important thing is to keep in mind all these great ways of showing resilience when we're feeling like we want to give up." He turned to Ms. Gooding. "Ms. Gooding has been counting up the votes from your nomination forms, so, as we line up to go to community meeting, she will tell us who is going to be this week's Commodore of the Week."

## BUILDING PERFORMANCE CHARACTER
## THROUGH ADVISORY

The most explicit lever through which Roxbury Prep seeks to influence the performance character of its students is Friday advisory. Advisory groups are structures in which an adult meets regularly with a small group of students to provide them with both academic and social-emotional support.[1] The central premise of advisory programming is that students are more likely to be successful when there is at least one adult in their school who knows them well.[2] Scholars have found advisory groups at the middle school level to be associated with an increased sense of trust and belonging on the part of students, increased levels of positive peer support, and improved relationships between students and teachers.[3] However, there is relatively little empirical research on the effects of advisory groups, in large part because of the wide variety of activities and objectives that are encompassed under the advisory label.[4] These objectives include community building, offering academic support, teaching life skills, exploring careers, discussing social issues, and engaging in community service learning.

At Roxbury Prep, advisory is focused primarily upon fostering students' performance character. As Will Austin explains, "When we talk about advisory, we're talking about that curricular time where folks are developing lessons for kids based on the creed. And what that looks like is an academic class that meets once a week. Like other classes at Roxbury Prep, there's a Do Now. It's highly structured, but the content is not necessarily academic. It usually isn't, because the goal is to develop some element of the school creed or character that we have selected for a group of kids."

Similar to Boston Prep's ethics program, Roxbury Prep's advisory programming meets once a week for an hour and immediately prior to the whole-school community meeting. Also similar to Boston Prep's ethics program, the curricular objectives for Roxbury Prep's advisory programming are differentiated by grade level. In the sixth grade, for example, the advisory curriculum is divided into three large units: "What it means to be an individual," "What it means to be a student at Roxbury Prep," and "What it means to be part of a movement." In the first of these units, one learning objective is "Students will understand the value of persevering in the face of challenges" and another is "Students will understand how their immediate actions have short- and long-term consequences." The eighth-grade advisory curriculum, on the other hand, is divided into two central units: "What it means to be a successful high school/college student" and "What it means to be a true leader." In the first of these units, one learning objective is "Students will be able to envision themselves in college" and a learning objective from the second unit is "Students will identify their own strengths and weaknesses as a leader, as well as create an action plan for improvement."

Recall that Boston Prep's ethics curriculum was developed and updated by a dedicated faculty member focused entirely on the ethics program. The advisory programming at Roxbury Prep is a more communal respon-sibility. At the start of the academic year, teachers on each of Roxbury Prep's grade-level teams take responsibility in pairs for planning two or three advisory lessons apiece. The teacher pairs share drafts of these advi-sory lessons with their colleagues several weeks in advance, make revisions based on feedback, and then distribute a final lesson plan and materials to the other members of their grade-level team a few days before the advisory lesson is to take place. These lessons are then archived in Roxbury Prep's electronic database so that teachers will be able to draw upon the most effective ones in subsequent years. Nonetheless, Will Austin notes wryly that there remains "an annual tradition of revamping the advisory curric-ulum." Though, Austin adds, "in some ways that is good. It's a reflection of the people teaching it because it needs to be authentic. And it's also re-flective of the kids who are there, so that it's authentic to them."

How do Roxbury Prep teachers and students feel about advisory? Sixth-grade teacher Chris Grover expresses the sentiment of a number of faculty members in his explanation that the challenge in teaching advisory is that "you don't have quite the same intimacy with how you're going to teach that lesson because you may not have been the one planning it." None-theless, faculty members also characterize advisory as an important learn-ing opportunity for their students. As teacher Marleny Abrams explains, "I just think it's so important. I think it's more important than some of the math problems I teach. The kids need it . . . It's the nonacademic skills they need for life—to be a good citizen and to be a successful individual. Things like persevering and what you do when you get knocked down." Teacher Stephanie Davis adds that advisory is "a little bit looser than their [academic] classes, so I feel like the kids who don't know the answers in math class will know some of the answers in advisory because it's asking general questions about motivation and goals and that kind of stuff." Both of these teachers characterize the focus of advisory as situated squarely in the realm of performance character development, as do sixth grader Loury, who explains that "they teach you to become a positive leader for other schools and in the future" and eighth grader Byron, who adds, "I feel like it's really helpful in terms of being street smart, not only like school smart." In the following sections, we delve into the particular mechanisms through which Roxbury Prep's advisory programming seeks to hone the performance character strengths of Roxbury Prep students.

## TEACHING PERSEVERANCE AND PERFORMANCE

Certainly the narrative at the outset of this chapter from a seventh-grade advisory lesson offers a window into the role of Roxbury Prep's advisory programming in teaching perseverance. The seventh-grade students in the Vanderbilt advisory worked to define resilience, discussed basketball star Michael Jordan's perspective on the value of failure, and reflected upon situations in their own lives that challenged their resilience. Almost two months later—just before the end of the first trimester—Roxbury Prep sixth graders engaged in a similar lesson focused on the merits of perseverance.

For this lesson, the sixth-grade advisors established four different stations within their classrooms, and their sixth graders traveled in groups of six from station to station, spending approximately fifteen minutes at each. The first station featured a video of President Barack Obama's 2010 graduation speech to students at Michigan's Kalamazoo Central High School. In the speech, Obama offered a number of examples to underscore his advice to graduates that lasting success "doesn't happen in an instant

. . . It's usually about daily effort"—everything from Thomas Edison trying out more than six thousand different materials for the light bulb to author J. K. Rowling persevering after her first Harry Potter manuscript was rejected by eleven publishers.[5] A second station gave sixth graders the opportunity to learn more from a Roxbury Prep eighth grader about the upcoming comps process. "Comps" are the comprehensive exams Roxbury Prep students take at the conclusion of each trimester. Going into their first ever round of comps, sixth graders had numerous questions about what comps mean and how to prepare for them. Chris Grover explains that the lesson gave his sixth graders the "chance of, one, talking with an older responsible peer about something that was coming up and then, two, internalizing some kind of external inspiration [about studying for comps]." He adds that his sixth graders benefited from this explicit guidance on "how do you go home and actually study for a big test when you've never had anything quite like that before?"

After the first round of comps ended and trimester two had begun, the seventh-grade advisory classes engaged students in developing their own inspirational superheroes. According to teacher Caroline Travers: "The beginning of trimester two, we usually try to make a big deal about like, 'This is a fresh start, it's a brand-new trimester. You have an A in everything right now, and what is your big area that you want to improve?'" Toward this end, teachers came up with superheroes for each subject area, and when seventh graders identified the particular class in which they wanted to aim for improved performance, their teachers assigned them a Roxbury Prep superhero. Travers continues, "We used pictures of actual superheroes like Batman, and then it had a Roxbury Prep name under it. And the kids got really into it." For students who chose English as the subject in which they wanted to improve, the superhero was the "Invincible Independent Reader." In advisory, students made ID cards for their superhero in which they identified that superhero's mortal enemies. For example, the Invincible Independent Reader's enemies included forgetting to take notes while reading, getting lazy, getting tired, and lying down while reading.

In a subsequent advisory lesson, students designed comic strips depicting their superheroes fighting off these enemies of improved performance, and then posted their artwork throughout the Roxbury Prep classrooms and hallways. For the remainder of the trimester, students could earn "superhero badges" by carrying out the superhero actions and avoiding the superhero enemies in their chosen subject areas. These superhero badges—as well as the advisory lessons described in the preceding paragraphs—served to clarify for Roxbury Prep students the notion that academic success is the result of hard work and perseverance, not some innate amount of "intelligence" that students either do or do not possess.[6] In this way, Roxbury Prep's advisory programming seeks to develop in students a framework for understanding academic achievement that maximizes their likelihood of success.

Other Roxbury Prep advisory lessons seek to teach students the so-called soft skills that will facilitate their achievement now and in the future. For example, a seventh-grade advisory lesson focused on *how* to ask for help from a teacher when students are struggling in a particular subject area. According to teacher Stephanie Davis: "We broke it down all the way to, 'Can we please script out how you're going to approach that certain teacher and ask for help?' So, rather than [saying] like, 'I don't get it' or 'This is hard,' really voicing your concerns and creating a dialogue." Chris Grover adds that the sixth-grade team developed a similar advisory lesson to tackle the question, "How do you deal with a grade that you're maybe not happy with? What are you going to do to follow up on that with the teacher?"

Other advisory lessons focused on improving students' time management skills. For example, an October seventh-grade advisory lesson sought to strengthen students' ability to prepare for their trimester-one comps. Students first considered their latest biweekly progress report and then reflected in writing upon their performance in each of their academic courses. When they were finished, their advisory teacher, Ms. Minardi, instructed, "Take out your agenda once you have passed up your reflection sheet. I am going to show you the upcoming comp schedule, so you can record these dates into your agenda." After these dates had been recorded, Ms. Minardi continued: "Now I'm going to let you work on a study plan with the person sitting next to you to fill out the study plan sheet." In the final portion of the class, Ms. Minardi asked different students to share their study plan for a particular academic subject and, finally, assigned students for homework to "choose the class you're doing the worst in, and make an appointment to get help from the teacher." Given that they had spent the previous week practicing for just such a conversation, Ms. Minardi believed her students were equipped to put this practice to good use just in time for their first-trimester comp exams.

All of these lessons sought to develop in Roxbury Prep students the self-advocacy skills that faculty members believe to be crucial to their success going forward. As teacher Marleny Abrams explains, "[These are] skills that I think every student should have, but in this case they're coming perhaps from an environment where they don't see it done all the time—where they don't have parents who have the time to teach them explicitly. And they can be brilliant mathematicians, brilliant writers, but if they don't have that, they're not going to be successful. Things like how to speak in public, how to interact with adults, how to shake hands." In short, Roxbury Prep faculty and administrators regard their students' pursuit of a college degree as requiring more than simply excellent academic skills. Rather, there are performance character skills such as public speaking ability, time management, and an ability to engage in self-advocacy that are crucial to students' pursuit of success as well. This perspective is supported by sociologist Annette Lareau's work on race, class, and family life.[7] In an ethnographic study of children raised in middle-class, working-class, and poor households, Lareau concluded that middle-class parents were far more likely than working-class and poor parents to engage in "concerted cultivation"—the active fostering of children's cognitive and social skills. As a result of this concerted cultivation, Lareau found that children raised in middle-class homes were more likely than their poor and working-class peers to develop the verbal skills, networking skills, and self-advocacy skills necessary to interact effectively in professional and institutional settings. Through its advisory programming, Roxbury Prep seeks to equip its largely low-income student body with the soft skills that are as important as academic skills in successfully navigating college and beyond.

## REFLECTING ON PERFORMANCE

Recall from chapter 3 that developmental psychologist Erik Erikson characterized adolescence as the period in which individuals confront for the first time the questions "Who am I?" and "How do I fit into the world around me?"[8] Recall also that a key component of Boston Prep's ethics curriculum was the treatise assignments in which Boston Prep students reflected upon the role of particular moral virtues in their own lives. These reflection assignments gave Boston Prep students an opportunity to think and write about who they are and what they value, which scholar Katie Davis characterizes as "support[ing] the critical task of identity formation by making it possible for individuals to form a theory of themselves and their role in society."[9]

Roxbury Prep's weekly advisory programming also provides students with opportunities to engage in reflection about who they are and what they value. At Roxbury Prep, however, this reflection is focused primarily upon students' performance character—the extent to which they are or are not achieving to their highest *academic* potential. For example, in an advisory class on the final day of school before spring break, progress reports were distributed in the seventh-grade advisories, and students were assigned to answer several reflection questions about their academic achievement thus far in the third trimester. These questions included: "In which class are you most proud of your performance? In which classes are you most concerned about your performance? What are some action steps you can take for raising your grades?" After several minutes of writing, Ms. Petrachos asked students to share their answers on the class about which they were most proud.

"I went from an F to a B– in math," volunteered one girl.

"I said English," said another, "because now I have a B+."

"I maintained my A– in science all three trimesters," said a third.

"History," explained a boy sitting in the front row, "because before I had a D, and now I have a B."

"All right," Ms. Petrachos told the class. "Now I want to hear some of your action steps for raising your grades in other classes."

"To do all my homework and study for tests," volunteered one boy.

"I actually have one goal," said a girl beside him. "I want to get tutored in history."

"Organizing my binder," volunteered another boy.

"In reading, I need to not worry about what I don't like and just do it," explained another.

"I want to do all the homework, so I can get higher grades. And not get distracted in class," said a fifth student.

Roxbury Prep eighth graders engaged in a similar discussion in the final weeks of their career as Roxbury Prep students. In this advisory lesson, the eighth graders entered the UMaine homeroom to find a packet waiting for them entitled "Gateway to Graduation—Final Comps!" The front page of the packet asked students to reflect silently upon four questions:

1. Your English and History comps are due the week before we go to Washington DC. What is your plan to finish them on time?

2. Which comps are you already feeling most prepared for?

3. Which comps are you most concerned about?

4. For each comp you are concerned about, list at least one thing you are going to do to prepare for the comp.

On the pages behind these warm-up questions were a schedule of the upcoming comps as well as a separate schedule of days that eighth-grade teachers had volunteered to remain late after school to work with students. After the UMaine eighth graders had spent several minutes responding to the four prompts, their advisory teacher, Ms. Ferrara, interjected: "Let's check in briefly on this. Believe it or not, this is the last part of your experience at Roxbury Prep as a student, and you will then graduate into alumni. Coming up first are your written comps. Anyone have a really good plan to get those done?"

"Don't procrastinate," volunteered one eighth-grade boy. "Like if you see the reading for history, you should probably have finished it this week. Start early or you're going to get overwhelmed."

Ms. Ferrara nodded. "Snap if you feel on pace with English and history." Her request was met with very few snaps. "Okay, we're going to work on that," Ms. Ferrara continued. "What are some things you're doing to make sure you're ready for these comps? Even little things you can do now?"

"I've been staying after school to get help from Ms. Leslie," volunteered one girl.

"Good," Ms. Ferrara told her. Then, to everyone: "You'll notice that the next page has your teachers' promises about when they'll be available to you. So this is for you."

In both of these examples, one can see Roxbury Prep using advisory as an explicit opportunity to engage students in reflection about the extent to which they are or are not meeting their full potential as scholars and, if not, about the specific steps they can take to strengthen their academic performance. Seventh grader Kyla volunteers that her favorite aspect of advisory is "when they show us our grades and then they give us a paper where we reflect on how we can do better and where we can do better in the next trimester." Likewise, classmate Desmond characterizes his favorite part of advisory as the lessons focused on "the goals we have." For both of these students, the opportunity in advisory to step back and take stock of their academic performance feels as or more valuable to them than the lessons seeking to address more specific performance skills such as public speaking or self-advocacy.

In *Smart & Good High Schools*, Thomas Lickona and Matthew Davidson write that one of the keys to promoting character development in schools is to "provide students with regular opportunities to self-assess and establish personal goals" and then to "help students use self-monitoring tools to gauge progress toward goals."[10] Roxbury Prep's advisory lessons provide explicit opportunities for students both to engage in self-assessment and goal setting as well as to monitor their success (or lack thereof) in achieving these goals.

## MAXIMIZING PRACTICE AND PERFORMANCE

In the mid-nineteenth century, eugenicist Sir Francis Galton argued that an individual's ability to engage in superior performance was most strongly predicted by that individual's innate mental capacities and talents.[11] Specifically, Galton asserted in *Hereditary Genius* that although individuals could improve their performance across a wide variety of endeavors through practice and experience, "maximal performance" was determined by heritable genetic traits. Galton's beliefs about performance remained prevalent for nearly a hundred years. Over the past several decades, however, the work of Anders Ericsson and other scholars has revealed that the primary predictor of expert performance is thousands of hours of sustained and deliberate practice.[12] Even child prodigies have been found to show gradual, steady improvement in their performance as a result of training and practice.

Of course, there is no magic amount of practicing that guarantees expert-level performance in a particular endeavor. Scholars have observed that many chess players can achieve grand master status after approximately ten years of sustained training and practice, while elite musicians often require twenty or thirty years of training to reach peak levels of performance.[13] Nonetheless, Ericsson argues that sustained and deliberate practice is a necessary prerequisite for achieving superior levels of performance in nearly any endeavor. Roxbury Prep's advisory programming not only asks students to reflect upon the importance of such sustained and deliberate practice, but also provides them opportunities to engage in it.

In the preceding chapter, we offered a glimpse into the Roxbury Prep community meeting that doubled as the school's "Powerful Speaking Extravaganza." As the Extravaganza emcees indicated, Roxbury Prep students had spent several weeks of advisory learning about the key elements of powerful public speaking and then *practicing* the pieces they had selected. As eighth grader Natasha explained in early February, "Right now [in advisory] we're practicing for PSE, which is Powerful Speaking Extravaganza, and we're practicing our hand motions, volume, and like what we need to improve on to be a powerful speaker."

In the final practice session before the Powerful Speaking Extravaganza, Mr. Marshall asked the students in his advisory, "What skills do you have to practice today?"

"Being louder," volunteered one student.

"When you emphasize words," said another.

"Accuracy," explained a third.

"Eye contact," a fourth student added.

"Whose greatest strength is volume?" Mr. Marshall asked. A few hands went up. "Emphasis?" A few more. He offered several more characteristics of powerful public speaking, pausing after each to allow students to volunteer their strengths. "Memorization? Eye contact? Hand gestures? Attitude? Posture? Tone? Pauses?" For this final practice session, Mr. Marshall challenged students to choose one of the areas that was *not* yet a strength and to try to make it one.

"What happens if you mess up and everyone laughs?" asked one student, voicing an anxiety shared by many of her classmates.

"If you do make a mistake, persevere," Mr. Marshall told the class. "Everyone wants to support you. It's a fantastic event." When advisory ended, the sixth graders lined up to head into the Powerful Speaking Extravaganza and to witness the impressive culmination of the entire school community's efforts. As Roxbury Prep codirector Will Austin reminded students at the Extravaganza's conclusion, "You need to work hard to be successful."

In Roxbury Prep's eighth-grade advisories, the first half of the academic year focused on preparing students for the high school placement process. With a full-time high school placement coordinator, Roxbury Prep aspires to help eighth graders win scholarships to prestigious independent schools or admission to esteemed magnet high schools such as the Boston Latin School. Toward that end, several advisory lessons sought to prepare students for the interviews that are a part of the admissions process at select private high schools. One of these lessons focused on dressing professionally for the interview, and what precisely that would look like. "Some students from other schools will show up at their interview in saggy jeans," one advisory teacher noted at the end of the lesson. Several students laughed. "And it's funny," she continued, "but it's also kind of sad because those students won't get in no matter how fabulous they are. So you may hate the uniform Roxbury Prep makes you wear, but you know how to dress professionally."

In another such advisory lesson, eighth-grade students practiced their responses to potential interview questions. "Where do you see yourself in five or ten years?" Ms. Ferrara asked eighth grader Byron, who had volunteered to role-play.

"Going to college, professional and sophisticated, but then have my other side still crazy and wild," Byron answered.

"Tell us what you mean by professional and sophisticated," Ms. Ferrara prodded.

"To act more like an adult than a child."

"I want more details," Ms. Ferrara pushed him. "Fill it in."

"Like mad straight, like paying attention."

"You're going to say, 'like mad straight'?"

"Taking notes in college," Byron amended.

"That's a lot better," Ms. Ferrara congratulated him. Later in the same advisory lesson, Ms. Ferrara and another teacher role-played a series of high school interviews. After a session in which Ms. Ferrara had played an unprepared student, the entire class discussed what the "student" in the scenario had done wrong.

"She's slouching and banging on the door [when she came in]," volunteered one girl.

"She said 'like' every other word," observed another.

"She said her favorite subject is gym, which is not very impressive," observed a boy.

"She kind of told this whole story about her morning that made her sound pessimistic."

"When they ask you about your favorite class, you should talk about something academic," another student recommended.

These advisory lessons served a dual purpose. On one hand, they represented another example of Roxbury Prep faculty working to develop in their students the verbal, networking, and self-advocacy skills that middle-class and affluent children learn implicitly from their parents or, in some cases, through expensive high school and college admissions consultants.[14] Simultaneously, these advisory lessons underscored for students the idea that high levels of performance come about only through perseverance and practice.

The culmination of this perseverance and practice was a dress-rehearsal mock interview with Roxbury Prep's high school placement coordinator in which students dressed professionally, participated in the mock interview, and then watched and reflected upon a video recording of their performance. In terms of the results of such practice, eighth-grade parent Tamara Oakley—whose daughter won admission to a Catholic college preparatory high school—explains, "She's grown so much in this school. Now she's able to speak in front of people and not be so timid. I mean, she's going to Trinity Catholic, and my husband and I went with her to the interview, and my husband and I were just so surprised with the way she was carrying herself. It was really amazing." As a result of these and other advisory lessons, students not only demonstrated improvement at the particular skills they were practicing, but also saw firsthand the direct relationship between practice and performance.

## PERSEVERING AND PERFORMING TOGETHER

A reasonable concern for educators contemplating an increased emphasis upon performance character development is that their students will become (even more) fiercely competitive with one another. However, it is important to note that Lickona and Davidson characterize performance character development as encouraging students to take on a "task orientation" in which they strive to surpass their own past performance rather than an "ego orientation" in which they aspire to surpass the performance of someone else.[15] Researchers have found a task orientation to be associated with greater levels of satisfaction, while an ego orientation is associated with higher levels of anxiety. For this reason, Roxbury Prep faculty work to make clear to their students through a number of different advisory lessons that performance character development is a collaborative, not individualistic, enterprise. As seventh-grade teacher Caroline Travers notes, "I think a lot of our advisory lessons are geared towards sort of, 'What does our advisory need to do better? How are we going to get our whole advisory to eighth grade?'" In other words, Travers characterizes Roxbury Prep's advisory programming as focused not only upon maximizing the performance of each individual student, but also upon engaging students in supporting the performance character development of their peers.

A seventh-grade advisory lesson near the end of the first trimester offers a prime example of this commitment to performance character development through collaboration. As Mr. Koenig explained to the students in his Boston University (Terriers) advisory, "We all just have so many strengths and, as a Terrier group, we can cover all six classes. So what I want you to do right now is to brainstorm some ideas that you can share with fellow classmates about how to have strength in all subjects." Mr. Koenig then divided his advisory into an English group, math group, science group, and history group, and each group put together a poster board of "tips for success" for that particular content area. In the final twenty minutes of the lesson, each group presented its tips for success and then took questions from classmates. For example, one student asked members of the English group, "What is the best way for me to edit my drafts in English?"

"Go back to the papers that Mr. Grover gives you," explained one young man in the English group. "Like he gave us a blue keynote that tells you what the symbols stand for."

"Who is going to tutor me if I need help?" asked another student.

"Mr. Grover can help you," explained another member of the group. "Miss Michelle can help you too." In this lesson, one can see evidence of Roxbury Prep's efforts to position character development as an endeavor with which its students can provide feedback and support to one another.

A different type of peer support was evident in an eighth-grade advisory lesson that took place just a few days before the administration of the MCAS exams—the high-stakes standardized tests required of all students in Massachusetts public schools. Ms. Ferrara explained to the students in her UMaine advisory, "As you know, the seventh grade has not been in a good place the past few weeks. They're kind of a mess. They're angry, confused, scared, and the seventh-grade team came to us and asked if we could do a little more than usual to be positive leaders. So remember how last year you received letters from the eighth graders about doing well on the MCAS? We're going to do the same thing." Before authoring these letters of encouragement, the advisory brainstormed different pieces of advice they might offer to seventh graders.

"To reread what you've written," volunteered one student.

"Don't put your head down," suggested another.

"Make sure you have breakfast that morning."

"Don't sit near your best friend for life."

"Restate the point."

Ms. Ferrara captured all of these suggestions on the whiteboard at the front of the classroom and then assigned each student a particular seventh grader to whom they should direct their letter. "You're doing [rough] drafts," she told her students, "because then a friend is going to read your draft to check for errors. Because think of the irony if you have advice on writing for a seventh grader, and then you have lots of mistakes yourself." In this lesson, Ms. Ferrara subtly underscored the importance of doing high-quality work at all times by insisting that her students write rough drafts of their letters while simultaneously emphasizing to students that members of the Roxbury Prep community have a responsibility to support the performance character development of their peers. Perhaps as a result of lessons like these, Roxbury Prep seventh grader Desmond shares, "We work as an advisory group in groups so that we can shout out [for help] so if maybe one of your classmates is good in that class, [he or she can] probably tell you 'Oh, I'm good,' and help you out, so that way you can be active and better." Likewise, his classmate Kyla notes that advisory provides an opportunity "for us to connect with other people in the advisory. Like, see what we need help on and stuff."

Much of the work that Roxbury Prep students will be expected to do in college and beyond will call for productive collaborations with colleagues and teammates. As educator Michael Fullan has noted, "The ability to collaborate—on both a large and small scale—is becoming one of the core requisites of postmodern society."[16] Through the advisory lessons described in the preceding paragraphs, Desmond, Kyla, and their classmates have learned to conceptualize their own performance character development not as a lone runner training on an empty stretch of road, but as a relay team in which each member offers support and feedback to the others. In so doing, these students demonstrate a sense of collective responsibility for each other's success that Lickona and Davidson characterize as "an essential part of an ethical learning community and necessary for optimal human development."[17]

## LEVERAGING POSITIVE LEADERS

Advisory is not the only lever through which Roxbury Prep seeks to foster the performance character development of its student body. Another is the characterization of Roxbury Prep eighth-grade students as positive leaders. As described in chapter 1, each time an eighth grader came up to the lectern to participate in community meeting, the entire school would chant in chorus "positive leaders!" followed by a series of rhythmic claps. And when eighth-grade advisor Ms. Ferrara explained to her students that they would be writing letters of encouragement to their seventh-grade peers, she noted that they were going to "do [even] a little more than usual to be positive leaders."

Codirector Will Austin characterizes "positive leaders" as a role highly specific to the eighth grade: "It's something that [emerged] when we thought about kids transitioning to high school, [and we asked ourselves] what were the types of skills or attributes that we wanted them to have before they moved on? And then if they're doing that, they're reflecting those attributes for their peers." Teacher Marleny Abrams adds, "I think how we leverage the eighth graders is incredible. This whole positive leader thing . . . [We tell them] you're the seniors, you're the big brothers. We have several of them either being mentors or tutors [to younger students], and they'll come to you and say, 'I want to tutor, I want to mentor.' . . . They serve as role models in the hall and in community meeting, and the sixth and seventh graders totally see it." Another Roxbury Prep teacher,

Ana Briggs, notes as well that the concept of becoming a positive leader as an eighth grader has become aspirational for Roxbury Prep's younger students: "Kids now talk about being a positive leader in sixth grade, [and] seventh-grade teachers at the end of the year will talk [to their students] about being positive leaders in training, so they are working towards earning that title in eighth grade." She adds that, as a result of this buildup, when a new class of eighth graders begins in September, "all of a sudden now they get the chant said for them [at community meetings], and before they were doing the chant for other kids. And I think they really step in with a sense of pride for that. It's kind of a unifying idea that the eighth-grade class, we are positive leaders."

How precisely does Roxbury Prep leverage this conception of eighth graders as positive leaders? For one example, we return to the advisory lesson in which eighth graders were assigned to write letters of support to anxious seventh graders. A few minutes into the drafting process, several of the eighth graders began trying to trade their assigned seventh graders with one another. Ms. Ferrara stopped class to reprimand her students: "I'm a little annoyed because I'm hearing people ask about trading people. This isn't a practice in writing to a close friend. This isn't a social enterprise. All of these [seventh-grade] students will know you as positive leaders, and this is about you offering them sage advice." With this reference to their responsibility as positive leaders, the UMaine homeroom snapped to attention and completed their assignment without further incident. On a similar note, Marleny Abrams says that "eighth graders hardly ever get in trouble and, when they do, all you have to say is, 'You're an eighth-grade positive leader; you have sixth and seventh graders watching you.' And that's it. 'I'm so sorry,' [they say]. They embrace it."

Ana Briggs recalls that, midway through the academic year, teachers felt like the entire student body was moving sluggishly during the passing time in between classes. In response, the dean of students simply spoke to the eighth-grade students in their advisories, telling them, "We need you positive leaders to step up and show your urgency to get to your classes. The sixth graders are watching you in the hallway." Briggs adds, "And they do [step up]. They respond to that."

In the run-up to the Powerful Speaking Extravaganza, Roxbury Prep students spent several weeks of advisory practicing their respective pieces with groups of students who had chosen a similar genre—poetry, comedy, drama, etc. These groups were mixed by grade level, and teachers frequently called upon the eighth graders in their respective groups to set an example for the other students. As noted earlier, in one such practice session Mr. Marshall challenged the students in his group to turn a weakness into a strength. When it was time for students to demonstrate to their peers what they had been working on, Mr. Marshall enthused, "Let's get some positive leaders [up here], Julian and Nancy!" The two eighth graders readily assented and, in so doing, set the standard for the rest of the students in their group.

Finally, parent Tamara Oakley notes that her daughter, Shainah, had to repeat the seventh grade at Roxbury Prep due to failing grades in several of her classes. According to Oakley, this was a harsh blow for her daughter but, now, as an eighth grader, Shainah serves as a mentor for two students who are repeating the seventh grade themselves. Oakley explains that "[Shainah] was saying that it's good she's able to let the kids know that it's okay, that you have to learn from the experience, and that you definitely need to work a little harder, but you can do it. And I mean, she did it. She's doing excellent in eighth grade now, so she just gives them the support they need." This parental perspective offers perhaps the clearest window of all into the tremendous influence of eighth graders as positive leaders—both upon their own sense of responsibility to model excellence and in the effect of this modeling upon younger students.

The benefits of Roxbury Prep's "positive leaders" mantra are underscored by a small but growing body of research on the importance of cross-age peer mentoring, which psychologist Michael Karcher characterizes as the fastest growing model of school-based youth mentoring.[18] Cross-age peer mentoring typically involves pairing an older youth with a younger youth, and meetings between the two almost always take place in the school context.[19] Programs that establish such cross-age mentoring relationships are grounded in the belief that peers serve as one of the primary socializing agents of youth and that this influence has the potential to be a highly positive one, particularly when adults structure such interactions.[20] Although researchers have only recently begun evaluating the outcomes of such relationships, a growing body of scholarship suggests that they can have positive effects upon the school connectedness, academic achievement, and social skills of the younger mentees as well as upon the school connectedness and self-esteem of the peer mentors.[21]

As previously noted, Roxbury Prep has established a number of "traditional" cross-age peer mentorship pairings, such as between Tamara Oakley's daughter Shainah and several seventh graders. Additionally, however, Roxbury Prep pushes *all* of its eighth-grade students to conceive of themselves as positive role models for the sixth- and seventh-grade students in terms of their attitude, academic achievement, and comportment. In numerous examples described in the preceding paragraphs, Roxbury Prep faculty and administrators called upon eighth-grade students to set a strong example for their younger peers by passing between classes with purpose and energy, volunteering to be the first participants in the Powerful Speaking Extravaganza, and so on. While few researchers have yet investigated the effects of this broader conception of peer mentorship, the impact of the positive leader role upon both Roxbury Prep eighth graders and the broader school culture suggests that this approach to peer mentorship is worthy of greater exploration.

All that said, Roxbury Prep teacher Ana Briggs rightly warns that the secret to the success of the "positive leaders" lever is not simply about a label: "You could say to any school, call your eighth graders 'positive leaders,' but [rather] it's this ingrained idea from sixth grade that you earn the title when you're in eighth grade. You have to build that culture and maintain that culture." One might say, then, that the effect of the "positive leaders" mantra is amplified by all of the other moments of the school day in which Roxbury Prep strives to promote a culture of performance and achievement.

## STRIVING FOR THE SPIRIT STICK

As described in chapter 2, every week at community meeting the Boston Prep faculty presents the DuBois Award to a student who has exemplified the integrity and scholarship of W. E. B. DuBois. This award represents Boston Prep's highest honor and underscores the school's commitment to developing the moral virtues of its student body. Roxbury Prep's equivalent to the DuBois Award is the Spirit Stick, which is also presented each week at community meeting to a deserving student. As befitting Roxbury Prep's intensive focus upon performance and performance character, however, the Spirit Stick is typically presented to a student who is not necessarily a top student academically, but who has demonstrated extraordinary levels of perseverance and self-discipline.

At one October community meeting, the Spirit Stick was awarded to a sixth-grade student, Ana Perez, who had only moved to the United States at the start of the school year from the Dominican Republic. Her teacher explained that Ana had fought to learn the language and adjust to the weather and an entirely new culture. "Ana still has a smile on her face," her teacher added, "at six o'clock p.m. after hours and hours of hard work . . . Thank you, Ana, for pushing yourself far beyond what is easy and for pushing everyone else to do the same." Likewise, at a March community meeting, the Spirit Stick was awarded to sixth grader Jerome Valdez. In presenting the award to Jerome, his teacher explained, "Jerome's discipline and consistent hard work inspire us. At the end of a long day, he is working on one of his homework [assignments], so he can have more time to himself in the evening. And I say to myself, if Jerome can go through seven classes and still do his homework, I should get going too."

At a community meeting near the end of the school year, the Spirit Stick was awarded to an eighth grader, Jocelyn, whose low grades had forced her to attend summer school the previous summer. As her teacher explained, "I asked Jocelyn if it was okay to share that Jocelyn was in summer school last summer. And if you miss more than two days, you repeat. And Jocelyn pretty quickly had two absences, and even though she put herself in a very difficult position, she found a way to move through it . . . So it's not always easy, but Jocelyn is someone we are proud to watch walk across that [graduation] stage on June 18th." In reflecting upon the impact of such selections for the Spirit Stick, teacher Chris Grover notes, "Last week the student that was selected for the Spirit Stick was a great kid named Hector who repeated last year and has worked incredibly hard this year and has brought his grades up from failing to Bs and Cs. So he was selected basically because of the way he does his hard work. And so I think showing kids that maybe are really struggling this year that positive example . . . and holding that person up as one type of kid that you can be, is really powerful for kids that maybe are having a tough time."

A number of Roxbury Prep students echo Grover's perception that the students chosen for the Spirit Stick winners inspire their peers to work harder. Eighth grader Natasha explains, "Sometimes I have bad weeks, but then like looking up to those people . . . makes me want to be just like them." Seventh grader Desmond adds, "It influences me because I want to be like that student and work hard and make sure I do all my work, so that way it will come to a point where I'll win it too." Finally, eighth grader Byron notes that seeing a number of his friends win the Spirit Stick has pushed him to work harder: "In seventh grade, I got used to the school and started slipping. So by seeing them get like leader of the month and the Spirit Stick, that like motivates me to want to do better."

Several Roxbury Prep parents also remark on the impact of the Spirit Stick upon their children. Glenda Washington explains that her seventh-grade daughter "told me a couple of kids in her class have gotten the Spirit Stick. She told me she hasn't gotten it yet, so I know she wants to get it. I told her, 'You've just got to keep working hard toward that goal of getting that Spirit Stick.' I think it's great." Likewise, Tamara Oakley—whose daughter did win the Spirit Stick—describes her daughter's obvious pride at her accomplishment: "She's like, 'You know, Mom, I had to work hard. Not everybody can get the Spirit Stick. You have to work hard.'" Finally, Gilbert Dunkel says that his son, Hector, taped to his bedroom wall the text of the speech that his teacher read about him before presenting him with the Spirit Stick, and notes, "We were all pretty excited!"

One can learn a lot about a company, organization, or school by the people it chooses to recognize. Roxbury Prep's awarding of the Spirit Stick week after week to students who are not the top students but who have demonstrated extraordinary perseverance reveals the extent to which the school values performance character strengths such as self-discipline and grit over pure intellect. And, as the students and parents cited in the previous paragraphs reveal, these Spirit Stick winners inspire their classmates to meet their potential as scholars and positive leaders as well.

## PERSEVERING WHEN PUSH COMES TO SHOVE

Recall from chapter 4 that Roxbury Prep students demonstrated, on average, higher levels of perseverance over the course of the academic year than their peers at Boston Prep and Pacific Rim. Our interviews with Roxbury Prep students and parents revealed that they too perceive the school to have had a significant effect upon their (or their children's) ability to persevere as scholars. Eighth grader Alanna explains that, since attending Roxbury Prep, "I think I've changed as a person. I think I've become more responsible, and I take my work more seriously, and I put my pride in it . . . 'Cause in elementary school, I'm not going to say I didn't really think about college, but I wasn't really that devoted to actually going to it and succeeding in college." Likewise, parent Bianca Medina says of her son: "I think he was not as focused as he is right now . . . He's not getting in as much trouble as before, he's doing his homework every night . . . I think with this school and how it's very structured, it really helped him change, and he's made a big, big improvement." And parent Nina Gomez says of both her children attending Roxbury Prep: "It surprised me that . . . they got to this place where there's so much homework that I thought they would be struggling, and it kind of surprised me that they got right on board . . . They didn't even complain about it. They just went on track with it and picked it up really quick."

Other Roxbury Prep students and parents focus on the school's impact upon their (or their children's) actual performance. For example, eighth grader Byron explains, "I think Roxbury Prep has definitely helped me. Like I may say that this school is a pain, but . . . I'm learning stuff that my parents don't know." Eighth grader Natasha adds, "You do get tired from the long days that we have and carrying those big binders around, but you learn more academically than in other schools . . . I know a lot of my friends [at other schools] and I talk about like things that we're learning in math, and they haven't learned that yet and we're in the same grade."

Parent Glenda Washington describes with astonishment the impact of Roxbury Prep upon her daughter's vocabulary and reading ability: "That school has made a big impact on the way she talks and thinks. Like she's forever correcting my English language, okay? And she's constantly telling me, 'Well, mom, that doesn't make sense. You have to put more thought into that. You have to be more specific in what you're saying.' And I'm like, 'Oh my goodness, this is just like a grown-up lady here talking to me!'" Similarly, parent Tamara Oakley says of her daughter: "She's grown so much. She's always been kind of a timid child, but ever since she's been in this school, she's more confident, you know . . . She has that feeling that 'I can do this, I can do anything that comes my way.'" Finally, parent Eldredge Williams seconds this description of Roxbury Prep's impact upon his own daughter's confidence: "Natasha's always been an assertive individual who really tackles the work. I think she's definitely gained more confidence in herself over the last year and a half. She's more apt to just want more. She's talking about going to boarding school to really excel. She's definitely looking to go beyond what I thought of at her age." These parents' observations serve as powerful evidence of the extent to which Roxbury Prep is strengthening students' motivation, confidence, and ability to achieve to their potential both inside and outside the classroom. These qualities that support achievement compose the definition of performance character as well as the character strengths that Roxbury Prep stakeholders believe will be the most important to their students' success in high school, college, and beyond.

# CIVIC CHARACTER
# AT PACIFIC RIM

## CHAPTER SIX

# Make a Contribution

"Today I am going to introduce you to a word you probably have not seen before," Ms. Rossing told the students in her sixth-grade character education class. "Your 'Do Now' is to take a guess about what this word means: *philanthropy*. Take a wild guess; take a silly guess. Your notebooks should be open, and you should start writing." The Pacific Rim sixth graders flipped open their notebooks and began jotting down their guesses.

A few minutes later, Ms. Rossing instructed her students to put their pencils down and share their responses.

"Is it a dance?" one student asked.

"Is it a crime?"

"A type of therapy?"

"A type of food?"

"A chemical?"

"A nice person that's crazy but needs therapy?"

"Those are all good guesses," Ms. Rossing told her sixth graders, "but none of them is correct. Philanthropy is when someone gives their time, talent, or treasure and takes action for the sake of others." She wrote the definition on the whiteboard behind her and then gave her students an opportunity to scribble it into their notebooks. When the majority of the class looked up again, Ms. Rossing continued. "Let me give you an example of philanthropy. Remember the earthquake last year in Haiti and how we had a bake sale to raise money for Haiti? That was us taking our time and treasure to do something for someone else."

A student raised her hand. "Like teachers, because you take the time to teach us?"

"With teachers, it's a little different," Ms. Rossing told her, "because we're being paid. Philanthropy is when you're not being paid."

Another student waved her hand. "What about when people do the walk for breast cancer?"

"That's right," Ms. Rossing told her. "That's practicing philanthropy."

Several other students began to offer examples of philanthropy from their own families, ranging from older siblings who had participated in canned-food drives to a mother who volunteered her time helping recent immigrants to learn English.

"Today we're going to read an article about Mark Zuckerberg, who is the founder of Facebook," Ms. Rossing told her students. "He is worth $4.9 billion all because of Facebook, and he just did something in September that is making a lot of news." She passed out to students an article from the *Christian Science Monitor* entitled "Mark Zuckerberg Makes Massive Donation to Newark Schools." As explained in the article, Zuckerberg had donated $100 million to the beleaguered public school system in Newark, New Jersey.[1]

After the students had finished the article, Ms. Rossing asked, "Is there a cause you feel really strongly about? Like, for me, public education is really important. For other people, it might be breast cancer. Tell me something that you are really passionate about."

A girl in the front row raised her hand. "Animals not getting harmed."

Another girl volunteered, "Kids that are given up for adoption."

Ms. Rossing called on a boy sitting in the middle of the classroom who had been doodling in his notebook. "Video games," the boy volunteered earnestly.

"How about a cause rather than a consumer product?" Ms. Rossing asked. "When people do philanthropy, it's for things they care about that are outside of them. So it's nice to buy video games, but how is that helping your community get better? So what do you care about outside of you?"

"More playgrounds?"

Ms. Rossing hesitated, but then another boy in the back of the class waved his hand. She nodded at him. "Going green?" he volunteered.

"That's a good one," she told him, before shifting to a different line of questioning. "So Mark Zuckerberg's passion is the public school system of Newark, New Jersey. Why do you think he donated so much money?"

A boy with a skeptical look on his face raised his hand. "I think he wants a bigger reputation. And I think he wants advertising."

A girl on the other side of the classroom spoke up, forgetting to raise her hand. "I respectfully disagree with Zach because it's not philanthropy if someone is doing it for themselves. I really don't think he did that because he could have given a lot less."

"Well, that's just a fraction of what he has," Zach countered.

The girl in the front row who had started the conversation waved her hand again. "Maybe 'cause he got a good education," she offered.

A boy who had not yet spoken raised his hand. "I have a question," he said after Ms. Rossing had nodded in his direction. "What if the kids don't want to learn? What if it's a waste of money?"

Ms. Rossing nodded her head. "As an educator, I'd say it's our responsibility as adults to make sure that kids learn. The idea that there are students who don't want to learn is unacceptable to me." She paused for a moment, then asked another question. "Do you guys have the ability to be philanthropists?" Her question was met with a chorus of yeses and nos.

When the hubbub subsided, Ms. Rossing began calling on students with their hands raised. "It takes a long time to learn to be nice," one girl explained.

"We don't have a lot of money," pointed out another boy.

"Remember," Ms. Rossing reminded her students, "philanthropy doesn't always involve money. We'll continue with this discussion next class. Please put away your character ed materials and stand for the call to order."

## CULTIVATING KAIZEN

As described in chapter 1, the Pacific Rim logo depicts two overlapping globes—one featuring the Eastern Hemisphere, and the other the Western

Hemisphere—and the school's website proclaims that Pacific Rim is a school where "East meets West." Founded in 1997 by two retired Boston School Committee members who were impressed by educational practices they had observed in Taiwan and Japan, the school aims to combine Eastern educational values and practices (high standards, discipline, and character education) with those of the West (diversity, creativity, and individualism).

When Pacific Rim opened its doors in 1997, one way in which the school's emphasis upon Eastern educational practices was conveyed to students was through the Japanese phrase *gambatte*, which means to persist or never give up. Both then and now, members of the Pacific Rim community use the phrase to exhort each other to persist in overcoming a variety of obstacles. For example, sixth grader Reginald explains that "the teachers, when you're taking a test, they'll say, 'Good luck and gambatte, don't give up.'" Likewise, middle school principal Carrie Sawyer describes sitting in the bleachers watching a Pacific Rim basketball game when both she and a parent overheard some nearby students talking about giving up on their goal of establishing a cheerleading squad at the school. Before Sawyer could say a word, the parent leaned over and told the students, "That's not really the gambatte attitude!" With this long-established focus on persistence—a performance character strength—it is not surprising that Pacific Rim students were nearly even with Roxbury Prep students in their demonstration of perseverance over the course of the 2010–2011 academic year.

Shortly after Pacific Rim opened its doors, Executive Director Spencer Blasdale introduced a second Japanese phrase, *kaizen*, which has become central to the school's approach to character development as well. According to Pacific Rim faculty, kaizen can be translated as a commitment to working for the continuous improvement of the community.[2] Principal Sawyer elaborates, "Striving for your individual best [only] covers half of what we want our students to do. We want them also to be working as a group and as a community."

In chapter 1, we defined *civic character* as "the knowledge, skills, virtues, and commitments necessary for engaged and responsible citizenship."[3] If moral character is situated in an individual's relationships and interactions with other individuals, civic character is situated in an individual's role within his or her local, national, and global communities. Likewise, if performance character consists of the qualities necessary for people to maximize their potential in individual endeavors ranging from art to academics to athletics, then civic character consists of the qualities necessary for people to be effective contributors to local, national, and global endeavors. Examples of civic character strengths include civic and political knowledge, an ethic of participation and service, and the numerous social skills necessary to work productively with others for the common good.[4] Over the course of the academic year, Pacific Rim sought to promote students' civic character development through lessons, activities, and practices focused on the concept of kaizen. The most consistent of these practices is the call-to-order ritual that Ms. Rossing utilized to conclude her character education class in the narrative that opened this chapter. At the conclusion of every middle school class period at Pacific Rim, teachers ask students to stand up and then provide feedback to the cohort on the extent to which they, as a group, demonstrated perseverance (gambatte) and worked cooperatively to maximize each other's learning (kaizen). On the wall of every middle school classroom are five-point rubrics for both gambatte and kaizen. The kaizen rubric reads:

- Did students speak respectfully to one another and their teacher?
- Listen respectfully to one another and their teacher?
- Transition smoothly and professionally through the different stages of the lesson?
- Display professional behavior?
- Maintain a clean and professional workspace?

As Principal Sawyer explains, "What we're asking students is, 'How well did you work together as a group, and here [is] a list of five things that meet that criteria.'" Based on these criteria, each middle school class receives a kaizen score between one and five. Cohorts that average a four or higher throughout the week across all of their classes are rewarded with a small treat such as a dress-down day or a class breakfast. Middle school teacher Victor Weaver notes that invoking the concept of kaizen after every class period allows Pacific Rim faculty to continually push students to reflect upon "how you affect your community and how your community affects you."

As for precisely how Pacific Rim students understand the concept of kaizen, sixth grader Tina says, "Kaizen, to me, means helping out your community in as many ways as you can. Like helping clean up trash outside is one example." Seventh grader Marco adds, "If there's an area in the classroom that's not clean, and it may not belong to you, you can still come in and help out others instead of just helping yourself." Finally, eighth grader Riley explains, "Even though you might work with people in a group that you don't like or want to work with, [you're supposed to] show kaizen and be helpful with them."

These descriptions of kaizen reveal students' development of increasingly complex understandings of what it means to possess responsibilities to one's community. Sixth grader Tina and seventh grader Marco understand kaizen in terms of keeping their classrooms tidy, while eighth grader Riley recognizes kaizen as including the ability to work effectively with a diverse set of classmates. As noted in chapter 2, such development aligns with Bärbel Inhelder and Jean Piaget's work on children's cognitive development.[5] Specifically, preadolescents such as Tina possess a limited capacity for theoretical thinking, and thus Pacific Rim's sixth-grade faculty are wise to focus on highly concrete examples of kaizen such as picking up the trash after lunch or lending a pencil to a classmate. As students move into eighth grade and early adolescence, however, they begin to develop a capacity for formal operational thinking that includes engaging in reflective thought and understanding abstract ideas. As a result, Pacific Rim's eighth-grade faculty can encourage their students to conceptualize kaizen in more complex ways.

Speaking to this point, middle school teacher Victor Weaver observes that sixth-grade students "get that kaizen is community building, and their big thing is, like, 'Well, we need to clean up [the classroom]. It needs to be clean.' . . . They're not getting the cosmic effect of how they affect their community quite yet, but as they get older, they do." He goes on to describe watching eighth-grade students at Pacific Rim reprimand a class-mate for not doing his homework: "They're not being bossy or rude, but they're starting to look at their peers and [say], 'Why didn't you do your homework? You know you had to do your homework. If you don't do your homework, we lose class score points.' This community, this kaizen, it comes together." Pacific Rim students' deepening understanding of kai-zen represents civic character development in action.

Pacific Rim high school students do not receive class scores at the con-clusion of every class. Several high school students explain that such a practice is unnecessary because they so deeply internalized the concept of kaizen during their middle school years. According to twelfth grader Al-vin: "Since we started the ninth grade, it doesn't like come up [in class]. It's like you just have it in yourself already." Twelfth grader Ezra agrees that teachers at the high school don't have to be so explicit about invoking kai-zen "because we had those three years of middle school where they were constantly doing that. It's more, like, rooted into us now." In this chapter, we consider the various practices through which Pacific Rim faculty and administrators work to develop this sense of civic responsibility within their students and also to extend it to students' perceptions of themselves as citizens of Boston, the United States, and the wider world.

## REWARDING KAIZEN

The emphasis upon civic character development at Pacific Rim is also ev-ident from the students the school chooses to recognize. Recall that at their respective community meetings each week, both Boston Prep and Roxbury Prep single out a student who has exemplified the school's core values. At Boston Prep, the DuBois Award is presented to a student who exemplifies the moral character strength of integrity, while Roxbury Prep awards the Spirit Stick to a student who has exemplified the performance character strength of perseverance. In so doing, these schools epitomize Thomas Lickona and Matthew Davidson's call for schools of character to "develop school traditions that express and strengthen commitment to excellence and ethics."[6] At Pacific Rim, the weekly award is the Kaizen-

Gambatte Award, which is presented to a student who has worked hard to contribute to the Pacific Rim community.

Similar to the two other schools, a different teacher presents the Kaizen-Gambatte Award each week, and offers a short story or description of the qualities possessed by the award winner. These narratives offer a valuable lens into the core values of the three different school communities. For example, at a middle school community meeting early in the school year, Pacific Rim middle school teacher Mr. Noble moved to the front of the cafeteria to present the Kaizen-Gambatte Award, holding five or six different hats. He then explained:

> Last year a store opened up near my house. It's a hat shop. And a few months later, I owned like ten hats. I want to share some of the reasons I get these hats. This is my sunny day hat, but the problem is that with this hat, if it rains, it's no good. So I have this wool hat for cold days and snowy days. My third hat is my gym hat. And this here is my favorite hat. It's my "wear it on special occasions" hat. So when I was thinking about today's Kaizen-Gambatte winner, I started thinking about hats. Because this person wears a lot of different hats. She doesn't actually wear a hat in class, but she does take on all of these roles. So on these bright sunny days in class, she is part of the reason—she's like the hat that tells us it's going to be a good day. And when it's not such a good day, she helps the class not get bogged down by a bad score and get back on track. And even in her own space, she's not afraid to dig in deeper for work and work really hard. And then in some ways she is sort of like the "going out" hat because almost every day I see her going above and beyond. She comes to me almost on a daily basis to ask what she can do to help out. And so the Kaizen-Gambatte Award goes to Nicolette!

Most notable about this explanation was its uniqueness to Pacific Rim. Such an explanation would not precede the awarding of the DuBois Award at Boston Prep or the Spirit Stick at Roxbury Prep. Mr. Noble's explicit focus on contributing to the community lies at the core of Pacific Rim's commitment to students' civic character development.

Pacific Rim also diverges from Boston Prep and Roxbury Prep in the extent to which faculty and administrators acknowledge that different types of students make different contributions to the school community.

At Boston Prep and Roxbury Prep, only one award is given out each week. At Pacific Rim's middle school community meeting, however, the Kaizen-Gambatte Award is followed by awards for artist of the week and athlete of the week. Likewise, at the high school community meeting, Principal Jenne Colasacco Grant explains that, in addition to the Kaizen-Gambatte Award, approximately a dozen students every month are recognized for their "meaningful contributions" to the school community. In a December high school community meeting, for example, Principal Grant began by acknowledging three different students' contributions to the thespian group, the mock-trial team, and the Gay-Straight Alliance, respectively, as well as applauding a fourth student for her commitment to being a good friend to her peers.

According to high school teacher Holly Anderson, what is unique about these contribution awards is that they aren't necessarily awarded each month to the classic academic achievers. As she explains, the award could just as easily go to a student whose "grades might not be that great, but they did a great job on the play and really took on leadership." Or, in Principal Grant's words, it might go to a student "running a really awesome pep squad with B grades and [who is] kind of in trouble sometimes." With its focus on performance character, Roxbury Prep might hesitate to reward an underachieving student. Likewise, Boston Prep's focus on moral character might disqualify the student who is "kind of in trouble sometimes." However, the emphasis on civic character development at Pacific Rim means that faculty and administrators more readily acknowledge and celebrate the varied contributions that different types of students make to the school community.

## CONNECTING COMMUNITY AND CHARACTER EDUCATION

Recall that at Boston Prep, the key pedagogical lever for introducing students to the school's moral character virtues is ethics class, whereas at Roxbury Prep, the primary means for bolstering students' performance character strengths is advisory. For middle school students at Pacific Rim, the key lever is character education class. All sixth-grade students at Pacific Rim participate in a weekly character education class, and in 2008, when the school began to admit students in the fifth grade, character education class was expanded to include them as well. Since both Boston Prep's ethics program and Roxbury Prep's advisory program are explicitly focused on character development, one could imagine character education classes at Pacific Rim resembling one or both of these programs. However, Pacific Rim's character education programming differs in some fundamental ways from the programming at the other two schools in both structure and content.

First, Boston Prep's middle school ethics classes and Roxbury Prep's advisory lessons are taught by students' advisors. At Pacific Rim, however, character education class is taught by a single faculty member, Angela Rossing, who also serves as the director of enrollment. Second, Roxbury Prep teachers divvy up the responsibility for designing advisory lessons, while Boston Prep has a dedicated faculty member responsible for creating both the lesson plans and materials for each ethics class. At Pacific Rim, Rossing takes responsibility for designing and executing the lessons for character education class, but other Pacific Rim faculty members offer input about topics or challenges that have arisen in their classes, and which they believe are most appropriate for further discussion in character education class. Finally, and most importantly, Boston Prep's ethics classes focus on the moral character virtues central to Boston Prep, while advisory at Roxbury Prep provides opportunities for students to hone their performance character strengths. Character education class at Pacific Rim is focused squarely on civic character development. As the narrative at the outset of this chapter illustrates, character education class seeks to deepen students' understanding of community and their investment in contributing to the communities of which they are a part.

For Pacific Rim sixth graders, the first two months of character education class focused on defining and exploring the value of community through a children's novel entitled *Seedfolks*.[7] The novel is set on a city street in Cleveland, Ohio, and begins when a young Vietnamese girl named Kim plants a few lima bean seeds in a vacant lot on the street. Each subsequent chapter is then narrated by another resident of the street, who belongs to a different ethnic group, and who ends up playing a role in the transformation of this vacant lot into a vibrant community garden. According to Rossing, "The whole story is centered around this whole community that comes together to raise this garden, and it's because everyone's inspired by the actions of somebody they see before them. The objective was that we all have a place in this community; we all have a responsibility to take care of the community; and we all have something to offer the community."

In one character education class, Pacific Rim students read the second chapter of *Seedfolks*, in which an elderly Romanian woman named Ana spots Kim planting the seeds in the vacant lot and initially assumes that she is up to no good. The key question with which Ms. Rossing began the class was, "How do prejudgments hurt a community?" After defining the terms *community* and *neighborhood*, the students discussed ways in which adults in the story had prejudged Kim:

MS. ROSSING: What do you think are the stereotypes that Ana may have been thinking about Kim when she prejudged her? And remember that the word *stereotype* usually uses the word *all*.

STUDENT 1: All kids are troublemakers.

MS. ROSSING: So what was the prejudgment?

STUDENT 2: That this little girl is a troublemaker.

STUDENT 3: She thought she was involved in drugs or guns or something like that.

MS. ROSSING: How do prejudgments hurt communities?

STUDENT 4: They spread from person to person.

STUDENT 5: People become less likely to trust one another.

STUDENT 2: People don't feel welcome or safe.

STUDENT 6: It causes people to feel bad about themselves.

Ms. Rossing then asked her students to consider whether they sometimes prejudged people themselves and whether that had an effect upon the Pacific Rim community:

MS. ROSSING: Do we all have feelings of prejudice?

STUDENT 4: I think we all do because we all wonder if someone new comes into the class whether that person might be dumb or might not be good. So anyone can have prejudices.

STUDENT 8: I think yes, because if you see someone walk up to you, and if they're dressed in all black, you think they must be either goth or emo.

MS. ROSSING: So how do we move past our prejudgments so that our community can thrive?

STUDENT 6: Get to know the person better.

STUDENT 9: Don't spread what you think.

STUDENT 1: See what you have in common with them.

STUDENT 10: I disagree a little, because what if the person doesn't want to get to know you?

STUDENT 1: But if you never try, how will you know?

In this excerpt from character education class, one can see ways in which the most explicit lever for character development at Pacific Rim differs from that of Boston Prep or Roxbury Prep. While ethics class at Boston Prep and advisory at Roxbury Prep focus on students' responsibilities as individuals, character education class at Pacific Rim engages students in reflection upon their roles and responsibilities as members of a community. In other words, the focus is on their civic character development rather than their moral or performance character development.[8]

Other lessons from Pacific Rim's character education class reveal this emphasis upon civic character development as well. A chapter midway through *Seedfolks* focuses on Gonzalo, a teenager from Guatemala who serves as the translator for all of the adults in his family because he is the only one who speaks English. In the character education class on this chapter, Ms. Rossing asked Pacific Rim sixth graders: "Do you think we sometimes underestimate people's value to the community based on whether or not they speak the language?"

In response, one student volunteered that when non-English speakers in the United States are excluded from participating in the community, "the community gets hurt because the person excluded might think you hate them, and you won't get everyone's ideas." Another student added,

"You make others feel bad, and you make the community a bad place to live." Other students expressed the opposite point of view. One student explained, "My friend's mom only speaks Spanish, and so I don't know when she's talking about me or anything."

These discussions of how prejudice can lead segments of a community to be ignored or discounted are particularly relevant to a school such as Pacific Rim with a diverse student body composed of white, African American, Latino, and multiracial students, and which is divided nearly evenly between poor and working-class families.[9] In recent scholarship on the relationship between socioeconomic status and political influence, researchers have found that the policy preferences of America's wealthiest citizens exert significantly more influence on the voting records of their elected representatives than the policy preferences of middle-class constituents, and that the policy preferences of America's poorest citizens exert no discernible influence at all upon legislators' voting records.[10] Likewise, political scientist Cathy Cohen has reported that there are significant differences between African American, Latino, and white youth in terms of their perceived relationships with the government.[11] Specifically, on a 2004 national survey asking youth (ages fifteen to twenty-five) to respond to the statement, "Leaders in government care very little about people like me," 56 percent of African American youth and 52 percent of Latino youth agreed with this statement as compared to only 44 percent of white youth. While statistics like these may be too complex to discuss with sixth graders, Ms. Rossing's character education class lays the groundwork for such discussions by engaging students in reflection upon the importance of soliciting the input and contributions of all members of a community.

In subsequent character education classes, Ms. Rossing further emphasized the concept of *contribution* to one's community. One example is the lesson profiled at the outset of this chapter in which students learned the definition of philanthropy and discussed the causes to which they would like to contribute. Likewise, in another class discussion of *Seedfolks*, Ms. Rossing asked students to describe the contribution *they* would make to the burgeoning community garden if they were characters in the book. The following week, the discussion turned to students' contributions to the Pacific Rim community. Ms. Rossing engaged her students in completing sentences for each of their classmates that began with the following: "1) One way I've seen you positively impact our community is . . . ; and 2) One way I think you could have even a greater impact on our community is . . ." Ultimately, the sentences that students generated became part of a giant bulletin board in the Pacific Rim cafeteria entitled "What's Your Contribution?" As noted in previous chapters, bulletin boards at Boston Prep focus on examples of moral character virtues such as compassion, and bulletin boards at Roxbury Prep feature slogans noting the role of hard work in cultivating success. Such bulletin boards exist at Pacific Rim as well; however, the majority of posters decorating the school's corridors focus on students' roles as members of both local and global communities.

## MAKING A CONTRIBUTION

Contribution is also a frequent theme of Pacific Rim's high school community meetings. For example, the tenth-grade advisory responsible for planning and executing a mid-March community meeting chose to focus their presentation on women's history in honor of women's history month. A dozen tenth graders lined up side by side at the front of the cafeteria, and each student stepped forward one at a time to address the Pacific Rim student body. A PowerPoint presentation beamed onto a giant screen reinforced each student's words with relevant phrases and pictures:

STUDENT 1: Before 1970, women's history was a subject rarely studied. Since then, however, today almost every university offers a women's studies course.

STUDENT 2: How did women's history develop? There was a movement in the 1960s, and there started being a growing number of female historians.

STUDENT 3: International Women's Day began in 1978 as Women's History Week in Sonoma, California.

STUDENT 4: Madame C. J. Walker lived during the 1800s and became a successful entrepreneur and inspiration.

STUDENT 5: Indira Gandhi was the third prime minister of India and started India's nuclear program.

STUDENT 6: Amelia Earhart was the first woman to fly solo across the Atlantic.

STUDENT 7: Maya Lin is an architect who designed the Vietnam Memorial and the Civil Rights Memorial.

STUDENT 8: Maya Angelou is a writer and a civil rights activist, and we're going to close our presentation by reading one of her poems, "Still I Rise."

Another Pacific Rim community meeting focused on the theme of contribution on a smaller scale. The presenting eleventh graders stood side by side at the front of the auditorium, and each student answered the question, "Who in our life gives our life meaning?"

STUDENT 1: My mother. She takes two jobs. She inspires me.

STUDENT 2: My sister, who is my best friend. I was bullied for six years and to have someone that gives me support, she's my inspiration.

STUDENT 3: My mother, she's a strong woman. She takes care of me and my sister. It's hard to explain.

STUDENT 4: My friends help me keep my grades up, because of competition with each other. And my whole class of 2012 inspires me to keep my grades up and be a leader.

STUDENT 5: My godfather, who knows just what to say to me to make feel good and proud of who you are.

After each of the presenting students cited a person who inspired them, Dean Diamond took the podium to offer a connection between the people who inspired these students and all of the work that Pacific Rim students do each day to achieve their academic goals. "Today," Dean Diamond told the student body, "we named friends, teachers, school members, and family for what they do for you. Get through this phase of your life so you can help and be ready for others to rely on you. Right now, they are making an impact on you, but you will have the tools and power to make an impact!"

Principal Grant had made a similar point at a community meeting a few weeks earlier in her presentation of the Kaizen-Gambatte award.

Before naming the deserving student, Grant offered a quotation found on the Westminster Abbey tomb of an Anglican bishop who died in the 1100s. The paraphrased quote read: "I dreamed of changing the world when I was very young; when I grew older, I dreamed of changing my country; in my twilight years I dreamed of changing my family . . . On my deathbed I realized if I had only changed myself, by example, I could have changed my family; and then maybe my family could have made a better country; and a better country could have changed the world." Principal Grant concluded with the observation that "with transformation of self, we make the world a better place," and she went on to describe a student who had recently made a "meaningful personal transformation" and, in so doing, was transforming the community around her.

At the high school level, character education class is replaced by a twice-weekly advisory that focuses, in large part, on the theme of contribution as well. For example, eleventh-grade teacher Holly Anderson describes one advisory lesson that began with students reading a newspaper article about a wealthy older couple who had started a series of free symphony concerts in Boston, with the goal of making beautiful music accessible to everyone. After her students read the article, Anderson—whose classroom includes a large sign above the whiteboard reading "Show up, Be Prepared, Contribute"—asked, "If you could do anything in the world and you could change anything, what would that change be?" Then, she recalls, "we went around the room and talked about what would you want to do. And it was just really interesting to hear the students' different dreams." Principal Grant adds that these discussions in the high school advisories then segued into "What could you do now that's a step closer to making that [dream] happen? Like, what organizations could you work with in the community that have similar goals?"

All of these examples reveal the extent to which the work taking place each day at Pacific Rim is framed around civic character development. Students are encouraged by their teachers to work hard now in order to transform themselves into scholars and professionals, so that they will be better able to contribute to the various communities of which they are a part. It is precisely this sense of purpose that Stanford psychologist William Damon has characterized as lacking in many high school and college students.[12] According to Damon, "the most pervasive problem of the day is a sense of emptiness that has ensnared many young people in long periods of drift during a time in their lives when they should be defining their aspirations and making progress toward their fulfillment."[13] Pacific Rim's emphasis on contribution makes the school an exemplar of Damon's claim that schools must explicitly work to develop in youth "a serious purpose that can give meaning and direction to life."[14]

## STRENGTHENING CIVIC CHARACTER IN CIVICS CLASS

Pacific Rim faculty and administrators have deliberately positioned character education class in students' first two years of middle school so that they have an opportunity to learn from the start about the ethic of kaizen that is so central to the school's ethos and practices. This experience is bookended six years later, when students participate during their senior year in a year-long civics course. Rather than focusing on the three branches of government or how a bill becomes a law, however, civics at Pacific Rim is designed to strengthen students' sense of civic responsibility for the roles that await them *outside* the walls of the Academy. As twelfth-grade student Gabby explains, "I think Pacific Rim has us taking civics because it kind of gets us all to start thinking about . . . how our communities are affecting us and how we're affecting our communities, and how Boston actually works. And I think it's for our senior year because we've [already] taken U.S. history and world history, and now we're working on, like, the present."

Particularly fascinating about Gabby's interpretation is that it parallels almost verbatim middle school teacher Victor Weaver's explanation that character education class starts Pacific Rim middle schoolers thinking about "the importance of being part of the community, and how you affect your community, and how your community affects you." In these comments, one can see that both sixth graders and twelfth graders at Pacific Rim are learning about their relationship with a community—all that has changed in the intervening years is the size and scope of the community about which they are learning.

As noted in chapter 3, psychologist Erik Erikson characterized adolescence as the period in the life span in which adolescents shift from a single-minded focus on "Who am I?" to a broader question of "How do I fit into the world around me?"[15] This second question becomes particularly relevant to adolescents in their final years of high school as they prepare to leave behind the familiar cocoon of their secondary school community and, often, to move away simultaneously from the family home in which they have spent their childhood. For all of these reasons, teenagers in late adolescence are particularly motivated by the opportunity to learn more about communities that lie beyond the walls of their high school and neighborhood—communities that they will shortly be entering as independent young adults.[16]

What precisely does Pacific Rim's civics class look like? The class is structured as a seminar in order to prepare students for the types of classes they will experience in college. As a result, the entire class—including the civics teacher, Tonya Batista—sits together in a tight circle and engages in more free-flowing discussions than Pacific Rim students have experienced in previous history courses. In one civics class, Pacific Rim seniors discussed the experiences of undocumented workers living in Boston. Students arrived for class having already read a research report on the needs of recent Hispanic immigrants to the Boston area, and the class began with students' reactions to the report:

STUDENT 1: They're being used. The meat-slicing guy, the situation he was in. After he got his finger cut, it's not a coincidence he stopped working. The companies use it against a person, and they know if something goes wrong, that person won't be able to do anything about it.

STUDENT 2: Yeah, if they try to speak up against their company, they can have them deported.

STUDENT 3: It's like they don't have a voice.

STUDENT 4: Isn't it like their fault they're getting misused? If the government or something finds out that a corporation is hiring undocumented workers, do they get in trouble?

MS. BATISTA: Yes, but why would a company do something like that?

STUDENT 5: Cheap labor, can't speak up for themselves.

STUDENT 6: And if you want to immigrate yourself, isn't it like a really long process and really expensive on top of that?

Although Ms. Batista's primary role in the preceding discussion was that of facilitator, this discussion also serves as an example of the willingness of Pacific Rim educators to provide a space for students to grapple with civic *and political* issues.

A subsequent civics class turned to the issue of gentrification. In preparation for this discussion, students had read a 2004 *New Yorker* article about the changing face of South Boston, a neighborhood that for many years had been a blue-collar Irish Catholic enclave, but was now gentrifying rapidly.[17] The article focused particularly on a church in South Boston that the Boston Archdiocese had sold to a real estate developer for conversion into condominiums. Ms. Batista began the class discussion with two overarching questions: "Whom does gentrification benefit? Whom does it harm?"

STUDENT 1: I was surprised they renovated a church. That felt a little weird to me because I consider a church sacred. I thought that was kind of disrespectful to do a thing like that just to make a profit.

STUDENT 2: I didn't find it that surprising because, for me . . . I thought this reading was about Southie losing its sense of community and turning into something else.

STUDENT 3: I don't think it's reasonable for people to be worried about a higher class of people moving in because that's what happens when you renovate. It's not crazy for people to want something new to come in there. It's not necessarily right, but it's the way it works.

STUDENT 4: The people getting moved out have fewer options than the people moving in. How do you just up and move someone out? How does that work?

STUDENT 5: Because like the people leave, and they abandon houses and stores and stuff, and the city is going to make it better so people come back.

STUDENT 6: It's not pro-community, in my opinion. It's just people helping themselves.

STUDENT 7: You can see how a community can get more and more expensive because the prices just keep going up and up and up.

MS. BATISTA: So who benefits from gentrification?

STUDENT 3: Realtors.

STUDENT 8: It makes the city look better, brings in more tourists.

STUDENT 1: The government, because they get all the tax money.

STUDENT 9: One guy said a grocery store was [now] close by, but he also said, "What's the point if you don't have the money to live there?"

In this discussion, Pacific Rim seniors worked together to deepen their understanding of a civic issue that will unequivocally impact them as young adults making their way in the world. According to Erikson, such a topic raises precisely the questions that individuals in late adolescence are seeking to answer.[18] For this reason, it is no surprise that Pacific Rim senior Alvin notes, "I feel really strongly about civics because I just like learning about Boston." Several of Alvin's classmates agree that civics is one of the most engaging classes they have taken at Pacific Rim.

## ENGAGING WITH SOCIAL ISSUES

Pacific Rim's focus on civic character development has also led the school to employ several levers beyond civics class to engage students in reflection upon civic and social issues. At the high school level, Principal Grant describes a number of advisory lessons that direct students' attention to the current events and challenges beyond the walls of the Academy. For example, one advisory lesson focused on an op-ed in the *Boston Globe* written after a spate of murders in Boston neighborhoods. The article was written by a Boston high school student as a letter addressed to the city of Boston. Grant explains that, in ninth- and tenth-grade advisories, students "could write back as if they were Boston or they could write a letter themselves to Boston." The students then shared their letters with one another and discussed their own perspectives on the safety (or lack thereof) in their respective neighborhoods.

Eleventh-grade advisor Holly Anderson describes another advisory lesson that took up the prevalence of racism in the city of Boston: "It was interesting to see which kids thought racism existed or did not exist in Boston. Clearly, kids who have experienced racial profiling said it does exist. And other kids were like, 'What are you talking about?' So that was a really interesting discussion to have. My advisory in particular really likes the deeper discussions. We just get into that." As noted earlier, political scientist Cathy Cohen has documented the divergent perspectives on discrimination among youth of different racial and ethnic backgrounds.[19] Pacific Rim's emphasis upon civic character development has prompted faculty to utilize advisory as another space for exploring issues imbued with civic and political meaning.

A variety of social issues were also the focus of Pacific Rim's men's and women's groups—extracurricular discussion groups that meet weekly during the lunch period. At a January community meeting, the faculty advisor to the men's group announced, "In the men's group meeting [today], we are going to talk about the [principal's] office, discipline, and behavior modification, including the number of students who are sent to the office, how those numbers break down by gender, race, [and] grade. Who gets sent to the office? And how is this connected to law enforcement outside of school?" This men's group discussion focused particularly on the role of racism in school disciplinary practices, which a number of scholars have found to exhibit the same discriminatory patterns as the criminal justice system.[20] Moreover, a women's group meeting in April focused on the topic of sexual abuse, and a joint meeting of the men's and women's groups in December considered the issue of community violence. A school less committed to students' civic character development might actively shy away from such charged discussion topics, but Pacific Rim explicitly establishes venues for addressing these topics head-on.

High school teacher Tameka Robinson explains that Pacific Rim's commitment to engaging students in reflection upon social issues is also embedded in the academic curriculum. As an example, Robinson—an English teacher—notes that her ninth-grade students are currently reading Richard Wright's *Native Son*, a novel about an African American man living in poverty on Chicago's South Side in the 1930s. According to Robinson: "They're reading it in the context of it being a protest novel by

Wright, but they're also thinking about big, essential questions like 'Is violence ever justified?' 'What are ways that people can incite change?' [and] 'How do writers have a political bias that they're coming to an issue with?' So just those conversations alone, sometimes the students will go into certain things that happen in their own communities and certain decisions they have to make and certain influences they have to push aside and not be influenced by." In this explanation, one can see that a primary lens through which Pacific Rim students explore Wright's novel is a civic one. Whereas an English class at Boston Prep might focus particularly on the moral issues embedded in the protagonist's decision to turn to crime to escape poverty, Pacific Rim faculty direct students' attention to the larger societal issues underlying the protagonist's decisions.

Finally, in the same way that Boston Prep faculty frequently invoke the school's five virtues in more informal interactions with students, Pacific Rim faculty do the same with civic and social issues. For example, Dean Diamond explains that he likes to display in his office pictures and quotations that encourage students to think more deeply about important social issues facing the communities in which they live. One picture on Dean Diamond's wall is a stenciled cartoon of a homeless man holding a piece of paper that reads, "You can keep your coins, I want change." According to Dean Diamond, pictures and quotations like these "are a great way for kids to just quickly take a gem of wisdom, and it will either impact them then or they'll think about it and when something happens, they can connect it, and I think that's largely the way we grow and learn."

Similarly, at an April community meeting, Dean Diamond told the students, "I want to share with you a poem that really made me think." He went on to read a poem about the state of poverty in America that concluded with the lines "Change will not come because we are good people. Change will not come because commissions are appointed, agencies established, speeches made . . . We can only count on the things we take or take back. There is only one real way to make change, and that is to fight back and to organize." Dean Diamond's call for engaged citizenship through activism and organization represents another example of the ways in which issues of civic character arise in Pacific Rim's informal teachable moments as well.

## DEVELOPING GLOBAL CITIZENS

Perhaps not surprising for a school explicitly founded with the goal of merging Eastern and Western cultures, Pacific Rim faculty and administrators are also committed to strengthening students' sense of *global citizenship*— that is, fostering in students a sense of responsibility for the well-being of fellow citizens across the globe and a desire to engage in behaviors and actions that benefit citizens beyond their own local, state, or national boundaries.[21] In his 2008 book *Five Minds for the Future*, psychologist Howard Gardner wrote of the pressing need for schools "to prepare youngsters so that they can survive and thrive in a world different from one ever known or even imagined before."[22] Likewise, Nancy Thomas asserted in a 2010 U.S. Department of Education report entitled *Strengthening Civic Learning and Democratic Engagement* that educational institutions must offer "learning experiences that will help students acquire and develop a global perspective they will need to thrive in a diverse, global society."[23]

One of the primary levers through which Pacific Rim strengthens students' sense of themselves as global citizens is the school's connection with China. From seventh grade through graduation, all Pacific Rim students study Mandarin Chinese, a language that has been characterized along with Arabic, Japanese, and Korean as among the most difficult for English speakers to learn and that is offered at fewer than 5 percent of the middle and secondary schools in the United States.[24] Dean Diamond offers this explanation: "I've had parents ask me why don't the kids learn Creole or French or Spanish, which will suit them better in their communities, and I say, well, in the larger world scale, knowing Mandarin is going to really put them ahead if they stick with it. And if they merge into business or scholarly work, that's the future."

Studying Chinese also allows for a robust exchange program between Pacific Rim and a secondary school in Beijing, China. Every year, twenty

Pacific Rim students travel to China for two weeks, and a handful of students spend a full trimester in Beijing attending classes and living with a host family. Pacific Rim high school teacher Tameka Robinson characterizes this opportunity to visit China as "part of the fabric of what we are and what we do here." She notes that the three students who had spent a trimester in China in 2010 "took all their courses in Mandarin there and came back really fluent in Mandarin." One of these students, twelfth grader Ezra, says, "I think it's a really good experience at such a young age to get to do stuff like that . . . It helps us to sort of break those boundaries, like a language barrier, and kind of make us see that we're all kind of teenagers, and we should get along." Such perspectives are particularly valuable given recent scholarship that has shown American youth lagging behind their international peers in their knowledge of world geography, current affairs, and international political relationships, and simultaneously more likely than their international peers to characterize their culture as superior to that found in other countries.[25]

Even the Pacific Rim students who never travel to China are influenced by this exchange. Pacific Rim plays host every January to twenty Chinese teenagers who attend classes at the school and are hosted by Pacific Rim families. High school teacher Shannel Tuzzo explains, "That experience of being in a foreign place [or] having exchange people come here that speak another language, you see they have the same cell phones and things with them, and that they like to hang out with their friends on the weekends. Some of those things are more obvious to our students." Ninth grader Julissa adds, "Recently, Chinese exchange students came here, and I got really close with one, and when she left, it was like really sad. But to think that you're going to keep in touch with somebody halfway across the world, it makes you feel like you have more connections to the world than an average student might have." With these words, Julissa offers a clear illustration of the ways in which Pacific Rim's exchange program allows students to conceptualize the roles and responsibilities of citizenship as extending beyond local or even national boundaries. As Dean Diamond notes, Pacific Rim's Chinese language offerings, and the exchange opportunities made possible by them, are "exposing kids to different characters, different ways of thinking, something so foreign to the way they live . . . I do think that it broadens them as people."

A second lever through which Pacific Rim fosters students' conception of themselves as global citizens is an English course open to eleventh- and twelfth-grade students on global citizenship. In another effort to prepare Pacific Rim students for the types of courses they will experience in college, the junior- and senior-year English courses at Pacific Rim are a series of seminars. English teacher Shannel Tuzzo characterizes the global citizenship seminar she teaches every year as her passion, saying, "I just think it's important that students see a world outside of themselves, and teenagers are, through no fault of their own, very focused on themselves. So I just think it's important to expose them to what's going on in the world. What are those countries out there in the world that we haven't talked about? And just sort of have a sense [that] these things affect them whether they're just paying their taxes or they're going to the grocery store or they're shopping for sneakers. They're global citizens. And it's just sort of bringing awareness of that to them."

Tuzzo has two primary learning objectives for her students. The first is developing an "awareness of how your actions are actually linked to other people, both people that you're meeting with or people that you might never meet." The second is gaining a clearer sense of how the United States fits into the wider world—in other words, for students "to know where countries are, [and] know how the U.S. trades with them or wages war with them, or supports their president." In these goals, Tuzzo echoes one of the core principles for global citizenship education established in 2005 by a blue-ribbon panel of America's leading civic education scholars— namely, that students should learn about the ways in which their local, national, and international communities are increasingly interdependent.[26]

Tuzzo recalls that, in the opening weeks of the school year, she gave students in her global citizenship seminar a questionnaire about what types of behaviors constitute global citizenship: "One [question] was buying a cup of coffee, and they're like, 'Oh, no, that's ridiculous.'" By the end of the semester, however, students had come to see how goods they buy, ranging from coffee to hair products, have implications for people's lives halfway across the globe. In Tuzzo's words, her students now recognize that "even if you're just buying your shoes, you can still be making a positive choice that would positively impact somebody, or you can be making a choice that you don't even think is positive or negative, and it could have negative consequences."

As part of Pacific Rim's global citizenship seminar, students read works such as the Iranian graphic novel *Persepolis* by Marjane Satrapi; Haitian novelist Edwidge Danticat's *Krik Krak*; Greg Mortenson's *Three Cups of Tea*; and Tracy Kidder's *Mountains Beyond Mountains*. This last selection depicts physician Paul Farmer's mission to improve the health outcomes of men, women, and children in Haiti. Tuzzo explains that she found the account of Farmer's work in Haiti to be a particularly useful teaching tool: "He's this kind of everyday white guy, right, who's going to this other country and immersing himself in it and ends up loving it better than his own country. So it's just sort of that letting himself be a part of this global world."

According to Tuzzo, another strength of the global citizenship course is its flexibility in accommodating learning and reflection about pressing international news. For example, the 2010–2011 academic year coincided with the Arab Spring—a period of historic protest and unrest throughout much of the Middle East. Tuzzo notes that current events are incorporated every semester into class discussions; however, "this year, through no planning of my own, the Egyptian revolution happened, and so the kids were curious. They started asking questions. They were like, 'Wait, I saw this on the news. I don't understand.' And so we started doing current events." Similarly, when the 2011 uprising to topple Colonel Muammar Gaddafi began in Libya, Tuzzo recalls that her students began arriving in class with questions like, "Why is Gaddafi a bad guy? He just seems like a president. What's the matter with it?" Through these class discussions, students gained deeper insight into the workings of the contemporary Middle East. Moreover, as philosopher Martha Nussbaum has pointed out, examining the unrest in these other countries, and the underlying social and political issues, provides a "useful mirror" for Pacific Rim students to reflect upon their own nation's beliefs and customs.[27] In all of these ways, Pacific Rim's global citizenship seminar is a powerful lever for promoting students' civic character development.

## SPEAKING CIVIC LANGUAGE

In chapter 2, we described the ways in which Boston Prep's ethics class creates a schoolwide vocabulary around five key virtues for discussing moral matters. Likewise, the culture of performance and achievement at Roxbury Prep results in a common vocabulary among the school's teachers and students around performance character strengths such as self-discipline and perseverance. These vocabularies play an important role in Boston Prep students' moral character development and Roxbury Prep students' performance character development because, according to psychologist Lev Vygotsky, identity and other types of psychological development are relational or "interpsychological" processes.[28] In other words, an individual's sense of his or her place in the world does not develop in isolation, but rather is influenced by the perspectives and ideas of those around him or her. A common vocabulary allows for these perspectives and ideas to be shared more effectively among members of a particular community.

At Pacific Rim, the focus on students' civic character development means that the common vocabulary invoked by both students and teachers to discuss important matters centers on community and citizenship. For example, at a December high school community meeting, Principal Grant announced, "A North Face jacket went missing [today]. This is the second jacket that went missing this year. This is obviously not the type of community we want to be. Please bring it back, no questions asked." Faculty responding to a similar incident at Boston Prep might have invoked individual moral character strengths such as compassion for the person missing a coat or integrity in coming forward to admit the theft. At Pacific Rim, however, the announcement of the missing coat focused on maintaining the type of school *community* in which faculty and students want to work.

Pacific Rim also stands out for its use of civic terminology to describe particular roles and practices within the school. For example, middle school students at Boston Prep, Roxbury Prep, and Pacific Rim all receive weekly (or biweekly) progress reports to be signed by their parents or guardians. At all three schools, these reports focus on students' academic grades as well as behavioral indicators such as merits, demerits, send-outs, absences, and tardies. Only Pacific Rim, however, refers to the sum of these behavioral measures as students' "citizenship scores." This framing of student behavior in terms of citizenship offers another example of how the school's focus on civic character development influences the language with which important matters are discussed.

On a similar note, in one character education class Angela Rossing divided her sixth-grade students into collaborative learning groups. Adhering to a common practice among educators, she then assigned her students to take on distinct roles within their respective groups. Interestingly, the roles that Ms. Rossing assigned to students corresponded to political roles within the White House: press secretary, director of communication, chief of staff, auditor, etc. She also explained the nature of these roles to her students in distinctly political terms. For example, she said of the press secretary: "Okay, at the White House, the press secretary spends his or her day running around, getting updates on how things are going, so that at the end of the day they can go to the press, and the press gets answers to questions. So [in each group] the press person is the one person who is going to be responsible for [reporting] what the group thinks." In a similar use of civic language to define students' roles, the eighth-grade students at Pacific Rim trained to give tours to visitors are officially referred to as the school's "ambassadors."

Perhaps the clearest example of the unique vocabularies through which the three schools in our study address important issues is their different approaches to bullying. As mentioned in earlier chapters, a 2010 law passed by the Massachusetts state legislature required all schools to adopt and implement antibullying curriculum at all grade levels. As we noted in chapter 2, Boston Prep incorporated these antibullying lessons into their ethical philosophy curriculum by discussing the behavior of bullies and bystanders through the character virtues of courage and compassion. Roxbury Prep sought to address bullying through performance—namely, assigning students to write and recite letters to victims of bullying. In character education class at Pacific Rim, students considered bullying through a civic lens. Specifically, in another of her character education classes, Ms. Rossing opened a discussion about bullying with her sixth-grade students by explicitly referencing the new Massachusetts law: "The Massachusetts Bullying Prevention Law was signed this past October in 2010. Why is this law in place?" This ensuing discussion focused on Phoebe Prince, a high school student in western Massachusetts whose suicide after several weeks of bullying had inspired the new legislation. Through a PowerPoint presentation, Ms. Rossing then walked her students through the specifics of the new law, including the legal consequences awaiting youth and adolescents found guilty of bullying. When students expressed surprise that the new law included the possibility of jail time for bullies, the conversation turned to appropriate legal consequences for such behavior:

MS. ROSSING: Tell me what you think is an appropriate punishment for bullying.

STUDENT 1: They should stay in a cell alone until their parents come to get them.

STUDENT 2: I think they should be suspended. They should [also] go to one of those talking doctors, a therapist.

STUDENT 3: Community service.

STUDENT 4: If it's to the point where someone committed suicide, they should go to jail for a pretty long time.

Ms. Rossing then turned to national statistics on bullying: "According to the Justice Department, 25 percent of kids will be bullied during their adolescence." The lesson concluded with students debating the veracity of that statistic and whether or not the incidents of bullying have actually risen over the past twenty years.

In this lesson, one can see that the lens through which Pacific Rim faculty addresses bullying with their students is quite different from that of Boston Prep or Roxbury Prep. At Pacific Rim, the focus is on the *civic* implications of bullying: *what motivated this new legislation? What precisely does the new legislation say? What impact will it have upon bullying at*

*Pacific Rim and in the United States more broadly?* As mandated by state law, each school in this study seeks to address the issue of bullying with its students, but does so through the lens and in the language particular to that school's own culture. At Pacific Rim, the lens and language is one of civic character, and the school's lessons and practices are focused upon strengthening students' connections to the various communities of which they are a part.

CHAPTER SEVEN

# Be the Change

"Thank you all for coming," Tonya Batista told the teachers, administrators, and Pacific Rim tenth graders who had crowded into her classroom to watch the seniors' legacy presentations. "As you know, seniors have been working third trimester on a research project slash action project. They've been working in the community on a topic of their choosing and doing research on their topic. And you'll see the incredible diversity of what they've been working on. They'll present for ten minutes and then take questions. The first presenter will be Gabby. Thank you for coming!" The audience applauded politely.

Gabby—a tall young woman with a confident demeanor—took Ms. Batista's place at the front of the classroom and brought to life the PowerPoint projector behind her. Her presentation was entitled "A Thousand Sisters: An In-Depth Look at Rape in the Congo."

"For my project, I wanted to look into rape in the Congo," she began. "Right now there is a conflict in the Congo, and it is considered the worst place in the world to be a girl or woman." Onto the screen behind her flashed a giant map of the Congo that was color-coded to indicate where the highest incidences of rape were occurring. "In Rwanda in 1994," Gabby continued, "there was a genocide between the Tutsis and the Hutus. When that genocide ended, all the Hutu fled Rwanda and took over this area in Congo." Gabby went on to explain that many of the incidences of rape in the Congo were being committed by former Hutu rebels, known as the Interahamwe, as well as by members of the Congolese army. "They're systematically attacking and humiliating and punishing women," Gabby explained. "There is a huge stigma against women who are raped, so once they are raped, their husbands kick them out of the village."

As part of her research, Gabby had read a book by author Lisa J. Shannon entitled *A Thousand Sisters: My Journey into the Worst Place on Earth to Be a Woman*. Drawing on this work, Gabby explained that first-world countries such as the United States have been reluctant to intervene in the internal politics of the Congo because they rely on the Congo for minerals that help to power electronics such as video games and telephones.

"What I did," Gabby continued, "was work with Grassroots International, which gives small grants to developing countries around the world. Their goal is to provide sustainable food and water to these countries. They [also] go after these big corporations to let them know how their products are affecting the rest of the world. Later on, I got involved with Congo Action Now, and they're working to try to stop the violence in the Congo."

Gabby clicked to a PowerPoint slide that read, "What You Can Do!" She explained, "People aren't expecting you to stop using computers, but you can go to RAISE Hope for Congo and write letters to Toshiba and Apple and let them know what is happening. And that is it!"

The entire audience applauded, with Gabby's fellow seniors expressing the greatest enthusiasm. A number of students raised their hands to ask questions.

One girl asked, "Do you know whether there are programs in the Congo that help women who've been raped recover?"

Gabby nodded. "There is one organization called Women for Women. It's a place where these raped women can go to get financial security and try to move on from their traumatic experience."

A tenth-grade girl asked, "You said men shun their wives after they've been raped. Do any men realize they should be helping?"

"The stigma with women who are raped is the biggest reason why a lot of women aren't going to the hospitals," Gabby explained, "because they're afraid to be shunned. The reason I started this project is because I saw this play called *Ruined* about a girl who had been brutally raped."

A senior boy asked, "Is there anyone in the Congo trying to help out?"

"The United Nations," Gabby explained. "[But] this is considered the UN's biggest failure because there are a lot of UN soldiers there, but the fighting still continues."

The young man asked a follow-up question: "So the Interahamwe is stronger than the UN soldiers?"

Gabby shook her head. "A lot of women aren't coming forward to say anything about the rape, and these rebel soldiers aren't in uniform. And these rebels often run back into the forest because the Congo has an enormous rainforest." A number of the young women in the classroom are visibly outraged by this information.

"Thank you," Ms. Batista said to Gabby, and everyone applauded again. "Our next presenter is going to talk to us about teen dating violence."

## MEASURING DARING

On the surveys that Roxbury Prep, Boston Prep, and Pacific Rim students completed at the beginning and conclusion of the academic year was a measure of courage that consisted of four survey items adapted from Nansook Park and Christopher Peterson's Values in Action Inventory of Character Strengths for Youth.[1] These items questioned students about their likelihood of engaging in actions such as defending a peer being treated unfairly and telling a friend if they believed that friend was making a poor decision. All together, these items formed a robust composite of the character strength of courage.[2] Within the Pacific Rim community, courage is typically referred to as *daring* and represents one of the core character strengths that faculty and administrators seek to foster in students.

We fit a series of multilevel regression models to compare the changes in daring of students across the three schools from the beginning to the end of the 2010–2011 academic year. We found no significant differences across the three schools at the middle school level. At the high school level, however, our analyses revealed that students at Pacific Rim demonstrated a significant ($p < .05$) shift in their commitment to daring behavior in comparison to their peers at Boston Prep.[3]

The mean daring scores for Boston Prep and Pacific Rim high school students at the beginning and conclusion of the academic year are presented in figure 7.1. As figure 7.1 shows, Boston Prep students demonstrated, on average, little change in their sense of daring over the course of the school year. In contrast, Pacific Rim students began the academic year with a marginally lower mean score on the daring measure than their peers at Boston Prep, but then showed a significant increase in their commitment to engaging in daring behavior over the course of the academic year. This effect of attending Pacific Rim upon students' commitment to daring can be characterized as a small one.[4]

In chapter 6, we focused on the academic and curricular levers through which Pacific Rim seeks to introduce students to the roles and responsibil-

FIGURE 7.1   Mean pre- and post-intervention daring scores for high school students at Boston Prep and Pacific Rim ($n = 279$)

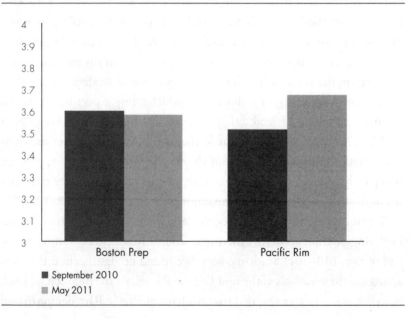

September 2010
May 2011

ities of citizenship at the local, national, and global levels. In this chapter, we focus on the ways in which Pacific Rim fosters civic character development by providing students with opportunities to not only learn about, but also actively engage in, the work of citizenship. We believe the numerous opportunities for Pacific Rim students to step into the role of civic *actor* within the school community, city of Boston, and wider world are responsible, in large part, for their significant increases in daring over the course of the school year.

## PROVIDING POWERFUL PARTICIPATORY EXPERIENCES

As noted in chapter 6, all Pacific Rim seniors participate in a civics course that introduces them to civic issues such as gentrification and illegal immigration. Civics class also provides Pacific Rim students with an opportunity to work alongside engaged citizens on a civic issue about which they feel passionate. Specifically, the culmination of civics class is a "legacy project" in which students identify a civic issue of personal importance to them; conduct research to learn more about the issue; and spend several weeks interning with an organization involved in addressing the issue. The narrative at the outset of this chapter came from field notes collected during twelfth grader Gabby's presentation of her legacy project focused on rape in the Congo. Directly following Gabby's presentation was a presentation by Camille, a twelfth-grade student who had chosen teen dating violence as the civic issue about which she wanted to learn. Her internship had taken place at the Boston Health Commission, an organization that, in Camille's words, "tries to educate teens about healthy relationships before they start dating." As part of her internship, Camille had participated in presentations to other high school students that offered tips and information about healthy dating relationships.

A third Pacific Rim senior, Alvin, had focused his legacy project on the issue of Haitian immigration. According to Alvin, "For my legacy hours, I worked at the Haitian Health Institute and also the Newcomers Academy. The Institute reaches out to meet the unmet needs of the Haitian community. For example, they've been raising money for the Haiti earthquake aftermath. I also worked at the Newcomers Academy, which is one of the best things I've ever done. I got really close to the kids because they couldn't really speak English." The Newcomers Academy, part of the Boston Public Schools, is a school for teenagers who have recently arrived in the United States with limited English proficiency. As Alvin explained at the conclusion of his presentation, this legacy project was a highly personal one for him because both of his parents had emigrated from Haiti before he was born and had experienced firsthand the poor conditions his civics class had discussed several months earlier.

In terms of the effects of these legacy projects, Gabby explains, "It's such a great way to end your career at Pacific Rim because you get to go out into the community and actually do something *you* want to do. And research a topic *you* found interesting. And really actually go into the community and do something." Likewise, another Pacific Rim senior, Ezra, says, "I think it really does get us open to, well, not the world, but our communities." As both students note, the internships embedded within the legacy projects give Pacific Rim students the opportunity to move beyond the familiar environs of their school, neighborhood, and families and take action alongside professionals committed to a cause in which they have expressed interest. Psychologist James Youniss has written that experiences like these can have a profound effect upon the civic identity development of adolescents because they offer adolescents powerful "participatory experiences" with both the recipients of the organization's efforts as well as the professionals working for the organization.[5] More specifically, Youniss has suggested that engaging in direct service through organizations like those described by Gabby, Camille, and Alvin "typically provide direct exposure to explicit ideological positions that can then be rejected or built into their developing ideologies."[6] In other words, Pacific Rim seniors interning at organizations such as Grassroots International and the Haitian Health Institute are exposed to new perspectives on both the particular social issues upon which they are working as well as civic responsibility more broadly. Whether students incorporate the perspectives they encounter at their internship sites into their own emerging worldviews, or reject these perspectives wholesale, the experience of considering new and different viewpoints is an important step in their own civic identity development. Or, as scholar Meira Levinson explains, "Participation promotes the inclusion of civic character into the [adolescent's] construction of identity that, in turn, persists and mediates civic engagement into adulthood."[7]

The internships in which Pacific Rim students engage as part of their legacy projects also represent an important foray into the professional sphere. Adolescent development scholars Michael Nakkula and Eric Toshalis have written that "powerful learning opportunities exist whenever we move beyond the safe and known," and that internships and job shadowing can be particularly beneficial in allowing students "to move beyond their immediate environments in their exposure to a world of work."[8] These types of powerful opportunities are more frequently presented to adolescents in affluent communities than to students from low-income backgrounds; however, the deep commitment to civic character development at Pacific Rim led Principal Jenne Colasacco Grant and Executive Director Susan Thompson to allocate the resources necessary to offer these opportunities to every Pacific Rim senior.[9] As a result, the legacy projects serve as a powerful lever for sharpening students' focus on the particular civic issues in which they will personally engage as young adults.

## BECOMING CIVIC ACTORS

The legacy projects represent the culmination of students' careers at Pacific Rim. On the other end of the spectrum, Pacific Rim faculty and administrators also present their youngest students with opportunities to engage in civic action. As discussed in chapter 6, Pacific Rim's sixth graders participate in a weekly character education class with content focused, in large part, on the themes of community and contribution. Another important component of character education class is the opportunity for sixth grade students to actively engage in the work of citizenship. Specifically, character education class serves as the site of monthly "town meetings," held by each sixth-grade class, in which students discuss and problem-solve the challenges facing their class communities. Thomas Lickona and Matthew Davidson cite such meetings as "a vehicle for recruiting students as partners in sharing responsibility for making the class the best it can be."[10]

In one character education class, Angela Rossing informed her students, "Today we are going to have a professional town meeting." Students brainstormed topics that their class community would benefit from discussing and then dove headlong into a conversation about whether or not classroom disruptions fell along gendered lines:

STUDENT 1 (FEMALE): Certain boys are being distracting during class.

STUDENT 2 (FEMALE): I agree with [Student 1], because it is distracting sometimes because some boys are fooling around and making noises.

STUDENT 3 (MALE): I think it's also the girls in the classroom sometimes.

STUDENT 4 (FEMALE): I respectfully disagree with [Student 3], because I think the distractions from the boys prevent the girls from paying attention to the teacher.

STUDENT 5 (MALE): I respectfully disagree. I think we've all contributed to the problems in the classroom because of how low our [class] scores are.

STUDENT 2 (FEMALE): Would it be okay if I comment again? I kind of respectfully disagree with [Student 5] because I think it's some boys and some girls.

STUDENT 6 (MALE): Even if you're not making noises but you laugh at those who are, you're still a problem.

In this town meeting, Ms. Rossing ultimately transitioned the class's conversation toward the question: "What are we doing to do to fix the problem?" Proposed solutions ranged from "keeping our thoughts in our head" to "pay more attention in class" to "tell each other to be quiet." These class meetings occur every month in character education class, and students discuss issues that include running in the hallways, the bathroom policy, treatment of substitute teachers, and rumor spreading. As Ms. Rossing noted at the outset of one meeting, "Today is not just a day to complain about what is going on. We are going to come up with actual solutions to actual problems."

Each town meeting concludes with a resolution upon which students vote thumbs up or thumbs down. For example, at the conclusion of a discussion about students bumping into each other on the playground at recess, the class approved a resolution stating, "We are going to be safer, apologize if we mess up, and pay attention to what we are doing." Through these meetings and resolutions, Ms. Rossing helped to clarify for her students that there were numerous responsibilities that accompany their membership within the Pacific Rim community and that one such responsibility is participation in discussions and decision making about the most effective ways for the community to function. Psychologist Marvin Berkowitz characterizes such town meetings "where students are empowered to make decisions, solve problems, and create class norms" as robust examples of a "pedagogy of empowerment."[11]

Visitors to these town meetings are often impressed by the language with which Pacific Rim sixth graders engage in civic (and civil) debate with one another. In preparation for these monthly town meetings, Ms. Rossing dedicates several lessons to teaching her students the civic skills necessary to work effectively as civic actors.[12] For example, one character education lesson began with the question "What happens when we communicate effectively?" Sixth-grade students offered responses to this question that ranged from "we have less arguments" to "our point gets across" to "people understand you more and hear you more."

For the lesson itself, Ms. Rossing divided the class into small groups and gave each group a handful of dry spaghetti sticks and gumdrops. She then challenged the groups to build the tallest structure possible using only the materials in front of them. The catch was that they could not speak to each other (or at all) as they built. After several minutes of work, Ms. Rossing stopped all of the groups and questioned students about the challenges of working cooperatively but silently. She then gave students a second opportunity to build together, but this time they were allowed to speak to one another. As the lesson came to an end, Ms. Rossing asked her students to compare the two experiences. One student explained, "When we weren't talking, we didn't know who had ideas and who didn't have ideas. So when we started talking, it was easier." Another student added,

"It was easier when we were talking because we were able to communicate and share our ideas." Through this lesson, Ms. Rossing sought to convey to her students the central role of good communication in working effectively together to solve a problem or confront a challenge.

Developmental psychologist Judith Torney-Purta has written that "schools achieve the best results in fostering civic engagement when they rigorously teach civic content and skills."[13] Likewise, Scott Keeter and his colleagues have found that civic engagement is significantly higher among Americans who have been explicitly taught civic skills, and that such learning is a much stronger predictor of civic engagement than participation in more generic coursework on social or political issues.[14] As for precisely what constitutes civic skills, authors Sidney Verba, Kay Lehman Schlozman, and Henry Brady define them as a series of "organizational and communication skills which allow the use of time and money effectively in a political arena."[15] These scholars offer a theoretical framework that divides civic skills into four broad categories: organization skills, communication skills, collective decision-making skills, and critical thinking skills. Ms. Rossing's character education lesson involving the spaghetti sticks and gumdrops explicitly sought to strengthen students' communication and collective decision-making skills.[16]

Another character education lesson introduced students to the specific phrases with which one engages in civic and civil debate. These phrases included "I respectfully disagree with so-and-so because," "I would like to add on to so-and-so's point," and "Would it be okay if I comment?" As a means of practicing these phrases, Ms. Rossing challenged her students to *respectfully* debate their opinions about who was the more talented pop singer, Miley Cyrus or Selena Gomez. The students grew remarkably passionate in their opinions about this topic; with some coaching, however, they learned to voice their opinions in a respectful manner and also to make certain that their comments were actually responding to those preceding them. Just prior to the aforementioned town meeting discussion on the role of gender in classroom disruptions, Ms. Rossing reminded students about these key phrases, posted them on the whiteboard at the front of the classroom, and instructed students to explicitly utilize them in the ensuing discussion. Through these lessons on civic discourse, Ms. Rossing explicitly works to strengthen her students' communication skills as well as their ability to engage in collective decision making.[17]

On the topic of these and other lessons on civic discourse, Pacific Rim middle school teacher Victor Weaver explains, "We're trying to teach them a lot of times to communicate with each other in a productive, pro-active manner." Likewise, Angela Rossing feels strongly that her students "need to be able to communicate with one another in a way that is effective and productive." She adds, "We can have disagreements; we can have situations where we're not seeing eye to eye. But as long as we're respectful toward one another, then, you know, I think it will all work out." These perspectives align closely with psychologist Larry Nucci's assertion that both civic and moral development occur "when students engage in forms of discussion where they work hard to take other points of view into account and wrestle with a solution that best resolves the moral problem."[18]

These town meetings exert a powerful effect upon participating students' civic development. Sixth grader Reginald says, "What I like about character ed is you get to share your own opinions about things that are going on in the class." His classmate Winnie adds, "If we have problems, like character ed actually helps us get away from those problems." Finally, parent Tamara Oakley says of her daughter's character education class: "That's so good for them to get together and discuss things as a class or as a community. I mean, it's their school too. So they should be a part of it, to respect it, and to help it achieve and succeed." Through character education class, Pacific Rim students not only learn what it means to contribute to one's community but also, through their monthly town meetings, take on the role and work of civic actors. In so doing, they exemplify Levinson's assertion that "simulated experiences may help students develop the civic skills needed to reduce the [civic] empowerment gap. But authentic experiences are necessary to help them develop the engaged and efficacious identities as well as the habits of action that predict civic engagement and empowerment."[19]

## AMPLIFYING STUDENT VOICE

Pacific Rim also provides opportunities for students to engage in active citizenship by incorporating student voice into decisions affecting the operation and governance of the school. In the narrative from Pacific Rim's high school community meeting in chapter 1, Dean Diamond briefly alluded to the role of the student government in determining school policy: "We used to have a 'no electronics' policy whatsoever. Thanks to your student government, we decided to let you use electronics such as headphones at certain points of the school day. But, to clarify, during the school day, when you're walking from place to place, you cannot use headphones." Embedded within Dean Diamond's admonition was the fact that Pacific Rim's faculty and administration had created a mechanism for students to exert their influence in policies governing everyday school practices.

Pacific Rim tenth grader Travis describes his role as a student government representative thusly: "I'm representing my grade. And so whatever the policies—the student policies, the teacher policies—if we want to change them, all they have to do is ask me, and I'll try to get it across to the [student government] president. And we'll make a proposal and bring it to Ms. Grant and the teachers." As for the school's motivation in offering the student body a voice in policy making, Dean Diamond explains, "One of the things that Principal Grant firmly believes in is student voice. And when you hear that voice, you can respond to issues . . . Through student leadership here and voice there, we try to help the students also learn to use it wisely and effectively."

Dean Diamond's explanation of the role of student voice in promoting character development is underscored by Berkowitz's assertion that "flattening the governance structures in schools, both among adults and with students, and empowering voices more horizontally, will promote generally healthier schools and promote student learning and development."[20] Likewise, Lickona and Davidson have written that schools of character "create a democratic school-wide governance system that gives students a voice in decisions affecting the whole school."[21] Finally, research on the effects of "just community" schools provides further evidence of the importance of promoting student voice in secondary schools. Originally founded in the 1970s and 1980s by Harvard psychologist Lawrence Kohlberg, just community schools were experiments in "radical democracy" in which "students, teachers, staff members, and principals come together on a regular basis in order to thoroughly discuss and democratically decide upon issues relevant to school life."[22] Researchers have found that students attending just community schools demonstrate significant gains in moral reasoning, empathy, and perspective taking.[23]

Soliciting student input regarding electronics policy may be a far cry from the "radical democracy" of Kohlberg's just community schools; however, one eleventh-grade advisory period revealed that Pacific Rim's student government has a hand in much larger school policy issues as well. For this advisory period, all three of the eleventh-grade advisories crowded into a single classroom so that representatives to the student government could update the entire grade on an important change in school policy. Specifically, Pacific Rim's student government had successfully petitioned for and developed a new conflict resolution system to resolve disputes between faculty and students.

When all of the eleventh graders were seated in Ms. Anderson's advisory on chairs they had carried into the room themselves, a stocky eleventh-grade boy stood up to explain the new school policy. "Thank you for your time," he began, sounding like a seasoned politician. "This is a student government presentation about resolving concerns between students and teachers. If you have a conflict with a teacher or about the school, you can fill out this form from Mr. Diamond's office. But not if you just got sent to the office, because then it will be out of anger. You have to wait until the next day or the end of the day, and then student government will review it. You put your name, date, grade, what happened, and it's supposed to help us grow as a community. Are there any questions?"

A male student raised his hand. "Say I got detention for being late once, can I write about that?"

The student representative nodded his head. "If you think the detention is unfair, and you've already talked to the teacher and it didn't solve the problem."

Another male student with a skeptical look on his face asked a follow-up question. "What if we fill out one of these, and we talk about a problem, and we see no change about that problem?"

"Student government will look over your form," his representative reassured him, "and you can list who you want to be involved in solving the problem. And then we'll try to go with your option."

"Do you have to have a personal meeting with that teacher?" a girl asked.

"Yes," the student representative told her. "You should try to work it out with the teacher before you fill out the form."

In this presentation, one can see evidence of Pacific Rim's student government stepping forward to involve itself in a significant dimension of school policy. As for how this new conflict resolution policy came about, Dean Diamond offers this background: "Student council was talking about the fact that students who are reprimanded sometimes feel like it was unwarranted. And while we do have some informal systems . . . they wanted a more public system for all students, so that way all students— those both socially stronger students and those students that might not have as much of a voice—have the ability to say when they feel wronged and feel like there should be some sort of follow-up."

Lawrence Kohlberg first established his just community schools out of a belief that students need to *engage* in democratic decision making rather than simply learn about abstract concepts such as democracy and justice.[24] While Pacific Rim does not give students the equal-partner status of the just community model, the school's emphasis upon student voice unequivocally allows its students to engage in, rather than simply learn about, the roles and responsibilities of active citizenship.

## PRACTICING CIVIC ENGAGEMENT

Just as Angela Rossing teaches her middle school students the communication and collective decision-making skills necessary to engage effectively with one another in civic discourse, Pacific Rim high school students receive explicit lessons in civic skill building as well. For example, in one eleventh-grade advisory lesson, students learned about engaging in "win-win" negotiation. Through a series of vignettes, Holly Anderson introduced her students to the concepts of "position" and "interests" within a negotiation. The class then applied these concepts of negotiation to an issue closer to home:

MS. ANDERSON: Here's another scenario. Imagine a school that doesn't have a dress code like Pacific Rim. A student is wearing an obscene T-shirt that the teacher doesn't want the student to wear. What are [the] positions? What are [the] interests?

STUDENT 1: The student broke a rule.

MS. ANDERSON: How could we create a win-win?

STUDENT 2: Put another shirt or sweater on top of it.

STUDENT 3: What if he doesn't have a sweater?

MS. ANDERSON: How could we allow him to keep wearing the shirt, but respect the teacher's desire?

STUDENT 4: Turn it inside out.

STUDENT 5: Jumping the teacher.

MS. ANDERSON: That would be an escalation of the problem.

STUDENT 6: What's the answer?

MS. ANDERSON: There's not one clear answer. Whatever's going to create a win-win, that's the answer. So what could you do in that moment? You could storm out of the classroom. You could do nothing. Let's identify the interest. That's how you can find the win-win. What's the interest of the student?

STUDENT 7: To not get in trouble, not get a detention.

MS. ANDERSON: What's the interest of the teacher?

STUDENT 8: To get the student in trouble.

MS. ANDERSON: I think it's to have order in the classroom. How can we maintain both of those interests and get a win-win situation?

STUDENT 5: What if the teacher is stubborn?

MS. ANDERSON: Great question! What has the student government created to deal with that?

STUDENT 9: A resolution for student-teacher conflicts.

MS. ANDERSON: And, if that conflict doesn't get worked out, it creates a lose-lose, right? Do you think it's good for me if I have a student in my class who is upset?

STUDENT 2: But you can send them to the office.

MS. ANDERSON: In the immediate. But it's a lose for me if I can't resolve it. What happens when you go to Mr. Diamond? He sits down with the teacher and student to try to work it out.

In this advisory lesson, Ms. Anderson taught her students to consider the positions and interests underlying a conflict—a civic skill that falls under the critical thinking category within Verba's framework—and also emphasized the importance of communicating effectively with one's negotiating partner. Simultaneously, she encouraged her students to conceptualize their school community as a space in which such civic actions have an important role to play and also reminded them about the conflict resolution system that their student government had put in place for instances when negotiations between teachers and students break down.

Finally, another Pacific Rim lever that provides opportunities for both civic skill building and civic action is the weekly community meeting. Recall from chapter 1 that Pacific Rim assigns high school students the responsibility of planning and executing the weekly community meeting. According to Dean Diamond: "We usually start with the older students so that they can set a good example and tone for the younger students. And then the younger students take that on. And it's just another level of student voice and another level of engagement. Students tend to listen to each other more than they do sometimes to adults. It practices public speaking skills; it gives kids an opportunity to express what's on their minds and what's important to them." The topics featured in Pacific Rim's high school community meetings have ranged from human rights to nutrition to global warming, and the format of these presentations has ranged from guest speakers to spoken word poetry to PowerPoint slideshows. As Principal Grant notes, "It's a community meeting; it shouldn't be run by the principal and the dean every week. That gets boring."

Each high school advisory at Pacific Rim is responsible for planning and leading two community meetings a year. Several students express appreciation for this opportunity to take on a leadership role within the school. For example, tenth grader Chelsea says of community meeting: "In the middle school, it was more teacher-run. Like the principal saying everything and mostly it was like 'We need to improve in this, we're tracking on this' . . . But here [at the high school] it's like we run the entire thing until the end." Her classmate Stan agrees that, in middle school, "it was teacher-run, and they kept telling us like what we're supposed to do. Now, in the high school, it's like we're just telling each other what we have to keep doing." Both of these students are enthusiastic about the opportunity to take a leadership role within the Pacific Rim community by expressing at community meeting what *they* believe is important and true rather than passively listening to their elders. As noted in previous chapters, psychologist Erik Erikson characterized adolescence as the developmental period in which individuals move beyond a blind adherence to the beliefs of their parents and teachers, and begin to seek out new and different ways of understanding the world.[25] Developing and executing the weekly community meeting gives Pacific Rim high school students an important opportunity to experiment with and express their emerging understandings of the world around them.

These student-run community meetings also offer students the opportunity to hone concrete skills related to civic leadership. Recall that the Pacific Rim community meeting featured in chapter 1 began with Dean Diamond coaching the students leading that day's meeting on projecting their voices. Likewise, Principal Grant explains, "One of the advisory lessons is actually how to make an announcement in community meeting. Because I think [students] know how to prepare for class, but they don't know how to stand up and say, like, there's going to be a meeting and where and when it is happening, and who should go. So it's been good to get them more comfortable being in front of the room." In short, the numerous and deliberate opportunities for amplifying student voice at Pacific Rim encourage students to take on the roles of civic actors. Levinson notes that these opportunities for students to "develop and practice empowering civic skills, habits, and attitudes" are especially important "for many low-income youth of color who, outside of school, rarely have the opportunity to practice such skills and are often treated not as future productive citizens but as likely criminals."[26]

## ENGAGING BEYOND THE CLASSROOM

A frequent drawback to schools such as Boston Prep, Roxbury Prep, and Pacific Rim is a dearth of extracurricular options. Because these schools have explicitly chosen to focus their efforts and resources on strengthening students' academic skills, and because they often feature extended school days, many "no excuses" schools offer little in the way of athletics, art, drama, music, etc. However, Pacific Rim's emphasis on civic character development has led the school to take a very different approach to extracurricular activities than many of its peer institutions. In a 2011 presentation to college students at Boston University, Principal Grant explained that she had attended an elite independent high school as a teenager, which afforded her a tremendous education both inside and outside of the classroom. At Pacific Rim, she aspires to offer her students a similarly powerful education in both domains. Toward this end, one of Grant's first structural changes to the high school upon becoming principal was to lengthen the daily lunch period to forty-five minutes so that extracurricular committees—Yearbook Committee, Black History Month Committee, Environmental Action Club, Student Government, etc.—could meet during lunch. Extracurriculars focused on performance—sports teams, dance troupes, the thespian group, art clubs, etc.—continued to meet after school. Principal Grant explains, "In the old schedule, kids had to always choose only one [extracurricular]. I really wanted kids to be able to do more than one thing. Like, most kids don't *only* want to be on Prom Committee. They want to be on Prom Committee and plan a dance and play soccer."

Because Grant believes engagement in extracurricular pursuits is so important to students' character development, she has made participation a graduation requirement. Similar to independent schools in which students are required each semester to play a sport or join an activity, all Pacific Rim students must earn eighteen credits for extracurricular activities prior to graduation. Certainly, there are students who resent this requirement to do something "extra"; however, the majority of students appreciate the variety of extracurricular opportunities available to them. For example, twelfth grader Gabby notes, "I think it's a great thing to make it required because it forces kids to participate and become part of the community, which helps the community out . . . I've been part of Save Darfur, International Human Rights Committee, the Environmental Action Club, [and] Model UN." Likewise, twelfth grader Alvin—who plays on the soccer team, works with the Black History Month Committee, and contributes to the student magazine—expresses appreciation that students' extracurricular participation "goes on your college application and everything because the colleges see what this school had and what you have done for the school." It is notable that both Gabby and Alvin frame their extracurricular involvement not in terms of personal growth, but as a means of contributing to the Pacific Rim community.

In *Smart & Good High Schools*, Lickona and Davidson assert that schools of character "use co-curricular activities to develop students' individual talents and the collective pursuit of excellence."[27] In this claim, Lickona and Davidson identify cocurricular activities as powerful opportunities to foster students' performance character development. However, other scholars have found that cocurricular activities impact students' civic character development as well. Specifically, in a 2007 analysis of National Educational Longitudinal Survey data, Daniel Hart and his colleagues reported that participation by high school students in extracurricular activities was associated with higher rates of volunteering and voting in early adulthood.[28] These authors concluded that "these activities provide opportunities for acquiring the skills of working collectively for a common purpose [and] taking a responsible role in one's community."[29] In short, then, there is evidence that Pacific Rim's emphasis on extracurricular participation serves as another powerful lever for strengthening student's civic character.

Just as character education class, community meeting, and extracurricular activities propel students to become active and engaged citizens within the school community, the Pacific Rim Enrichment Program (PREP) pushes students to spend their summers engaging and contributing to the other communities of which they are a part. Specifically, Pacific Rim high school students are required each summer to spend a minimum of seventy-five hours "performing community service, exploring career possibilities through internships, or broadening their academic horizons through college prep summer programs."[30] Although there are Pacific Rim students who resent the school's extension of its graduation requirements into the summer months, eleventh grader Klarens sums up many students' attitudes toward PREP with this acknowledgment: "The good side to it is like it helps students do something they've never done before, and it gets them out of their comfort zone."

What do students' PREP experiences look like? Twelfth grader Ezra spent one summer working as a counselor-in-training at a summer camp and the next summer taking classes at the Boston Architectural Center, and feels that "it was a really good experience because it kind of gave me a sense of what jobs I kind of want to look for." Tenth grader Chelsea, who interned with Boston's Freedom Trail Foundation for her first PREP experience, says, "I kind of liked it because you stay focused. It's summer vacation, but you don't blank out . . . It's like you're still doing summer reading and going to PREP. And it looks really good on college applications when you say, 'Oh, I dedicated my summer to this and that.'" When discussing his PREP experiences working as a counselor at the Hyde Park Community Center, tenth grader Stan echoes Chelsea's thoughts on the college admissions benefit: "When you're applying, you know you can go in and say that you actually did something."

Through PREP, Pacific Rim faculty and administrators achieve three interconnected purposes. First, PREP pushes Pacific Rim students to gain experience in a new academic or professional context. As noted earlier, such experiences allow students to "move beyond their immediate environment in their exposure to a world of work."[31] Second, these experiences encourage Pacific Rim students to become active and engaged citizens in a community outside the familiar walls of Pacific Rim. Through their interactions in these communities, students are exposed to new and different worldviews that contribute to their development of a mature adult identity.[32] And, finally, as Chelsea and Stan mention in the preceding paragraph, PREP pushes Pacific Rim students to seek out the types of summer enrichment experiences that will increase their competitiveness in the college admissions process. Former Amherst College president Anthony Marx has observed that "colleges reward students for overseas travel and elaborate community service projects . . . [but] don't recognize, in the same way, if you work at the neighborhood 7-Eleven to support your family."[33] Pacific Rim's PREP requirement pushes students to seek out summer experiences that allow them to compete with more affluent peers.

A final way in which Pacific Rim engages students in the work of active citizenship is through community service. Among the three schools in our study, Pacific Rim presents students with the greatest number of opportunities to engage in community service and community service learning. The Pacific Rim community meeting featured in chapter 1 began with an announcement from the student government about a school-wide clothing drive "for students in orphanages who don't have warm clothes for the winter." Certainly, fundraisers and clothing drives like this one take place at Boston Prep and Roxbury Prep as well; however, these types of service opportunities are ubiquitous at Pacific Rim. For example, at one high school community meeting, a student made an announcement seeking volunteers for a bake sale sponsored by student group Humans Helping Humanity, the proceeds of which would be donated to a charity focused on human rights. In an eleventh-grade advisory in early December, the advisor and her students discussed plans to volunteer on the following Saturday at a Christmas party for homeless youth sponsored by Toys for Tots, and for which they had also collected dozens of presents from the rest of the high school advisories. At a high school community meeting in the spring, a student raised his hand during the announcements to explain, "I'm doing a walk called Walk for Music. It's this organization in East Boston that offers a lot of free programs, and my personal goal is to raise $300. If you can, please find me to sponsor me. No amount is too small." Finally, eleventh grader Sasha explains of Pacific Rim's extracurricular offerings: "There's a whole lot of social justice, social advocacy–type things." These include student groups such as the International Human Rights Committee, Save Darfur Committee, Gay-Straight Alliance, Black History Month Committee, Hispanic Heritage Committee, and Environmental Action Club.

Researchers have found the participation of adolescents in community service learning experiences to be highly predictive of a host of civic outcomes that include future engagement in community service, likelihood of making charitable contributions, voting participation in local and national elections, awareness of societal problems, and commitment to social justice.[34] In short, then, the many opportunities for students to take part in community service at Pacific Rim can be characterized as another powerful lever through which faculty and administrators seek to engage students in active citizenship and, in so doing, promote their civic character development.

## CIVIC CHARACTER AND DARING

At the outset of this chapter, we reported that Pacific Rim students demonstrated significant shifts over the course of the school year in their commitment to acting courageously in comparison to their peers at Boston Prep. Moreover, we asserted that this deeper commitment to courageous behavior—or daring—can be explained, in large part, by the numerous opportunities present at Pacific Rim for students to take on the role of civic actor both within and beyond the school's walls. Specifically, at Pacific Rim, students possess both the opportunity and the responsibility to be active participants in their class's town meetings, to develop the agenda and lead a schoolwide community meeting, to help determine school policy, to engage in internships at nonprofit organizations and government agencies, to participate in extracurricular activities, to learn Chinese and interact with peers from China, and to participate in meaningful community service.

As explained throughout this chapter, all of these opportunities for civic engagement play an important role in fostering the civic character development of Pacific Rim students. For example, the town meetings in which middle school students participate are important spaces for developing the communication and decision-making skills that Verba and his colleagues have identified as crucial to working effectively in a civic or political arena.[35] Likewise, the internships in which Pacific Rim seniors engage through their legacy projects promote students' civic identity development by exposing them to new ideological positions and perspectives on a civic issue about which they feel passionate.

While these and other experiences at Pacific Rim are explicitly designed to promote students' civic character development, they simultaneously provide opportunities for Pacific Rim middle and high school students to practice engaging in daring behaviors. Psychologists Nakkula and Toshalis have characterized "positive risk taking" as an important mechanism through which adolescents carry out the identity exploration that ultimately results in their development of a mature adult identity.[36] According to these scholars, healthy development entails adolescents seeking out experiences "that test the boundaries of self-understanding, relationships, and social conventions." In other words, a successful transition from adolescence to adulthood requires adolescents to exhibit a sense of daring by seeking out experiences that take them beyond their traditional comfort zones.

Speaking one's mind at a town meeting in front of one's peers represents a daring act for nearly all pre-adolescents. As sixth-grade student Fletcher explains, it is sometimes difficult in these town hall meetings "to point out people and say, like, 'Zach is not turning in his homework.'" Yet, according to Pacific Rim faculty member Victor Weaver, one of the key civic lessons that students learn through these town meetings is "ways to communicate with each other in a productive, proactive manner." Holding monthly town meetings in character education class offers Pacific Rim sixth graders regular opportunities to practice engaging in daring behavior.

Studying Chinese—one of the most difficult languages for English speakers to learn—also requires a sense of daring. As parent Tamara Oakley explains of her sixth-grade daughter, who will begin taking Chinese next year as a seventh grader, "She is a little nervous about it just because Chinese is a hard language. But I know quite a few kids that have gone to Pacific Rim who have graduated who have done just fine." As Oakley notes, the opportunity to meet a genuine challenge head-on represents an opportunity for students both to practice—and see the benefits of—engaging in daring behavior. Moreover, learning Chinese presents Pacific Rim students with the opportunity to travel abroad to China or to host a Chinese exchange student in their own homes—both of which push students far beyond their typical comfort zones and, in so doing, strengthen their sense of daring.

Pacific Rim students are also encouraged to press beyond their comfort zones by the school's requirement of extracurricular involvement. Ninth grader Julissa explains that getting involved in the drama club allowed her to "meet a lot of new people" that she didn't think she would meet. Likewise, eighth grader Justin adds, "I was sort of afraid to go for sewing this year for an extracurricular because of what people would say, but I actually went for it, and it was sort of fun." Left to their own devices, neither Julissa nor Justin would necessarily have engaged with an unfamiliar portion of the Pacific Rim student body; however, the school's requirement that students be engaged members of the community afforded Julissa the opportunity to meet "new people" and Justin the opportunity to do something he'd "never really done before." For both of these students, Pacific Rim's focus on civic character development has provided opportunities for engagement in the community that have simultaneously strengthened their sense of daring.

The internships in which students engage as part of their legacy projects also push students to take a positive risk by interacting with professionals in Boston's government agencies and not-for-profit organizations. Venturing into the professional sphere can be a daunting experience for all adolescents, but particularly those whose orbits have not brought them into contact with significant numbers of high-powered professionals. To this point, sociologist Annette Lareau has observed that an important difference in the child-rearing practices of middle class and poor families is that, on average, middle-class families are significantly more likely to teach their children how to question and advocate for themselves in the presence of educators, doctors, and other professionals.[37] Lareau asserts that this "concerted cultivation" by middle-class parents of their children's familiarity with professional settings represents an important form of social capital that these children carry with them into adolescence and adulthood. The numerous internships required of Pacific Rim students push these students to step outside their comfort zones and, in so doing, strengthen both their sense of daring and their access to the social capital typically reserved for adolescents from more affluent communities.

In a number of ways, Pacific Rim high school students articulate their recognition of the school's impact upon their own sense of daring. As mentioned in chapter 1, the character strengths championed by Pacific Rim are spelled out in the acronym KG-PRIDE, which is short for kaizen, gambatte, purpose, respect, integrity, daring, and excellence. One of the yearly traditions at Pacific Rim is to record a video in which every graduating senior responds to the question, "Which character virtue means the most to you and why?" This video is then incorporated into Pacific Rim's graduation ceremony. According to Principal Grant, "daring and gambatte are the ones the kids talk about the most—and I actually think daring is really important."

Likewise, in a November high school community meeting, a number of Pacific Rim high school students expressed their recognition of the numerous ways in which the school's focus on civic engagement had strengthened their sense of daring. Ninth grader Tracy explained to her high school peers that she hadn't wanted to be a part of the Pacific Rim community when she first started attending the school as a sixth grader. That feeling changed when she began actively engaging in the Pacific Rim community through a variety of extracurricular activities. According to Tracy, those opportunities opened her mind, and now she's "embracing new things and meeting new people." Likewise, twelfth grader Nakia explains that, when she began at Pacific Rim as a sixth grader, she was incredibly shy and determined to keep to herself. However, over the course of seven years at Pacific Rim, she developed the courage to speak her mind in venues ranging from a schoolwide community meeting to a conference sponsored by the nonprofit organization at which she had conducted her legacy internship. As Nakia explained to the audience of Pacific Rim faculty and students, "Just the fact that I'm standing here right now is because of Pacific Rim. I would never have imagined being able to do this when I was younger."

In chapter 6, we focused on the various levers through which Pacific Rim engages students in reflection upon the importance of community and contribution. In this chapter, we have turned our attention to the numerous opportunities for Pacific Rim students to push beyond their comfort zones and exhibit the daring necessary to engage in the actual work of contributing to their various communities. This combination of learning, reflection, and action uniquely positions Pacific Rim students to move forward into college and beyond with both the commitment and skills to fulfill their responsibilities as citizens of a university, city, nation, and world.

# CONCLUSION

## CHAPTER EIGHT

# Building Powerful School Culture Through Character Development

In 2010, the Institute of Education Sciences (IES)—the research arm of the U.S. Department of Education—published a report on one of the most robust studies of character education to date.[1] This longitudinal study considered the effects of seven school-based character education programs upon the social and character development of six thousand elementary school students enrolled in eighty-four different schools in six states. These seven character education programs included the Academic and Behavioral Competencies Model, Competence Support Program, Love in a Big World, Promoting Alternative Thinking Strategies, the 4Rs, Positive Action, and Second Step. These programs purported to "enhance students' social competencies and behavior," "strengthen students' emotional literacy," "promote conflict resolution and inter-group understanding," "reduce anti-social behavior" and "promote [students'] positive relationships with their teachers and peers."[2]

Researchers randomly assigned half of the participating schools to implement one of the character education programs and then assessed the effects of each program upon participating students over a three-year period. For many advocates of character education, the results of this study were discouraging. Researchers found that, on average, none of the seven programs exerted a significant effect upon participating students' social or emotional development, behavior, academic achievement, or perceptions of school climate. Certainly, these null effects should raise educators' wariness about trusting a particular character education program to deliver the outcomes that it promises. That said, what this landmark study most conclusively demonstrated was that "copying and pasting" a character education program into a school's existing culture and practices is not likely to be successful. Context matters.

## DEVELOPING HOMEGROWN CHARACTER EDUCATION

In contrast to the schools featured in the 2010 IES study, all three schools profiled in *Character Compass* represent examples of what Marvin Berkowitz and Melinda Bier refer to as "homegrown or grassroots character education."[3] In other words, stakeholders at Boston Prep, Roxbury Prep, and Pacific Rim have developed character education curriculum and practices that meet the needs of their particular mission, school context, and goals for students.

For example, Boston Prep was able to sequence its ethics curriculum to address the developmental and seasonal needs of its particular student body, and to make additional adjustments as necessary. According to Head of School Scott McCue, "There's certain things that we just know are going to come up at certain points of the year." For example, Boston Prep has learned through trial and error to begin the sixth-grade ethics curriculum with lessons on respect so as to support its youngest students in making the "startling transition" from their respective elementary schools. Likewise, Boston Prep faculty and administrators have learned to begin the ninth-grade ethics curriculum with a unit on integrity in order to counteract the increased academic pressure students feel upon entering the high school grades. As McCue explains, "I think that we've learned about the emotional journey that a Boston Prep student takes, and that has influenced how we think about when we deploy what virtue." Such *customized* character education has led to Boston Prep students demonstrating significantly higher levels of integrity and empathy—two moral character strengths—than their peers at Roxbury Prep and Pacific Rim.

Whereas Boston Prep focuses on students' moral character development, stakeholders at Roxbury Prep prioritize students' performance character development. Rather than turning to existing programming, Roxbury Prep has also sought to develop its own performance character curriculum and practices that fit into the school's weekly advisory program. For example, in the month preceding the school's Powerful Speaking Extravaganza, advisory lessons offered direct instruction on the key elements of public speaking and then engaged students in the "sustained and deliberate practice" necessary to deliver polished public speaking performances.[4]

Other Roxbury Prep advisory lessons engage students in goal setting and reflection upon the perseverance with which they approach their academic work. Similar to the ethics lessons at Boston Prep, these opportunities for goal setting and reflection are deliberately timed to align with the Roxbury Prep calendar as well as the natural ebb and flow of students' motivation. By utilizing advisory for lessons on how to strengthen performance, reflection on students' performances, and as a venue for sustained and deliberate practice, Roxbury Prep has fostered in students higher levels of perseverance—a performance character strength—than their peers at Boston Prep or Pacific Rim.

Finally, Pacific Rim has sought to nurture students' civic character development through a number of different "homegrown" levers that range from character education class for its sixth graders to civics and global citizenship courses for its eleventh- and twelfth-grade students. For example, the final six weeks of civics class entail each senior choosing a civic issue of personal interest and then interning with a government agency or nonprofit organization dedicated to addressing the issue through service or advocacy. These forays into the professional sphere strengthen students' sense of daring and promote their civic identity development. It is no surprise, then, that Pacific Rim high school students have scored significantly higher in daring behavior than their peers at Boston Prep.

Each of these descriptions reveals substantial differences between the approaches to character education of the three schools profiled here and the eighty-four schools selected to participate in the 2010 IES study.

Schools in the IES study were randomly assigned to incorporate a packaged character education program into their existing culture and practices, while our three schools have developed curriculum and pedagogy to support a vision of character development embedded in their respective mission statements. When one considers the null effects reported in the IES study and the significant effects witnessed at Boston Prep, Roxbury Prep, and Pacific Rim, a number of takeaways emerge for educators, parents, and policy makers interested in character education. First, there is no guarantee that character education programming that boasts a past record of success will be equally successful with a different group of students in a different school context. Second, stakeholders committed to effective character education in their school community must start by determining their overarching objectives for students' character development and *then* seek out (or create themselves) the highly customized curriculum and practices that will allow students to achieve those objectives.

## ACCOUNTING FOR CONTEXT

One upshot of advocating for homegrown character education is that our portraits of character development at three Boston schools are not intended to serve as templates for character education programming in other school contexts. No school community, for example, would be well served by simply adopting wholesale Boston Prep's five virtues, ethics class, and DuBois Award, or Roxbury Prep's creed deeds, advisory programming, and Spirit Stick. Copying and pasting these character education practices would likely yield the same null effects reported by the Institute of Education Sciences.

Rather, *Character Compass* lays out three distinct approaches to character education with the goal of promoting reflection and discussion among educators, parents, and policy makers regarding the "goodness of fit" of each approach to stakeholders' own school and community contexts. Particular curricula and practices should be considered only after members of a school community have come to a decision about the overarching approach to character education that best suits their particular students and context.

An example of such decision making in action can be found at the brand-new Grove Hall Preparatory Charter School (Grove Hall Prep). Just as the research for this book was concluding, Roxbury Prep leaders received a charter from the Massachusetts Department of Elementary and Secondary Education to open a new middle school in Grove Hall, a Boston neighborhood adjacent to Roxbury. This new middle school—Grove Hall Prep—is fewer than five miles away from Roxbury Prep, is staffed by a principal and faculty who all came directly from Roxbury Prep, and serves a student body nearly identical to Roxbury Prep in terms of students' gender, race/ethnicity, socioeconomic status, and academic preparedness. Many of the practices at Grove Hall Prep—from the school uniform to students' class schedules—are closely modeled after those at Roxbury Prep; however, the founding director and faculty of Grove Hall Prep wisely chose *not* to copy Roxbury Prep's ten creeds, but rather to develop their own set of core values that reflect their particular aspirations for students' character development.

Grove Hall faculty ultimately settled upon seven creeds that together form the acronym STRIDES: scholarship, time, responsibility, integrity, dignity, excellence, and stamina. Through these creeds—six of which can be characterized as performance character strengths—Grove Hall faculty and administrators signaled their intention to focus even more narrowly than Roxbury Prep upon students' performance character development. Such clarity allows Grove Hall faculty to develop its advisory programming, community meetings, and other character development practices with a laser-like focus upon the particular type of character development the school has chosen to privilege.

That is not to say that every educator or school must reinvent the wheel when it comes to character education. Once a particular school community has determined its overarching goals for character development, there is great value in its stakeholders reaching out to schools with a similar character focus and adapting practices that are already working well for other educators and students. Grove Hall Prep will undoubtedly adopt a number of the character education practices currently working well at Roxbury Prep. Likewise, Pacific Rim adopted from a Rhode Island high school its practice of replacing the traditional graduation valedictory speech with a video recording of Pacific Rim seniors responding to the question, "Which character virtue means the most to you and why?" Finally, Boston Prep borrowed from Pacific Rim the practice of providing regular character feedback to middle school students through class scores. Whereas class scores at Pacific Rim focus on kaizen and gambatte, Boston Prep developed a rubric for determining class scores that reflects its own moral character focus. Certainly, then, there is great value in connecting with other educators and stakeholders around best practices in character education. Moreover, the emergence of Web sites such as BetterLesson.com and ShareMyLesson.com—which allow educators to share lesson and unit plans with one another—greatly facilitates such connections.

## CHOOSING AN APPROACH

As for determining which type of character development to emphasize, one approach is to privilege the type that stakeholders believe to be most important for students' growth and development. All three schools studied here are focused on preparing students from low-income urban communities to succeed in college; however, the Boston School Committee members who founded Pacific Rim asserted from the outset that a key lever for college readiness was instilling in students a sense of global citizenship. Stakeholders at Boston Prep, on the other hand, envisioned their students' success as built upon a commitment to moral character strengths such as integrity and compassion. Finally, Roxbury Prep stakeholders aspired to instill in students the character strengths necessary to outperform peers in more affluent communities. Certainly, then, a wise starting point for educators, parents, and policy makers committed to incorporating character development into their students' schooling is an inclusive conversation about the conception of character most valued by their particular community and context.

A second approach to determining which type of character development to privilege might entail focusing upon those qualities that educators, parents, and policy makers believe their students most need to *strengthen*. In considering the role of schools and communities in preparing the next generation of civic and professional leaders, psychologist Howard Gardner has argued that schools and communities must develop in young people a commitment to doing work that is *excellent* in quality, carried out in an *ethical* manner, and *engaging* to the young people themselves.[5] Gardner refers to these qualities as the "three Es of good work" and asserts that students in different communities struggle with different dimensions of this trichotomy. In other words, one school community might find that its biggest challenge is fostering students' commitment to approaching their school work ethically—that is, with honesty and integrity. Another school community might find that its biggest challenge is helping students to develop the literacy, computational, and analytic skills necessary to do work that is excellent in quality. Finally, a third school community might find that its students demonstrate little appetite or enthusiasm for taking on the responsibilities of work and citizenship that lie ahead of them.

Gardner's three Es map neatly onto the moral-performance-civic character model that has served as our conceptual framework for exploring character development.[6] Specifically, developing a commitment to doing excellent work aligns with performance character; carrying out work in an ethical manner aligns with moral character; and actively taking on the roles and responsibilities of citizenship aligns with civic character. A school community that perceives its student body to be particularly lacking in one of the three Es might choose to privilege the type of character development that most directly addresses this dimension of students' development. For example, Roxbury Prep's intensive focus upon performance character development stems from the fact that the majority of its students arrive for sixth grade with academic skills that lag far behind those of peers in more affluent communities. As a result, Roxbury Prep faculty and leaders perceive their most important role to be strengthening students' capacity for carrying out work that is excellent in quality. Recall that scholars such as Angela Duckworth and Martin Seligman have described performance character strengths such as self-discipline as the "royal road to building academic achievement."[7] Taking this definition to heart, Roxbury Prep has chosen to focus on students' performance character development out of a belief that it is the surest way to strengthen students' capacity for doing excellent work.

Boston Prep and Pacific Rim share Roxbury Prep's commitment to developing their students' academic skills; however, both schools have focused their character education efforts upon the *ends* to which their respective student bodies will apply their burgeoning academic skills. Specifically, Boston Prep has chosen to privilege students' moral character development out of a belief that formal training in ethical philosophy will promote students' ability to approach their work and relationships in an ethical manner. Likewise, Pacific Rim has chosen to emphasize students' civic character development in order to deepen students' commitment to engaging fully in the various communities they will join upon graduating from Pacific Rim. In each of these three schools, stakeholders have privileged the type of character development that they believe will best equip their students to be positive and productive family members, professionals, and citizens.

## LAUNCHING, REORIENTING, OR REBOOTING

All three schools in this study have incorporated character development programming into their culture and practices since their respective beginnings, but existing schools can also decide to incorporate a more explicit character focus into their current work or reorient a longstanding approach to character education. For example, as we've noted, Pacific Rim opened its doors in 1997 with a narrow character focus on gambatte— the performance character strength of persistence. According to Principal Sawyer, it was only several years later that the school's stakeholders realized that "striving for your individual best only covers half" of what we want our students to do. Sawyer continues, "We want them also to be working as a group and as a community." It was only then that kaizen became a part of the school's culture, practices, and ethos. In other words, Pacific Rim's privileging of civic character development occurred several years after the school's founding. And the decision to incorporate "daring" into the school's core values occurred nearly a decade after that.

If Pacific Rim reoriented its character focus by incorporating *new* character strengths into its core values, then Roxbury Prep serves as an example of a school that has modified its character education focus by *narrowing* the character strengths it has chosen to privilege. As we've discussed, Roxbury Prep opened its doors in 1999 with a set of ten core values that included scholarship, perseverance, and investment but also peace, social justice, and community. While all of those values remain an official part of Roxbury Prep's creed, the school has chosen to focus its character education efforts upon the core values most tightly connected to students' performance character development. Recall from chapter 4 that the creeds Roxbury Prep teacher Stephanie Davis sees "being rewarded the most are scholarship, perseverance, and responsibility." And her fellow teacher Chris Grover observes that although the school faculty and administrators believe strongly in "peace and social justice," they are no longer emphasized in the school's advisory curriculum. These adaptations underscore that the school portraits offered in *Character Compass* are by no means applicable only to parents, policy makers, and educators *founding* a new school upon a character foundation but also to stakeholders interested in launching, reorienting, or rebooting their existing character education efforts.

## PRIVILEGING MULTIPLE CHARACTERS

A logical question is whether schools must privilege a single type of character or can instead emphasize multiples types of character development. The three schools in this study certainly had their respective character emphases, but stakeholders at each school would point out that they did not focus *exclusively* on one type of character development. As evidence of this claim, recall that perseverance—a performance character strength—is one of Boston Prep's five key virtues, despite the school's heavy emphasis upon moral character development. Likewise, integrity—a moral character strength—is a core value at both Roxbury Prep and Pacific Rim, schools that privilege performance character and civic character, respectively.

More than just paying lip service to these character strengths, Boston Prep students conclude each and every community meeting by joining hands and declaring "effort determines success!"—a performance character mantra. Likewise, the community meeting at Roxbury Prep featured in chapter 1 concluded with the presentation of the Spirit Stick to an eighth-grade student, Shawn Patterson, who was not yet succeeding academically but was nonetheless an important contributor to the well-being of the Roxbury Prep community. The teacher presenting the Spirit Stick explained to Shawn and the entire student body: "Shawn makes it his mission to make people laugh, so I just wanted to thank you because this was a month where we needed you to make us laugh. So I would ask all of us to leave today appreciating Shawn, and people like Shawn, in our community. And I would ask all of you—what role do you want to play in our community? Because Shawn has decided he is going to lift people up, and I invite you to join that fight with him." In this teacher's words, one can hear unequivocal evidence of Roxbury Prep recognizing and celebrating the importance of civic character.

In short, nearly every school strives to varying degrees to promote its students' moral, performance, *and* civic character development. And a strong argument can be made that all three forms of character development have unique contributions to make to student success. In fact, when we merged our survey data across all three schools, we found the strongest predictors of students' academic achievement to be perseverance, community connectedness, and receipt of demerits (a negative predictor). This means that, across all three schools, the students most likely to receive high academic marks were those who demonstrated high levels of perseverance, felt highly connected to their school community, *and* engaged in few disruptive or antisocial behaviors. Perseverance is one of the quintessential performance character strengths; community connectedness is related to civic character; and avoiding the behaviors that result in demerits draws primarily upon moral character strengths such as integrity and respect. Certainly, then, educators and schools are rightly motivated to foster each of these types of character in their students. That said, the year we spent observing and assessing character development practices at these three schools raised questions about any school's ability to give *equal* weight to moral, performance, and civic character development without dramatically reducing its impact upon any of these character dimensions. These questions stem from two circumstances common to middle and secondary schools across a diverse range of communities.

First, effective character education takes time, but time in schools is a scarce commodity. As we have covered in previous chapters, the foundations for character development at Boston Prep, Roxbury Prep, and Pacific Rim are laid in ethics class, advisory class, and character education class, respectively. The character foundations established through these curricular levers allow each school's faculty to infuse further opportunities for character development into content classes, community meetings, extracurricular activities, and more informal interactions with students. However, at all three schools, these initial crucibles of character development convene only for about one hour per week, or about forty hours over the course of the academic year. The fact that three schools that conceptualize character education as central to their mission can allocate only forty hours apiece for direct character instruction points to a challenge facing educators in every school context: finding the instructional minutes for all of the different kinds of learning from which students will benefit. The difficulty of facilitating in just forty hours students' development of valuable skills or deep knowledge in even a single content area calls into question whether a school community can *effectively* introduce students to multiple conceptions of character within such a tight window of time.

Second, the impact of character education programming at each of the three schools in our study stemmed, in large part, from the development of a common vocabulary with which faculty, students, and parents could discuss important matters. At Boston Prep, that common vocabulary centers upon moral character strengths; at Roxbury Prep, it is grounded in the language of performance; and at Pacific Rim, it rests on mutual understandings of community, contribution, and civic responsibility. Even if a school community *could* allocate the time to introduce several of these character vocabularies, adolescent literacy researchers have found that the most effective vocabulary instruction emphasizes depth over breadth.[8] In other words, such a school would likely be sacrificing quality for quantity and, in so doing, diluting the power of a common language to facilitate authentic interactions between students, faculty, and parents.

Put another way, the common character vocabularies at Boston Prep, Roxbury Prep, and Pacific Rim play a similar role to the expectations established by classroom teachers in all types of schools in the opening days of the school year. These classroom expectations foster a common understanding of how teaching and learning will proceed in that particular classroom community. Researchers have found that teachers with the best-managed classrooms offer students "a small number of positively stated rules," while the least effective classroom managers "have either no rules at all or else have so many rules that the rules become overly specific and essentially meaningless."[9]

Such is the case with character education as well. At all three schools, students benefit from an intensive focus upon a tightly focused set of character strengths. In contrast, schools placing equal emphasis upon multiple *types* of character might find that, like the least effective classroom teachers just described, they inadvertently render their multiple character emphases "essentially meaningless." This does not mean that schools or educators should ignore or disavow other types of character development, but rather that a particular school is well served by emphasizing a particular approach to character development.

Could stakeholders in a particular school community privilege a very small number of character strengths that cut across the different character types? For example, imagine a school community that chooses to focus its character education efforts upon cultivating students' perseverance (a performance character strength) and integrity (a moral character strength). Could such an approach to character development be effective? Unfortunately, the results of the present study shed relatively little light upon the feasibility of such an effort. On one hand, recall that despite an intensive focus on civic character development, Pacific Rim also emphasizes the performance character strength of gambatte, or persistence. Perhaps as a result, Pacific Rim lagged only a bit behind Roxbury Prep in students' demonstration of perseverance over the course of the school year. On the other hand, Boston Prep's character education programming homed in on five key virtues, which cut across the moral, performance, and civic dimensions of character. Yet, despite this relatively narrow character focus, students at Boston Prep demonstrated significant shifts only in their empathy and integrity—the moral character strengths that represent the school's top priority for students' character development. Ultimately, more research is needed to arrive at firmer conclusions about the effectiveness of educators privileging a small number of character strengths that cut across multiple strands of character.

## LOOKING BEYOND MORAL, PERFORMANCE, AND CIVIC CHARACTER

The three schools profiled in *Character Compass* represent three distinct and powerful approaches to character education; however, this trichotomous character framework is neither intended to be all-encompassing, nor to imply that stakeholders interested in character education are limited to choosing between moral, performance, and civic character development alone. Take, for example, Fenway High School, a pilot high school in the Boston Public Schools that focuses primarily upon cultivating students' *intellectual character*.

Intellectual character can be defined as the "overarching conglomeration of habits of mind, patterns of thought, and general dispositions toward thinking that not only direct but also motivate one's thinking-oriented pursuits."[10] Scholar Ron Ritchhart identifies six central qualities of intellectual character: curious, open-minded, reflective, strategic, skeptical, and truth seeking.[11] Certainly, Boston Prep, Roxbury Prep, and Pacific Rim seek in various ways to strengthen these qualities in their students. For example, Roxbury Prep rewards intellectual feats such as the memorization of pi; Pacific Rim features seminar-style classes in which students participate in rich discussions of their assigned reading; and Boston Prep's ethics lessons often engage students in philosophical puzzles and dilemmas. Yet the central purpose of Pi Day at Roxbury Prep seemed to be the rewarding of self-discipline and performance; the seminar format at Pacific Rim is characterized as an important means of preparing for university coursework; and the philosophical dilemmas and puzzles at Boston Prep are primarily tools for cultivating students' integrity, compassion, and other moral character strengths.

At Fenway High School, on the other hand, promoting intellectual curiosity might be characterized as the faculty's highest goal for student development.[12] Seniors at Fenway High School spend an entire semester on an individualized science project that they personally develop and carry out; the math curriculum emphasizes students' exploration of mathematical concepts over the application of procedures or formulas; and humanities courses pose an essential question each year that becomes the focus of students' reading and writing assignments for the entire school year at every grade level. Finally, Fenway High School features a Project Week every spring, during which classes are suspended and students and faculty are divided into small learning teams. These teams then explore together, through both research and field trips, a topic of pure intellectual curiosity ranging from "how does the restaurant business work?" to "what happens to trash after you throw it away?"

Fenway High School is a prime example of a school focused on a form of character development that falls outside the moral-performance-civic character trichotomy. Likewise, one might describe parochial and other types of religious schools as privileging a *spiritual* character development, which shares some of the features of moral character development but in other ways is quite distinctive. There are also Afrocentric and Greek schools—many of which are structured as addenda to children's traditional schooling experiences—that privilege students' *cultural* (or ethnoracial) character development in ways that overlap with civic character development but also possess distinctive elements. For example, at an Afrocentric school such as the Benjamin Mays Institute for Boys—a charter school in Hartford, Connecticut—student learning is built upon the foundation that "blacks have historically been a great and self-sustaining people and they can and should continue this legacy of collective achievement and self-determination."[13] As all of these examples reveal, stakeholders in a particular school community are by no means limited to moral, performance, or civic character in deciding upon a character emphasis that will honor their community's core values or support the particular needs of its young people.

## STRUCTURING CHARACTER EDUCATION

As noted previously, Boston Prep, Roxbury Prep, and Pacific Rim each dedicate approximately forty hours per school year to direct instruction in character education through ethics class, advisory, and character education class, respectively. Each of these curricular decisions raises an important topic of debate within the character development scholarship about whether character education should be taught as a separate subject or infused into all academic classes.

On one hand, one of the Character Education Partnership's core principles of effective character education is that "the school uses a comprehensive, intentional, and proactive approach to character development," which scholars Thomas Lickona, Eric Schaps, and Catherine Lewis interpret as a call to "integrate character education into academic content and instruction."[14] Taking this advice to heart, faculty and leaders in the Knowledge is Power Program (KIPP) charter school network deliberately engage in what KIPP founder Dave Levin refers to as "dual-purpose instruction"—that is, "the practice of deliberately working explicit talk about character strengths into every lesson."[15] A KIPP English teacher, for example, might explicitly focus students' discussion of a novel upon a particular character's optimism or grit, and a KIPP math teacher might incorporate character strengths such as perseverance into students' word problems. Faculty at Boston Prep, Roxbury Prep, and Pacific Rim engage in similar examples of dual-purpose instruction throughout the school day as well; however, the effectiveness of these teachable moments is built upon the character foundation established in students' standalone ethics, advisory, and character education classes. In this way, the three schools have responded to the question of whether to position character education as a standalone course or a form of learning infused throughout the entire academic curriculum by taking a "both/and" approach rather than an "either/or" approach.

A related question is *who* should be responsible for character education within a school community. The short answer is "everyone." In order for teachers to effectively infuse character content into their own classes and interactions with students, they need to be fluent in the character language of that school community. Berkowitz has lamented that "professional development is ubiquitous in schools, [but] it also tends to be focused more on academic instruction than on character education."[16] Boston Prep, Roxbury Prep, and Pacific Rim can be characterized as exceptions to this pattern in that educators at all three schools engage in several weeks of orientation prior to every school year that focuses, among other things, on deepening teachers' knowledge and familiarity with the school's core character values. Of the school's teacher orientation, Pacific Rim middle school principal Carrie Sawyer explains, "The first week is exposing them to the culture of the Academy and also the academic expectations. So they're really exposed to that right from the beginning—the emphasis on kaizen, on what it means, and how that translates into the classroom." Such exposure is crucial for teachers to be able to amplify in their own classes the learning that students are doing in ethics class, advisory, and character education class.

In terms of who should assume responsibility for direct instruction in character education, it is notable that Boston Prep, Roxbury Prep, and Pacific Rim each take different approaches. Boston Prep assigns a dedicated faculty member, Alex Leverett, to design the ethics lessons for all grade levels. Leverett and Head of School Scott McCue teach the high school ethics classes themselves, but every middle school teacher is responsible for teaching eight to ten advisees the grade-specific ethics lessons that Leverett has designed for them. In contrast, at Roxbury Prep, faculty members on each grade level team divvy up the responsibility for designing advisory lessons, workshop these lessons at team meetings, and then utilize the finalized lessons with their respective advisories. Finally, at Pacific Rim, one educator is responsible for designing the curriculum and teaching the character education courses at the middle school level, and a second faculty member takes responsibility for the high school civics classes.

Each of these approaches had benefits and drawbacks. Every member of Roxbury Prep's grade-level teams contributes to the development of advisory lessons, which increases the entire faculty's investment and familiarity with the character objectives and lessons taking place in advisory. Moreover, this collaborative authoring of advisory lessons means the lessons themselves hew closely to the school's vision for character development rather than being skewed toward a single educator's worldview, biases, or experiences. On the other hand, because advisory lessons are developed by different faculty members each week, they are not always tightly connected to one another. Put another way, Roxbury Prep's advisory lessons do not always feel as if they are building toward an overarching objective in a methodical and sequential way.

Pacific Rim, on the other hand, has assigned a single educator to plan and teach character education classes at the middle school level and another to plan and teach civics at the high school level. As a result, both of these learning experiences possess the methodical and sequential buildup toward an overarching goal—developing civic character—that advisory lessons at Roxbury Prep sometimes lack. At the same time, the single instructor for character education class and civics class means that both courses are influenced by the particular perspectives and worldviews of those two instructors. Moreover, other Pacific Rim faculty members have weaker understandings of precisely what students are learning in these courses. As a result, Pacific Rim's middle and high school faculty are not as effective as Roxbury Prep faculty at amplifying through content instruction the civic character foundation established in character education class and civics class.

Perhaps the most effective structure for direct character instruction is that of ethics class at Boston Prep's middle school. As a result of assigning a single dedicated faculty member to develop the ethics curriculum at every grade level, Boston Prep boasts an ethics program that is not only coherent and sequential over the course of a single school year, but that seeks to build upon students' prior knowledge of ethics as they advance from one grade to the next. At the same time, engaging Boston Prep's middle school faculty in teaching the weekly ethics lessons means that each of these faculty members has a close familiarity with the content of ethics class—a familiarity that allows them to readily integrate this ethical content into their own academic subjects. For example, sixth-grade geography teacher Shauvon Ames notes that her students "are writing an essay right now on the Chernobyl power plant accident and which virtue was broken to cause this amount of destruction." Ames's familiarity with the ethics curriculum allows her to integrate ethical content into students' study of the Chernobyl disaster. Such integration would seem to be a truly authentic example of dual-purpose instruction.

## INTEGRATING FEEDBACK FROM FACULTY

A legitimate question about Boston Prep's approach to ethics class is whether the school's faculty members have reservations about teaching ethics lessons that they have not designed themselves. Such a sentiment seems reasonable, and yet the majority of Boston Prep faculty members express relief at having one less responsibility on their already overflowing plates. For example, eighth-grade teacher Jeffrey Granderson says, "I was [initially] a little bit skeptical about teaching an ethics curriculum that was created by someone else . . . but I've come to really enjoy it. I think it's great to have that framework every week and then be able to sort of tweak it as it needs it." Likewise, eighth-grade teacher Kelsey Morales says of Leverett's work designing the ethics curriculum: "I love it because I just don't have the time. If I didn't have the schedule I have, I would love to be a part of it. But at this school, it is absolutely impossible. So it's great to have somebody thinking through the whole year." Finally, Shauvon Ames acknowledges that she, like Granderson, also adapts the weekly ethics lesson to suit her particular teaching style: "I am a natural storyteller . . . so I'll just infuse stories into [the ethics lesson]." The perspectives of these teachers reinforce existing scholarship on advisory programming in middle and secondary schools that have found that teachers working in schools with advisory programs "wanted more resources in the form of guidebooks or lesson plans that would provide structure and content to depend on."[17]

In her comments on the existing structure of Boston Prep's ethics curriculum, Kelsey Morales adds, "I really wish we could meet maybe once a month to be able to say, 'These are some of the things that have been coming up. Do we need to add in an extra [ethics] lesson about X, Y, or Z?'" This suggestion points to perhaps an even more effective model that draws on elements from all three schools—namely, a dedicated faculty member designs the curriculum and lessons, every faculty member plays a role in teaching the lessons, and there is an explicit forum for faculty members to offer feedback and insights on the direction of the curriculum. Incorporating this third step into the process would draw upon an important element of Roxbury Prep's collaborative authoring model, and, in so doing, increase the likelihood of alignment between a school's character education programming and its stakeholders' character development goals. Such a procedure would also allow schools to take advantage of the nimbleness and adaptability that contribute greatly to the impact of home-grown character education programming.

## UNDERSTANDING PARENTAL PERSPECTIVES

One might expect that parents who have enrolled their children in a school with an explicit character focus would feel strongly about that school's commitment to promoting character development. Our interviews with parents, however, revealed that the schools' character education efforts were not truly on parents' radar screens when they made the decision to send their children to one of the three schools. Rather, what was foremost in parents' minds were the schools' reputations as safe schools within the city of Boston as well as their focus upon preparing students for college.

Despite this initial lack of familiarity with the schools' character education programming, very few parents or teachers at any of the schools described cases of conflict over character education practices. Boston Prep middle school principal Amanda Gardner notes, "We've had very little to any pushback on what the content of the ethics class is, or any of that.

Over the [last] seven years, I can think of maybe two conversations that I've had with families that have been difficult, and those were sort of misunderstandings about what was actually taught." Likewise, Pacific Rim middle school principal Carrie Sawyer explains, "One parent told me a couple years ago that it wasn't my place to be teaching her child to be a good person, but [otherwise] there's been very limited pushback from parents in terms of 'Hey, you're teaching my kid values, and is that really appropriate for you to do that?'" Much more common are parents such as Karen Clements, who says of Boston Prep's character education programming: "I think it's great because, again, they have to be able to carry what they're learning outside of school. And if a parent is not able to appreciate them having an ethics class, then I think there is something going on because we all have a value system . . . And they mimic the same thing that I feel we should all be living up to." Clements's perspective is supported by national surveys that have found 85 percent of American parents expect schools to teach values to their children.[18]

Certainly, parents, students, and teachers at all three schools raise questions from time to time about their respective school's character education programming. During the 2010–2011 school year, members of the Pacific Rim parent advisory board expressed reservations about the school's PREP program *requiring* students to take a positive risk each summer by participating in an internship, job, or volunteer experience. Principal Gardner recalls a conversation with an irate Boston Prep parent whose child had interpreted an ethics lesson on the achievement gap to mean that students of color were less capable than their white peers (when the lesson had been intended to convey the opposite message). A handful of students at each school expressed frustration with aspects of their respective school cultures that ranged from the use of demerits to the requirement of school uniforms. Likewise, there are individual faculty members at all three schools who described elements of their respective school's character emphases with which they do not feel personally aligned. Any school that commits to a particular approach to character education will experience similar rumblings of resistance, and the voices of these stakeholders deserve to be heard and considered.

Would such rumblings be even louder in other school communities? Whether potentially controversial lessons—such as Boston Prep's ethics class about the integrity of gay rights activist Harvey Milk, or Pacific Rim's civics class about the experiences and exploitation of undocumented workers in Boston—would face resistance from students, faculty, or parents in other school communities is, of course, highly specific to the particular school and community in question. As a result, every school community—whether public, private, or parochial; urban, suburban, or rural—will need to fashion the character education programming that fits its particular context.

## CONCLUSION

*Character Compass* has presented portraits of three distinct approaches to character education and the disparate effects of these approaches upon students at the Boston Preparatory, Roxbury Preparatory, and Academy of the Pacific Rim charter schools. One of the most effective means of highlighting distinctions in these approaches was a comparison of the schools' individual responses to school bullying. We return to that topic now in our conclusion.

Just before this research study began, the tragic suicides of several American teenagers who were victims of school bullying led the Massachusetts state legislature to mandate that every public school in the state implement antibullying curriculum at every grade level.[19] Perhaps not surprisingly, dozens of educational consultants, nonprofit organizations, and education researchers stepped forward to offer programming purporting to satisfy the state mandate.

Speaking to the effectiveness of such programs goes beyond the scope of this volume; however, middle and secondary educators should be wary about simply inserting such programming into their existing school practices and expecting to see significant effects upon students. Adolescents—those being bullied, those doing the bullying, and those who are bystanders to bullying—already possess an intimate knowledge of the issue, and it is unlikely that squeezing a few antibullying lessons into an existing advisory program or convening a single whole-school assembly will guide students to a deeper understanding of this problem. As emphasized throughout this final chapter, effective character education cannot be copied and pasted from one school context to the next.

In contrast, a school such as Boston Prep—which had already expended significant time and effort to develop a common vocabulary and ethical framework through which students and faculty could discuss moral issues—was ideally positioned to discuss the issue of bullying and one's ethical response to it. Likewise, Roxbury Prep was able to take on the topic of bullying using the language of performance, and Pacific Rim did the same by invoking the language of community and social responsibility. The discussions of bullying at all three schools were greatly aided by the prior establishment of a framework and vocabulary through which faculty and students could reflect together in a "language" authentic to their community. The ability of students, faculty, parents, and other stakeholders to engage together in authentic discussions of important matters is perhaps the ultimate indicator of a school community with a powerful character foundation upon which to build. In presenting portraits of three school communities engaged in such authentic discussions, we have sought to provide, if not a blueprint, then a starting point for parents, students, educators, and other stakeholders to engage in meaningful conversations of their own about the role of character education in supporting students' success.

# A Note on Research

*Character Compass* is the result of a yearlong mixed methods study of character education programming at the Boston Preparatory, Roxbury Preparatory, and Academy of the Pacific Rim charter schools during the 2010–2011 academic year. The seeds of this project were first sown when I learned informally from Boston Prep middle school principal Amanda Gardner about the school's ethical philosophy curriculum. Such programming was of particular interest to me because, for nearly a decade now, my research program has focused on the civic development of adolescents and emerging adults. Moreover, I had just completed a research study that considered the impact of a community service learning program at Boston College that combined academic learning in philosophy and theology with a yearlong community service project focused on combating the effects of poverty. I had found this combination of service and philosophy to have a profound effect upon participating college students' civic development, so I was intrigued to learn more about the effects of philosophical study upon middle and secondary students.[1]

The original objective of the research study, then, was to consider the impact of Boston Prep's ethical philosophy program upon participating students. In the process of seeking out apt comparison schools for such a study, I encountered Roxbury Preparatory Charter School and Academy of the Pacific Rim Charter Public School. The schools were located within a few miles of Boston Prep, served similar student populations, achieved similar results on state assessments, and also positioned character development as central to student success. What quickly became apparent, however, was that the three schools conceptualized character development in very different ways. *Character Compass* emerged from my interest in assessing how these different character emphases across the three schools impacted their respective student bodies.

My research team and I took a mixed methods approach to this assessment. Specifically, the student bodies at all three schools completed quantitative surveys at the beginning and conclusion of the 2010–2011 academic year that sought to measure attitudinal shifts on a number of different character measures. We also carried out qualitative interviews with students, faculty, administrators, and parents associated with each school and conducted observations of the schools' character education programming and practices. Finally, we made use of each school's internal data on student achievement and conduct. Triangulation of the various data allowed for more robust conclusions about the results of our quantitative and qualitative analyses.

## STUDY PARTICIPANTS

This study's participants consisted of 653 middle school students (grades six through eight) and 279 high school students (grades nine through twelve) attending Boston Prep, Roxbury Prep, and Pacific Rim. The summary statistics for these students in terms of gender and race/ethnicity are presented in table A.1.

As shown in table A.1, the student bodies of all three schools are evenly divided between male and female students. In terms of race/ethnicity, Boston Prep and Roxbury Prep are composed almost entirely of students of color, while Pacific Rim has a more sizable population of white students (21 percent of the student body). In terms of socioeconomic status across the student bodies of all three schools, 73 percent of Boston Prep students qualify for free or reduced-price lunch (a proxy for low socioeconomic status) as compared to 76 percent of Roxbury Prep students and 54 percent of Pacific Rim students.

TABLE A.1    Summary statistics for Boston Prep, Roxbury Prep, and Pacific Rim students by gender and race/ethnicity (n = 936)

| | Grades 6–8 | Grades 9–12 | Gender | | Race/ethnicity | | | |
|---|---|---|---|---|---|---|---|---|
| | | | Male | Female | Black | Latino | White | Multi-racial |
| **Boston Prep** | 189 | 126 | 158 (50%) | 157 (50%) | 190 (60%) | 59 (19%) | 16 (5%) | 50 (16%) |
| **Roxbury Prep** | 231 | N/A | 101 (44%) | 130 (56%) | 112 (49%) | 91 (40%) | 0 (0%) | 28 (11%) |
| **Pacific Rim** | 233 | 157 | 188 (48%) | 202 (52%) | 223 (57%) | 41 (11%) | 84 (21%) | 42 (11%) |

As I'll describe in greater detail shortly, approximately one thousand students across the three schools completed character development surveys at the beginning and conclusion of the academic year. In addition, my research team and I conducted qualitative interviews with fifty-one students from across the three schools and at every grade level. All of these students are identified by pseudonyms.

We also carried out interviews with twenty-two faculty members and administrators from Boston Prep, Roxbury Prep, and Pacific Rim. All of the faculty members are identified by pseudonyms. With their permission, we have used the actual names of administrators at the three schools throughout the book, as their positions within their respective schools made it impossible to effectively conceal their identities.

Finally, we conducted qualitative interviews with sixteen parents of children at Boston Prep, Roxbury Prep, and Pacific Rim. One parent—Tamara Oakley—had a daughter in the eighth grade at Roxbury Prep and another daughter in the sixth grade at Pacific Rim. All of these parents are identified by pseudonyms.

## DATA COLLECTION

As noted previously, we collected several different types of data from the students, faculty, and parents participating in this research study: quantitative surveys, qualitative interviews, participant observations, and archival achievement and behavioral data. Here we describe each in turn.

### Surveys

Students at all three schools completed surveys in the opening weeks of the school year in September 2010 ($T_1$), and then completed a similar survey at the conclusion of the academic year in May 2011 ($T_2$). The survey consisted of a number of character measures adapted from the Youth Social Responsibility Scale, Children's Empathy Questionnaire, Values in Action Inventory of Character Strengths for Youth, Academic Motivation & Integrity Survey, Aristotelian Ethical Identity Questionnaire, and Sense of Community Connectedness Scale.[2] These measures were chosen because they aligned with core values cited by one or more of the schools in their mission statements or mottoes. For example, the Academic Motivation & Integrity Survey was included in our survey tool because all three schools cite integrity as a core value.

### Interviews

At each of the three schools in the study, a faculty member served as a point person for the research study, and these point people were instrumental in recruiting parents, students, and other faculty for participation in the qualitative interviews.

The twenty-two faculty members and administrators from Boston Prep, Roxbury Prep, and Pacific Rim who participated in qualitative interviews for this study were recruited via the point person at each school. Specifically, the point person sent out an email to his or her respective faculty soliciting volunteers to be interviewed about their perspective and experiences with the school's character education programming. These interviews with faculty and administrators were all conducted in person at the three school sites (with the exception of one interview conducted over the phone with a Roxbury Prep faculty member). Each interview lasted approximately one hour and followed a semistructured interview protocol that questioned faculty and administrators on the following topics:

- Key levers within the school for promoting character development
- The relationship between character development and academic achievement
- The character development witnessed in students over the course of the academic year
- The perceived value of community meeting
- The effect upon students of receiving the DuBois Award/Spirit Stick/Kaizen-Gambatte Award
- Students' responses to merits and demerits
- The transferability of lessons in ethics class/advisory/character education class
- Particularly effective and ineffective lessons in ethics/advisory/character education class
- The effect of the school's core values/virtues/creeds upon school culture

The sixteen qualitative interviews with parents of students attending Boston Prep, Roxbury Prep, and Pacific Rim were all conducted over the telephone. Again, the faculty point person from each school reached out to a diverse set of parents (in terms of their children's grade levels and academic achievement) to request their participation in the research study. These interviews lasted approximately forty minutes and followed a semistructured interview protocol that questioned parents on the following topics:

- Their decision to send a child to this school
- The impact of the school upon their child's character development
- How their child has changed since attending the school
- The extent to which their child talks about the school's core values
- The extent to which their child talks about ethics/advisory/character education class
- The extent to which their child talks about the DuBois Award/Spirit Stick/Kaizen-Gambatte Award

- Their discussions about students' weekly progress reports with their child

Finally, the fifty-one students who participated in qualitative interviews were also identified by each school's faculty point person, with the goal of establishing a diverse sample of interview participants at each school in terms of grade level and academic achievement. Administrators at all three schools were understandably reluctant to allow students to miss class time in order to participate in these interviews. As a result, all students were interviewed during their lunch periods. Each interview lasted approximately thirty minutes and followed a semistructured interview protocol that questioned students about their perceptions of the impact of the following school practices upon themselves and their classmates:

- Ethics/advisory/character education class
- Community meeting
- Merits and demerits
- The DuBois Award/Spirit Stick/Kaizen-Gambatte Award
- Their school's core values/virtues/creeds
- Their own character development
- Their school's aspirations for their character development
- The school practices they would incorporate into their own ideal school

### Participant Observation

Finally, a doctoral research assistant and I conducted more than one hundred fifty observations across the three schools of community meetings, ethics classes, advisory periods, character education classes, civics classes, and academic content classes. At Boston Prep, we observed twenty-six middle school ethics lessons, thirty-one high school ethics lessons, and twenty-nine community meetings. At Roxbury Prep, we observed fourteen advisory lessons and twelve community meetings. Finally, at Pacific Rim, we observed thirteen character education classes, fifteen community meetings, three civics classes, and three high school advisory lessons.

We compiled extensive field notes for each of these observations. In these field notes, we sought to transcribe as closely as possible the entire lesson or community meeting, including questions and comments made by individual students and faculty members within the class.

### Internal School Data

At the conclusion of the academic year, we also collected from administrators at the three schools student-level data on academic achievement (GPA per term) and student behavior (demerits and merits received per term).

All three schools grade students academically on a traditional 100-point scale in which 90–100 represents an A, 80–89 represents a B, 70–79 represents a C, 60–69 represents a D, and grades falling below 60 are failing. At all three schools, students are issued demerits from their classroom teachers for a variety of misbehavior that includes disrupting class, using inappropriate language, exhibiting disrespectful behavior, chewing gum, violating the uniform policy, etc. Receiving a particular number of demerits (which varies by grade level) results in an afterschool or Saturday detention.

Middle school students at all three schools can also receive merits from their classroom teachers for engaging in various forms of prosocial behavior. For example, students might receive a merit for working diligently with classmates on a cooperative learning assignment, helping to explain a challenging problem to a confused classmate, writing a get-well note to an ill classmate, or taking a "positive risk" by contributing to a class discussion. Merits can be turned in for prizes such as school supplies, books, or movie tickets either at the school store or at a quarterly creed deed auction.

## DATA ANALYSIS

To analyze the *quantitative surveys*, we first conducted a principal components analysis to form composites from the survey items completed by this study's participants for the following constructs: daring, empathy, community connectedness, ethical identity, integrity, perseverance, and respect. Before carrying out the analysis of interest for each variable, we conducted preliminary checks to ensure that there was no violation of the assumptions of normality, linearity, homogeneity of variances, homogeneity of regression slopes, and reliable measurement of the covariate.

We then began our analyses by fitting unconditional multilevel regression models for each of the aforementioned character measures, with students' post-intervention ($T_2$) scores on these measures as the dependent variable. Next, we built a baseline control model by adding a number of individual-level demographic predictors including gender, race/ethnicity, grade level, academic performance, receipt of merits, and receipt of demerits. We then added to the model a level one (individual-level) and level two (school-level) control predictor. The level-one control predictor accounted for students' pre-intervention ($T_1$) scores on the particular measure being tested, and the level-two control predictor accounted for the participants being nested within particular ethics, advisory, and character education classes within their particular schools. Finally, we added to the model school-level dummy variables representing students' affiliation with Boston Prep, Roxbury Prep, or Pacific Rim in order to assess whether school affiliation significantly predicted students' shifts on any of the character measures. For those measures that did demonstrate statistically significant results, we calculated effect size using Cohen's *d*.

The *qualitative interviews* with students, teachers, and parents were recorded and transcribed verbatim. Our analysis of these interviews was an iterative process consistent with research methods focused on *emic perspectives*—descriptions of behaviors or beliefs by participants in a study in language that is culturally specific to those participants.[3] First, our research team worked collaboratively to develop a codebook based on the different ways in which interview participants described 1) the ways in which their respective schools sought to influence the character development of attending students; and 2) what they perceived to be the effect of such character education upon their own beliefs and values (or those of their students or children). In so doing, we also worked to ensure that all members of the research team shared a common understanding of our codes. The codebook was seven pages in length and contained descriptions of 109 discrete codes ranging from "race talk" to "schoolwide events" to "global citizenship."

Next, each qualitative interview was coded independently by two members of the research team. For each member of the team, the coding process involved two separate readings of the transcribed interviews. The first reading focused on descriptions by participants of the elements of character education present at their respective schools. The second reading of each interview transcript focused on descriptions by participants of the perceived effects of such character education practices upon their own beliefs and values (or those of their students or children).

After coding each interview independently, two members of the research team then compared their analyses of each interview transcript, recoded, and then compared again until all coding discrepancies were resolved. An identical process was carried out with the field notes recorded during observations at all three schools of ethics classes, advisory classes, academic classes, community meetings, and special events. *Character Compass* presents the key themes and patterns identified in these interviews and field notes about character education practices and their perceived effects at each of the three schools in the study.

In considering these emergent themes, we also drew upon findings from our quantitative survey data about students' shifts over the course of the academic year on a number of moral and performance character strengths. We believe that such triangulation of quantitative and qualitative data offers a robust window into the effects of the different character education practices utilized at Boston Prep, Roxbury Prep, and Pacific Rim.

## RESULTS

The key results of our quantitative analyses are reported in chapters 2, 3, 4, and 7. Here, we provide additional details regarding the final fitted models for each of our character measures.

### Integrity

In chapter 2, we stated that Boston Prep middle and high school students demonstrated significantly higher levels of integrity over the course of the school year than their peers at Roxbury Prep and Pacific Rim. The final fitted models for students' $T_2$ integrity scores are presented in tables A.2 and A.3.

After controlling for students' initial integrity scores, we found that being a student at Boston Prep was associated with higher levels of integrity over the course of the school year. Additionally, for middle school students, being in the sixth grade was found to be a positive predictor of students' $T_2$ integrity scores, and receipt of demerits was found to be a negative predictor of students' $T_2$ integrity scores. In other words, being a Boston Prep student, being a sixth grader, and earning few demerits were all significant predictors of high levels of integrity at the conclusion of the academic year. At the high school level, being in the ninth grade was found to be a positive predictor of students' $T_2$ integrity scores. In other words, ninth-grade students at both Boston Prep and Pacific Rim demonstrated, on average, higher levels of integrity than the upperclassmen.

TABLE A.2    Effects of attending Boston Prep upon the integrity of its middle school students

Final fitted model for the effects of attending Boston Prep upon the integrity of participating middle school students, controlling for select background characteristics of the cohort in which students are grouped for ethics/advisory/character education class ($n$ sections = 31, $n$ students = 541).

| Fixed effect | Coefficient | Se | T-ratio | p-value |
|---|---|---|---|---|
| Intercept | 1.54 | .22 | 7.07 | .0001 |
| **School level** | | | | |
| Boston Prep | .13 | .06 | 2.06 | .03 |
| **Individual level** | | | | |
| $T_1$ integrity | .62 | .05 | 13.41 | .0001 |
| Sixth grade | .15 | .06 | 2.49 | .01 |
| Total demerits | −.0004 | .0001 | −2.81 | .005 |
| Random effect | Variance component | Se | Z | p-value |
| Random effect of student ($r_{ij}$) | .37 | .02 | 15.57 | .0001 |
| Random effect of cohort ($u_{0j}$) | .0001 | .01 | .08 | .47 |

Note: −2LL = 869.1

TABLE A.3    Effects of attending Boston Prep upon the integrity of its high school students

Final fitted model for the effects of attending Boston Prep upon the integrity of participating high school students, controlling for select background characteristics of the cohort in which students are grouped for ethics/advisory (*n* sections = 22, *n* students = 279).

| Fixed effect | Coefficient | Se | T-ratio | p-value |
|---|---|---|---|---|
| Intercept | .13 | .21 | 3.54 | .002 |
| **School level** | | | | |
| Boston Prep | .33 | .12 | 2.66 | .008 |
| **Individual level** | | | | |
| $T_1$ integrity | .75 | .05 | 15.19 | .0001 |
| Ninth grade | .45 | .17 | 2.69 | .007 |
| Random effect | Variance component | Se | Z | p-value |
| Random effect of student ($r_{ij}$) | .43 | .04 | 9.99 | .0001 |
| Random effect of cohort ($u_{0j}$) | .03 | .02 | 1.19 | .11 |

*Note:* –2LL = 434.4

## Empathy

In chapter 3, we noted that Boston Prep high school students demonstrated significantly higher levels of empathy over the course of the school year than their peers at Pacific Rim. The final fitted model for students' $T_2$ empathy scores is presented in table A.4.

After controlling for students' $T_1$ empathy scores, we found that being a high school student at Boston Prep was a positive and significant predictor of students' empathy at the conclusion of the academic year. Table A.4 also reveals, however, that aside from students' initial empathy scores, none of the individual-level demographic predictors (e.g., gender, grade point average) was a statistically significant predictor of students' year-end empathy scores.

## Perseverance

We stated in chapter 4 that Roxbury Prep middle school students demonstrated significantly higher levels of perseverance over the course of the

TABLE A.4    Effects of attending Boston Prep upon the empathy of its high school students

Final fitted model for the effects of attending Boston Prep upon the empathy of participating high school students, controlling for select background characteristics of the cohort in which Boston Prep and Pacific Rim students are grouped for ethics class/advisory ($n$ sections = 22, $n$ students = 279).

| Fixed effect | Coefficient | Se | T-ratio | p-value |
|---|---|---|---|---|
| Intercept | 1.73 | .13 | 13.85 | .0001 |
| School level | | | | |
| Boston Prep | .16 | .08 | 2.03 | .04 |
| Individual level | | | | |
| $T_1$ empathy | .20 | .04 | 5.28 | .0001 |

| Random effect | Variance component | Se | Z | p-value |
|---|---|---|---|---|
| Random effect of student ($r_{ij}$) | .31 | .02 | 9.96 | .0001 |
| Random effect of cohort ($u_{0j}$) | .002 | .01 | 0.15 | .44 |

*Note:* −2LL = 382.0

school year than their peers at Boston Prep or Pacific Rim. The final fitted model for students' $T_2$ perseverance scores is presented in table A.5.

After controlling for students' initial levels of perseverance, we found that being a student at Roxbury Prep was associated with higher levels of perseverance on the $T_2$ survey. Additionally, students' grade point average was found to be a significant positive predictor of perseverance, and receipt of demerits was found to be a significant negative predictor of perseverance. In other words, being a student at Roxbury Prep, earning a high grade point average, and receiving few demerits were all associated with high levels of perseverance at the conclusion of the academic year.

## Daring

Finally, in chapter 7 we noted that Pacific Rim high school students demonstrated significantly higher levels of daring over the course of the school year than their peers at Boston Prep. The final fitted model for students' $T_2$ daring scores is presented in table A.6.

After controlling for students' initial daring scores, we found that being a student at Pacific Rim is a significant and positive predictor of stu-

TABLE A.5    Effects of attending Roxbury Prep upon the perseverance of its middle school students

Final fitted model for the effects of attending Roxbury Prep upon the perseverance of participating middle school students, controlling for select background characteristics of the cohort in which students are grouped for ethics/advisory/character education class ($n$ sections = 31, $n$ students = 541).

| Fixed effect | Coefficient | Se | T-ratio | p-value |
|---|---|---|---|---|
| Intercept | .61 | .30 | 2.01 | .04 |
| **School level** | | | | |
| Roxbury Prep | .13 | .06 | 2.13 | .03 |
| **Individual level** | | | | |
| $T_1$ perseverance | .59 | .03 | 16.96 | .0001 |
| Grade point average | .01 | .003 | 2.79 | .005 |
| Total demerits | −.001 | .0001 | −5.41 | .0001 |
| Random effect | Variance component | Se | Z | p-value |
| Random effect of student ($r_{ij}$) | .38 | .02 | 15.60 | .0001 |
| Random effect of cohort ($u_{0j}$) | .005 | .011 | .45 | .32 |

*Note:* −2LL = 920.5

dents' end-of-year daring. Additionally, students' grade point average and feelings of (school) community connectedness were found to be significant and positive predictors of their $T_2$ daring scores. In other words, being a high school student at the Pacific Rim, earning a high grade point average, and feeling highly connected to one's school community were all associated with high levels of daring at the conclusion of the academic year.

## LOOKING AHEAD

The call for more longitudinal research is a familiar refrain in educational arenas, but the need for such research is particularly vital in the fields of character development and character education. As noted in chapter 3, Aristotle observed in *Nicomachean Ethics* that the purpose of studying ethics is not "as it is in other inquiries, the attainment of theoretical knowledge: we are not conducting this inquiry in order to know what virtue is, but in order to become good, else there is no advantage to studying it."[4] One could make a similar point about all three types of character development

TABLE A.6    Effects of attending Pacific Rim upon the daring of its high school students

Final fitted model for the effects of attending Pacific Rim upon the daring of participating high school students, controlling for select background characteristics of the cohort in which Boston Prep and Pacific Rim student are grouped for ethics class/advisory (*n* sections = 22, *n* students = 279).

| Fixed effect | Coefficient | Se | T-ratio | p-value |
|---|---|---|---|---|
| Intercept | .14 | .38 | .37 | .72 |
| School level | | | | |
| Pacific Rim | .17 | .08 | 2.13 | .03 |
| Individual level | | | | |
| $T_1$ daring | .53 | .05 | 10.99 | .0001 |
| Grade point average | .008 | .004 | 1.96 | .05 |
| Community connectedness | .28 | .05 | 5.84 | .0001 |

| Random effect | Variance component | Se | Z | p-value |
|---|---|---|---|---|
| Random effect of student ($r_{ij}$) | .31 | .03 | 9.77 | .0001 |
| Random effect of cohort ($u_{0j}$) | .002 | .009 | .18 | .43 |

*Note:* –2LL = 351.6

presented in *Character Compass.* There is great value in assessing the impact that Boston Prep, Roxbury Prep, and Pacific Rim are having upon their students' character development in the present, but equally important is the question of whether these effects will persist going forward. Will Roxbury Prep students possess the self-discipline necessary to succeed in college when they are expected to complete their school work with far greater independence than is expected of them now? Will Pacific Rim students go on to become active and engaged citizens in the communities in which they settle after graduating from high school? Will Boston Prep students approach their professional endeavors with a deep commitment to acting with integrity? Several Boston Prep high school students noted that they find it easier to act in virtuous ways inside the school walls than out in the "real world." Thus, the relationship between the schools' character education efforts and students' longer-term outcomes remains an important and, as yet, unanswered question.

# Notes

## Foreword

1. David Halberstam, *The Best and the Brightest* (New York: Random House, 1972).

## Introduction

1. B. Edward McClellan, *Moral Education in America: Schools and the Shaping of Character from Colonial Times to the Present* (New York: Teachers College Press, 1999).
2. Lawrence Kohlberg, "A Just Community Approach to Moral Education in Theory and Practice," in *Moral Education: Theory and Practice*, eds. Marvin W. Berkowitz and Fritz Oser (Hillsdale, NJ: Erlbaum, 1984), 27–82; William J. Bennett, *The Book of Virtues* (New York: Simon & Schuster, 1996).
3. Colette T. Dollarhide and Matthew E. Lemberger, "'No Child Left Behind': Implications for School Counselors," *Professional School Counseling* 9, no. 4 (2006): 295–304; Deborah Meier et al. *Many Children Left Behind* (Boston: Beacon Press, 2004).
4. Paul Tough, "What if the Secret to Success Is Failure?" *New York Times Magazine*, September 14, 2011, http://www.nytimes.com/2011/09/18/magazine/what-if-the-secret-to-success-is-failure.html?pagewanted=all.
5. Jonah Lehrer, "Don't: The Secret of Self-Control," *New Yorker*, May 18, 2009, http://www.newyorker.com/reporting/2009/05/18/090518fa_fact_lehrer; Tough, "Secret to Success."
6. Thomas Lickona and Matthew Davidson, *Smart & Good High Schools* (Washington, DC: Character Education Partnership, 2005).
7. Tough, "Secret to Success," 7.
8. Angela L. Duckworth and Martin E. P. Seligman, "Self-Discipline Outdoes IQ in Predicting Academic Performance of Adolescents," *Psychological Science* 16, no. 12 (2005): 939–944; Angela L. Duckworth and Martin E. P. Seligman, "Self-Discipline Gives Girls the Edge: Gender in Self-Discipline, Grades, and Achievement Test Scores," *Journal of Educational Psychology* 98, no. 1 (2006): 198–208.
9. Angela L. Duckworth et al., "Grit: Perseverance and Passion for Long-Term Goals," *Journal of Personality and Social Psychology* 92, no. 6 (2007): 1087–1101.
10. K. Anders Ericsson, Ralf Th. Krampe, and Clemens Tesch-Römer, "The Role of Deliberate Practice in the Acquisition of Expert Performance," *Psychological Review*

100, no. 3 (1993): 363–406; Michael J. A. Howe, *Genius Explained* (Cambridge: Cambridge University Press, 2001); Lewis Madison Terman and Melita H. Oden, *The Gifted Child Grows Up: Twenty-five Years' Follow-up of a Superior Group* (Palo Alto, CA: Stanford University Press, 1947); Ellen Winner, *Gifted Children: Myths and Realities* (New York: Basic Books, 1997); Warren W. Willingham, *Success in College: The Role of Personal Qualities and Academic Ability* (New York: College Entrance Examination Board, 1985).

11. Anna M. Phillips, "New York City Charter School Finds That a Grade of 'C' Means Closing," *New York Times*, January 12, 2012, http://www.nytimes.com/2012/01/12/education/new-york-city-plans-to-close-a-charter-school-for-mediocrity.html.

12. Joshua D. Angrist et al., *Student Achievement in Massachusetts' Charter Schools* (Cambridge, MA: Harvard University Center for Education Policy Research, 2011).

13. United States Department of Agriculture, "Income Eligibility Guidelines," http://www.fns.usda.gov/cnd/governance/notices/iegs/iegs.htm.

14. S. Paul Reville, "High Standards + High Stakes = Success in Massachusetts," *Phi Delta Kappan* 85 (April 2004): 591–597.

15. *Boston Globe*, "2011 MCAS Results," http://www.boston.com/news/special/education/mcas/scores11/index.htm.

16. *CNN/Money Magazine*, "Best Places to Live," http://money.cnn.com/magazines/moneymag/bplive/2010/top25s/financial/.

17. *Boston Globe*, "Highest, lowest median incomes in Mass.," http://www.boston.com/business/gallery/medianincomesinmass.

18. New Leaders for New Schools, "The EPIC Incentive Awards Program," http://http://www.newleaders.org/what-we-do/epic; Katherine K. Merseth et al., *Inside Urban Charter Schools* (Cambridge, MA: Harvard Education Press, 2009).

19. A more thorough description of this study's research methods is presented in the appendix.

## Chapter 1

1. Boston Preparatory Charter Public School, "School Overview," http://www.bostonprep.org/school-overview.shtml.

2. Roxbury Preparatory Charter School. "Roxbury Prep" http://roxburyprep.uncommonschools.org/.

3. Roxbury Preparatory Charter School, "Roxbury Prep Student and Family Handbook," http://roxburyprep.uncommonschools.org/sites/default/files/pdf/student_and_family_handbook.11-12.rpc_.pdf.

4. Academy of the Pacific Rim Charter Public School, "Character Education," http://pacrim.org/apps/pages/index.jsp?uREC_ID=88708&type=d.

5. Marvin W. Berkowitz and Mary Anne Hoppe, "Character Education and Gifted Children," *High Ability Studies*, 20, no. 2 (2009): 131; Bryan W. Sokol, Stuart I. Hammond, and Marvin W. Berkowitz, "The Developmental Contours of Charac-

ter," in *International Research Handbook on Values Education and Student Wellbeing*, eds. Terence Lovat et al. (Berlin: Springer, 2010), 579.

6. Merle J. Schwartz, *Effective Character Education: A Guidebook for Future Educators* (Boston: McGraw-Hill, 2008).

7. B. Edward McClellan, *Moral Education in America: Schools and the Shaping of Character Since Colonial Times* (New York: Teachers College Press, 1999).

8. Due to the inherent difficulty of masking their identities, all Boston Prep, Roxbury Prep, and Pacific Rim administrators are referred to by name if they participated in qualitative interviews for this research study and agreed to be identified. All other teachers, students, and parents are referred to by pseudonyms.

9. Marvin W. Berkowitz, "Moral and Character Education," in *APA Educational Psychology Handbook, Volume 2: Individual Differences and Cultural and Contextual Factors*, eds. Karen R. Harris et al. (Washington, DC: American Psychological Association, 2011): 3.

10. Merle J. Schwartz, *Effective Character Education*.

11. Lawrence Kohlberg, *The Psychology of Moral Development: The Nature and Validity of Moral Stages* (San Francisco: Harper & Row, 1984); Kevin Ryan and Karen E. Bohlin, *Building Character in Schools* (San Francisco: Jossey-Bass, 1999); Howard Gardner, *Frames of Mind: The Theory of Multiple Intelligences* (Philadelphia: Basic Books, 1983); Robert L. Selman et al., "A naturalistic study of children's social understanding," *Developmental Psychology* 19 (1983): 82–102.

12. Stephen J. Thoma, James R. Rest, and Mark L. Davison, "Describing and testing a moderator of the moral judgment and action relationship," *Journal of Personality and Social Psychology* 61, no. 4 (1991): 659–669.

13. William Bennett, *The Book of Virtues* (New York: Simon & Schuster, 1983); Ryan and Bohlin, *Building Character*.

14. Ryan and Bohlin, *Building Character*, 46.

15. Gardner, *Frames of Mind*; Selman, "Naturalistic study."

16. Selman, "Naturalistic study."

17. Martin L. Hoffman, *Empathy and Moral Development: Implications for Caring and Justice* (New York: Cambridge University Press, 2000); Samuel P. Oliner and Pearl M. Oliner, *The Altruistic Personality: Rescuers of Jews in Nazi Europe* (New York: Free Press); Nel Noddings, "Conversation as Moral Education," *Journal of Moral Education* 23, no. 2 (1994).

18. Nancy Eisenberg and Paul A. Miller, "The Relation of Empathy to Prosocial and Related Behaviors," *Psychological Bulletin* 101, no. 1 (1987): 91–119; Hoffman, *Empathy*.

19. Oliner and Oliner, *Altruistic Personality*, 3.

20. Ibid., 168.

21. Nel Noddings, *Educating Moral People: A Caring Alternative to Moral Education* (New York: Teachers College Press, 2002), 20.

22. Virginia A. Hodgkinson et al., *Giving and Volunteering in the United States, Volume 2: Trends in Giving and Volunteering by Type of Charity* (Washington, DC: Independent Sector, 1995).

23. Sheldon Berman, *Children's Social Consciousness and the Development of Social Responsibility* (Albany, NY: State University of New York Press, 1997); Helen Haste, "Moral creativity and education for citizenship," *Creativity Research Journal* 6, no. 1–2 (1993): 153–164; Mimi Michaelson, "A model of extraordinary social engagement or 'moral giftedness,'" in *New Directions for Child and Adolescent Development* 2001, no. 93, eds. Mimi Michaelson and Jeanne Nakamura (Marblehead, MA: John Wiley & Sons, 2001): 19–32.

24. Angela L. Duckworth and Martin E. P. Seligman, "Self-Discipline Outdoes IQ in Predicting Academic Performance of Adolescents," *Psychological Science* 16, no. 12 (2005): 939–944; Angela L. Duckworth and Martin E. P. Seligman, "Self-Discipline Gives Girls the Edge: Gender in Self-Discipline, Grades, and Achievement Test Scores," *Journal of Educational Psychology* 98, no. 1 (2006): 198–208; Benjamin S. Bloom, ed., *Developing Talent in Young People* (New York: Ballantine Books, 1985); K. Anders Ericsson, Ralf Th. Krampe, and Clemens Tesch-Römer, "The Role of Deliberate Practice in the Acquisition of Expert Performance," *Psychological Review* 100, no. 3 (1993): 363–406; Herbert A. Simon and William G. Chase, "Skill in chess," *American Scientist* 61, issue 4 (1973): 394–403.

25. Raymond N. Wolfe and Scott D. Johnson, "Personality as a Predictor of College Performance," *Educational and Psychological Measurement* 55 (1995): 177–185; Warren W. Willingham, *Success in College: The Role of Personal Qualities and Academic Ability* (New York: College Entrance Examination Board, 1985).

26. Berkowitz, "Moral and Character Education."

27. Thomas Lickona and Matthew Davidson, *Smart & Good High Schools* (Washington, DC: Character Education Partnership, 2005).

28. David Light Shields, "Character as the Aim of Education," *Phi Delta Kappan* 92, no. 8 (2011): 48–53.

29. Lickona and Davidson, *Smart & Good High Schools*, 18.

30. Sokol, Hammond, and Berkowitz, "Developmental Contours," 108.

31. Lickona and Davidson, *Smart & Good High Schools*, 18.

32. Marvin W. Berkowitz and William Puka, "Dissent and character education," in *Reclaiming Dissent*, ed. Mordechai Gordon (Amsterdam: Sense Publishers, 2009), 108.

33. Bruce O. Boston, *Restoring the Balance Between Academics and Civic Engagement in Public Schools*, eds. Sarah S. Pearson and Samuel Halperin (Washington, DC: American Youth Policy Forum, 2005), 7.

34. Shields, "Character"; Judith Torney-Purta and Susan Vermeer Lopez, *Developing Citizenship Competencies from Kindergarten through Grade 12: A Background Paper for Policymakers and Educators* (Denver: Education Commission of the States and National Center for Learning and Citizenship, 2006).

35. McClellan, *Moral Education.*

36. Lickona and Davidson, *Smart & Good High Schools*, 22.

37. Shields, "Character," 52.

38. Larry P. Nucci, *Education in the Moral Domain* (Cambridge: Cambridge University Press, 2001), 128.

39. Berkowitz, "Moral and Character Education"; Sokol, Hammond, and Berkowitz, "Developmental Contours."

40. Lickona and Davidson, *Smart & Good High Schools*, xxi.

41. Ibid.

## Chapter 2

1. Jason M. Stephens, Michael F. Young, and Thomas Calabrese, "Does Moral Judgment Go Offline When Students Are Online? A Comparative Analysis of Undergraduates' Beliefs and Behaviors Related to Conventional and Digital Cheating," *Ethics & Behavior* 17, no. 3 (2007): 233–254.

2. A principal components analysis revealed that a single construct was being measured by this scale, accounting for 56 percent of the variance (eigenvalue = 2.83) and showing good internal consistency reliability (Cronbach's $\alpha$ = .80).

3. A more detailed description of the data analytic strategy and research methods is offered in the appendix.

4. The estimates and statistics for the final fitted model of students' post-intervention integrity scores are offered in the appendix.

5. Cohen's $d$ = .20.

6. Allen Ruby and Emily Doolittle, *Efficacy of Schoolwide Programs to Promote Social and Character Development and Reduce Problem Behavior in Elementary School Children* (Washington, DC: National Center for Education Research, Institute of Education Sciences, U.S. Department of Education, 2010).

7. Thomas Lickona and Matthew Davidson, *Smart & Good High Schools* (Washington, DC: Character Education Partnership, 2005).

8. Paul Tough, "What if the Secret to Success Is Failure?" *New York Times Magazine,* September 14, 2011, http://www.nytimes.com/2011/09/18/magazine/what-if-the-secret-to-success-is-failure.html?pagewanted=all.

9. Abby Goodnough, "The Examined Life, Age 8," *New York Times,* April 16, 2010, http://www.nytimes.com/2010/04/18/education/edlife/18philosophy-t.html?pagewanted=all.

10. Matthew Lipman, "The Cultivation of Reasoning Through Philosophy," *Educational Leadership* 42, no. 1 (1984): 51–56; Matthew Lipman, *Philosophy Goes to School* (Philadelphia: Temple University Press, 1988).

11. Gareth B. Matthews, *Philosophy & the Young Child* (Cambridge, MA: Harvard University Press, 1980); Gareth B. Matthews, *The Philosophy of Childhood* (Cambridge, MA: Harvard University Press, 1994).

12. Bärbel Inhelder and Jean Piaget, *The Growth of Logical Thinking from Childhood to Adolescence* (New York: Basic Books, 1958).

13. Sharon Daloz Parks, *Big Questions, Worthy Dreams: Mentoring Young Adults in their Search for Meaning, Purpose, and Faith* (San Francisco: Jossey-Bass, 2000), 40.

14. Lev Vygotsky, *Thought and Language* (Cambridge, MA: MIT Press, 1962).

15. Ibid.

16. Robert Kegan and Lisa Laskow Lahey, *How the Way We Talk Can Change the Way We Work* (San Francisco: Jossey-Bass, 2001).

17. Emily Bazelon, "Bullies Beware: Massachusetts just passed the country's best anti-bullying law," *Slate*, April 30, 2010, http://www.slate.com/articles/life/bulle/2010/04/bullies_beware.html.

18. danah boyd, "Identity Production in a Networked Culture: Why Youth Heart MySpace" (paper presented at the annual meeting of the American Association for the Advancement of Science, St. Louis, Missouri, February 16–19, 2006); Susannah R. Stern, "Expressions of Identity Online: Prominent Features and Gender Differences in Adolescents' World Wide Web Home Pages," *Journal of Broadcasting and Electronic Media* 48, no. 2 (2004).

19. Katie Davis, "Coming of Age Online: The Developmental Underpinnings of Girls' Blogs," *Journal of Adolescent Research* 25, no. 1 (2010): 145–171; David Huffaker, "Teen Blogs Exposed: The Private Lives of Teens Made Public" (paper presented at the American Association for the Advancement of Science, St. Louis, Missouri, February 16–19, 2006); Lois Ann Scheidt, "Adolescent Diary Weblogs and the Unseen Audience," in *Digital Generations: Children, Young People, and New Media*, eds. David Buckingham and Rebekah Willett (Mahwah, NJ: Lawrence Erlbaum, 2006), 193–210.

20. Davis, "Coming of Age," 146.

21. Erik H. Erikson, *Identity: Youth and Crisis* (New York: W. W. Norton & Company, 1968).

## Chapter 3

1. Aristotle, *The Nicomachean Ethics*, trans. David Ross, eds. J. L. Ackrill and J. O. Urmson (Oxford: Oxford University Press, 1998).

2. Mark H. Davis, "Empathic Concern and the Muscular Dystrophy Telethon: Empathy as a Multidimensional Construct," *Personality and Social Psychology Bulletin* 9, no. 2 (1983): 223–229.

3. Gerald R. Adams, "Social Competence During Adolescence: Social Sensitivity, Locus of Control, Empathy, and Peer Popularity," *Journal of Youth and Adolescence* 12, no. 3 (1983): 203–211; Kimberly A. Schonert-Reichl, "Empathy and Social Relationships in Adolescents with Behavioral Disorders," *Behavioral Disorders* 18, no. 3 (1993): 189–204.

4. Gianluca Gini et al., "Does Empathy Predict Adolescents' Bullying and Defending Behavior?" *Aggressive Behavior* 33, no. 5 (2007): 467–476; Jane L. Ireland, "Provictim attitudes and empathy in relation to bullying behaviour among prisoners," *Legal and Criminological Psychology* 4, no. 1 (2007): 51–66; Darrick Joliffe and David

P. Farrington, "Examining the Relationship Between Low Empathy and Bullying," *Aggressive Behavior* 32, no. 6 (2006): 540–550.

5. Lynnette Unger and Lakshmi Thumuluri, "Trait Empathy and Continuous Helping: The Case of Voluntarism," *Journal of Social Behavior and Personality* 12, no. 3 (1997): 785–800; Patricia A. Oswald, "Does the Interpersonal Reactivity Index Perspective-Taking Scale Predict Who Will Volunteer Time to Counsel Adults Entering College?" *Perceptual and Motor Skills* 97 (2003): 1184–1186; Hannah Paterson, Renate Reniers, and Birgit Vollm, "Personality Types and Mental Health Experiences of Those Who Volunteer for Help Lines," *British Journal of Guidance & Counselling* 37, no. 4 (2009): 459–471; Mark Wilhelm and René Bekkers, "Helping Behavior, Dispositional Empathic Concern, and the Principle of Care," *Social Psychology Quarterly* 73 (2010): 11–32.

6. Helene Borke, "Interpersonal Perception of Young Children: Egocentrism or Empathy?" *Developmental Psychology* 5, no. 2 (1971): 263–269; Francine Deutsch and Ronald A. Madle, "Empathy: Historic and Current Conceptualizations, Measurement, and a Cognitive Theoretical Perspective," *Human Development* 18 (1975): 267–287; C. Daniel Batson, "Prosocial Motivation: Is It Ever Truly Altruistic?" *Advances in Experimental Social Psychology,* 20 (1987): 65–122; Paul A. Miller and Nancy Eisenberg, "The Relation of Empathy to Aggressive and Externalizing/Antisocial Behavior," *Psychological Bulletin* 103, no. 3 (1988): 324–344.

7. Nancy Eisenberg, "Prosocial Development in Early and Mid Adolescence," in *From Childhood to Adolescence, A Transitional Period?*, eds. Raymond Montemayor, Gerald R. Adams, and Thomas P. Gullotta (Thousand Oaks, CA: Sage Publications, 1990), 240–268.

8. Jason J. Barr and Ann Higgins-D'Alessandro, "Adolescent Empathy and Prosocial Behavior in the Multidimensional Context of School Culture," *Journal of Genetic Psychology* 168, no. 3 (2007): 231–250.

9. Jeanne Funk et al., "The development of the Children's Empathic Attitudes Questionnaire using classical and Rasch analyses," *Journal of Applied Developmental Psychology* 29, no. 3 (2008): 187–196.

10. A principal components analysis indicated that a single construct was being measured by this scale, accounting for 43 percent of the variance (eigenvalue = 2.60) and showing acceptable internal consistency reliability (Cronbach's $\alpha$ = .73).

11. The estimates and statistics for the final fitted model of students' post-intervention empathy scores are offered in the appendix.

12. Cohen's $d$ = .27.

13. Bärbel Inhelder and Jean Piaget, *The Growth of Logical Thinking from Childhood to Adolescence* (New York: Basic Books, 1958).

14. Ibid.

15. James Bentley, *Martin Niemoller: 1892–1984* (New York: Free Press, 1984).

16. John McCain, *Character Is Destiny* (New York: Random House, 2005).

17. Sampson Davis, George Jenkins, and Rameck Hunt, *The Pact: Three Young Men Make a Promise and Fulfill a Dream* (New York: Riverhead Trade, 2003).

18. Jacqueline Mroz, "Sharing Their Stories," *New York Times,* October 17, 2008, http://www.nytimes.com/2008/10/19/nyregion/new-jersey/19docsnj.html?pagewanted=all.

19. Deanna Palmeri Sams and Stephen D. Truscott, "Empathy, Exposure to Community Violence, and Use of Violence Among Urban, At-Risk Adolescents," *Child & Youth Care Forum* 33, no. 1 (2004): 33–50; Klaus Schreiber, "The Adolescent Crack Dealer: A Failure in the Development of Empathy," *Journal of the American Academy of Psychoanalysis* 20, no. 2 (1992): 214–249.

20. Steven L. Berman et al., "The Impact of Exposure to Crime and Violence on Urban Youth," *American Journal of Orthopsychiatry* 66, no. 3 (1996): 329–336; Karyn Horowitz, Stevan Weine, and James Jekel, "PTSD Symptoms in Urban Adolescent Girls: Compounded Community Trauma," *Journal of the American Academy of Child & Adolescent Psychiatry* 34, no. 10 (1995): 1353–1361.

21. Michael J. Nakkula and Eric Toshalis, *Understanding Youth: Adolescent Development for Educators* (Cambridge, MA: Harvard Education Press, 2006), 90.

22. Erik H. Erikson, *Identity: Youth and Crisis* (New York: W. W. Norton & Company, 1968).

23. Ibid.

24. Erik H. Erikson, *The Challenge of Youth* (New York: Doubleday, 1965), 24.

25. Epictetus, *Discourses and Selected Writings*, trans. Robert Dobbin (New York: Penguin Classics, 2008).

26. Sharon Daloz Parks, *Big Questions, Worthy Dreams: Mentoring Young Adults in their Search for Meaning, Purpose, and Faith* (San Francisco: Jossey-Bass, 2000).

27. Nakkula and Toshalis, *Understanding Youth*, 48.

28. Eisenberg, "Prosocial Development."

29. Nakkula and Toshalis, *Understanding Youth*, 48.

30. Robert L. Selman, *The Growth of Interpersonal Understanding: Developmental and Clinical Analyses* (New York, Academic Press, 1980).

31. Erikson, *Identity*; Parks, *Big Questions*.

32. Samuel Casey Carter, *"No Excuses: Lessons from 21 High-Performing, High-Poverty Schools* (Washington, DC: Heritage Foundation, 2000); Joshua D. Angrist et al., "Who Benefits from KIPP?" *NBER Working Paper No. 15740* (Cambridge, MA: National Bureau of Economic Research, 2010).

33. Erikson, *Identity*; Nakkula and Toshalis, *Understanding Youth*.

34. Nakkula and Toshalis, *Understanding Youth*, 3.

35. Ibid., 24.

36. Aristotle, *The Nicomachean Ethics*, 30.

## Chapter 4

1. Nansook Park and Christopher Peterson, "Moral Competence and Character Strengths among Adolescents: The Development and Validation of the Values in

Action Inventory of Strengths for Youth," *Journal of Adolescence* 29, no. 6 (2006): 891–909.

2. A principal components analysis indicated that a single construct was being measured by this scale, accounting for 57 percent of the variance (eigenvalue = 2.29) and showing acceptable internal consistency reliability (Cronbach's α = .77).

3. The estimates and statistics for the final fitted model of students' post-intervention perseverance scores are offered in the appendix.

4. Cohen's *d* = .16.

5. Thomas Lickona and Matthew Davidson, *Smart & Good High Schools* (Washington, DC: Character Education Partnership, 2005), 18.

6. Samuel Casey Carter, *On Purpose: How Great School Cultures Form Strong Character* (Thousand Oaks, CA: Corwin Press, 2010), 16.

7. Lickona and Davidson, *Smart & Good High Schools*, 114.

8. Carol S. Dweck, *Mindset: The New Psychology of Success* (New York: Random House, 2006).

9. Carol S. Dweck, *Self-Theories: Their Role in Motivation, Personality, and Development* (London: Psychology Press, 2000).

10. Carter, *On Purpose*, 15–16.

11. Lewis Madison Terman and Melita H. Oden, *The Gifted Child Grows Up: Twenty-five Years' Follow-up of a Superior Group* (Palo Alto, CA: Stanford University Press, 1947); Ellen Winner, *Gifted Children: Myths and Realities* (New York: Basic Books, 1997).

12. Benjamin S. Bloom, ed., *Developing Talent in Young People* (New York: Ballantine Books, 1985), 544; Michael J. A. Howe, *Genius Explained* (Cambridge: Cambridge University Press, 1999), 15.

13. Angela L. Duckworth and Martin E. P. Seligman, "Self-Discipline Outdoes IQ in Predicting Academic Performance of Adolescents," *Psychological Science* 16, no. 12 (2005): 939–944; Angela L. Duckworth and Martin E. P. Seligman, "Self-Discipline Gives Girls the Edge: Gender in Self-Discipline, Grades, and Achievement Test Scores," *Journal of Educational Psychology* 98, no. 1 (2006): 198–208.

14. Duckworth and Seligman, "Self-Discipline Outdoes IQ," 944.

15. Peter Unger, *Living High & Letting Die* (Oxford: Oxford University Press, 1996).

16. Joshua Greene, "From neural 'is' to moral 'ought': what are the moral implications of neuroscientific moral psychology?" *Nature Review Neuroscience* 4 (2003): 847–850.

17. Lickona and Davidson, *Smart & Good High Schools*, 22.

18. Lickona and Davidson, *Smart & Good High Schools*.

## Chapter 5

1. Rachel A. Poliner and Carol Miller Lieber, *The Advisory Guide: Designing and Implementing Effective Advisory Programs in Secondary Schools* (Cambridge, MA: Educators for Social Responsibility, 2004).

2. Paul S. George and William M. Alexander, *The Exemplary Middle School* (Fort Worth, TX: Harcourt Brace, 1993); Anthony W. Jackson and Gayle A. Davis,

*Turning Points 2000: Educating Adolescents in the 21st Century* (New York: Teachers College Press, 2000).

3. Suzanne Ziegler and Linda Mulhall, "Establishing and Evaluating a Successful Advisory Program in a Middle School," *Middle School Journal* 25, no. 4 (1994): 42–46; Linda R. Ayres, "Middle School Advisory Programs: Findings from the Field," *Middle School Journal* 25, no. 3 (1994): 8–14; Samuel Totten and William Nielsen, "Middle level students' perceptions of their advisor/advisee program: A preliminary study," *Current Issues in Middle Level Education* 3, no. 2 (1994): 9–33.

4. John P. Galassi, Suzanne A. Gulledge, and Nancy D. Cox, "Middle School Advisories: Retrospect and Prospect," *Review of Educational Research* 67, no. 3 (1997): 301–338.

5. Barack Obama, "Remarks by the President at Kalamazoo Central High School Commencement," Western Michigan University Arena, June 7, 2010, transcript, http://www.whitehouse.gov/the-press-office/remarks-president-kalamazoo-central-high-school-commencement.

6. Carol S. Dweck, *Mindset: The New Psychology of Success* (New York: Random House, 2006).

7. Annette Lareau, *Unequal Childhoods: Class, Race, and Family Life* (Berkeley: University of California Press, 2003).

8. Erik H. Erikson, *The Challenge of Youth* (New York: Doubleday, 1965); Erik H. Erikson, *Identity: Youth and Crisis* (New York: W. W. Norton, 1968).

9. Katie Davis, "Coming of Age Online: The Developmental Underpinnings of Girls' Blogs," *Journal of Adolescent Research* 25, no. 1 (2010): 146.

10. Thomas Lickona and Matthew Davidson, *Smart & Good High Schools* (Washington, DC: Character Education Partnership, 2005), 29.

11. Francis Galton, *Hereditary Genius* (London: Macmillan and Company, 1869).

12. K. Anders Ericsson, Ralf Th. Krampe, and Clemens Tesch-Römer, "The Role of Deliberate Practice in the Acquisition of Expert Performance," *Psychological Review* 100, no. 3 (1993): 363–406; K. Anders Ericsson and A. C. Lehmann, "Expert and Exceptional Performance: Evidence of Maximal Adaptation to Task Constraints," *Annual Review of Psychology* 47 (1996): 273–305.

13. William G. Chase and Herbert A. Simon, "Perception in Chess," *Cognitive Psychology* 4, no. 1 (1973): 55–81; K. Anders Ericsson, "The Influence of Experience and Deliberate Practice on the Development of Superior Expert Performance," in *Cambridge Handbook of Expertise and Expert Performance*, eds. K. Anders Ericsson et al. (New York: Cambridge University Press, 2006): 683–704.

14. Peter Demerath, *Producing Success: The Culture of Personal Achievement in an American High School* (Chicago: University of Chicago Press, 2009); Denise Clark Pope, *Doing School: How We Are Creating a Generation of Stressed-Out, Materialistic, and Miseducated Students* (New Haven, CT: Yale University Press, 2001).

15. Lickona and Davidson, *Smart & Good High Schools*.

16. Michael Fullan, *The New Meaning of Educational Change* (New York: Teachers College Press, 2001), 197.

17. Lickona and Davidson, *Smart & Good High Schools*, 53.

18. Michael J. Karcher et al., "Mentoring Programs: A Framework to Inform Program Development, Research, and Evaluation," *Journal of Community Psychology* 34, no. 6 (2006): 709–725.

19. Michael J. Karcher, "Cross-Age Peer Mentoring," *Mentor* 7 (2007): 3–23.

20. Judith Rich Harris, *The Nurture Assumption* (New York: Free Press, 1998); Michael J. Karcher, Michael J. Nakkula, and John Harris, "Developmental Mentoring Match Characteristics: Correspondence between Mentors' and Mentees' Assessments of Relationship Quality," *Journal of Primary Prevention* 26, no. 2 (2005): 93–110; Thomas A. Kindermann, "Natural Peer Groups as Contexts for Individual Development: The Case of Children's Motivation in School," *Developmental Psychology* 29, no. 6 (1993): 970–977.

21. Patrick Akos, "Mentoring in the Middle: The Effectiveness of a School-Based Peer Mentoring Program" (PhD diss., University of Virginia, 2000); Michael J. Karcher, "Cross-Age Peer Mentoring," in *Handbook of Youth Mentoring*, eds. David L. Dubois and Michael J. Karcher (Thousand Oaks, CA: Sage Publications, 2005), 206–285; Stacy Shannon Ikard, "Peer Mentoring as a Method to Enhance Moral Reasoning Among High School Adolescents" (PhD diss., University of Alabama, 2001); Keoki Hansen, *BBBS Jack-in-the-Box Partnership Report: Summary Statistics for the Jack-in-the-Box High School Bigs Pilot Program for School Year 2001–2002* (Philadelphia: Big Brothers Big Sisters of America, 2006); Ann Devries Stoltz, "The Relationship Between Peer Mentoring Program Participation and Successful Transition to High School" (PhD diss., University of California, Davis, 2005).

## Chapter 6

1. Beth DeFalco and Samantha Henry, "Mark Zuckerberg Makes Massive Donation to Newark Schools," *Christian Science Monitor*, September 23, 2010, http://www.csmonitor.com/USA/Latest-News-Wires/2010/0923/Mark-Zuckerberg-makes-massive-donation-to-Newark-schools.

2. Literal translations of *kaizen* often focus only on the concept of improvement; however, as explained by Pacific Rim faculty, the term is often utilized in Japan to refer to the commitment to improvement of a business or organization in which every member of the organization is effectively playing his or her part to bring about this improvement.

3. Bruce O. Boston, *Restoring the Balance Between Academics and Civic Engagement in Public Schools*, eds. Sarah S. Pearson and Samuel Halperin (Washington, DC: American Youth Policy Forum, 2005), 7.

4. David Light Shields, "Character as the Aim of Education," *Phi Delta Kappan* 92, no. 8 (2011); Judith Torney-Purta and Susan Vermeer Lopez, *Developing Citizenship*

*Competencies from Kindergarten through Grade 12: A Background Paper for Policy-makers and Educators* (Denver: Education Commission of the States and National Center for Learning and Citizenship, 2006).

5. Bärbel Inhelder and Jean Piaget, *The Growth of Logical Thinking from Childhood to Adolescence* (New York: Basic Books, 1958).

6. Thomas Lickona and Matthew Davidson, *Smart & Good High Schools* (Washington, DC: Character Education Partnership, 2005), 38.

7. Paul Fleischman, *Seedfolks* (New York: Harper Trophy, 2004).

8. Marvin W. Berkowitz, "Moral and Character Education," in *APA Educational Psychology Handbook, Volume 2: Individual Differences and Cultural and Contextual Factors*, eds. Karen R. Harris et al. (Washington, DC: American Psychological Association, 2011).

9. Fifty-four percent of Pacific Rim's student body qualifies for free or reduced-price lunch (a proxy for low socioeconomic status). The school's demographics in terms of race and ethnicity can be found in table 9.1 in the appendix.

10. Larry M. Bartels, *Unequal Democracy: The Political Economy of the Gilded Age* (Princeton, NJ: Princeton University Press and Russell Sage Foundation, 2008).

11. Cathy J. Cohen, *Democracy Remixed: Black Youth and the Future of American Politics* (Oxford: Oxford University Press, 2010).

12. William Damon, *The Path to Purpose* (New York: Free Press, 2008).

13. Ibid., xii.

14. Ibid., 7.

15. Erik H. Erikson, *Identity: Youth and Crisis* (New York: W.W. Norton, 1968).

16. Scott Seider, "Literature, Justice, and Resistance: Engaging Adolescents from Privileged Groups in Social Action" (EdD diss., Harvard University, 2008).

17. Susan Orlean, "The Outsiders: Reinventing a Part of Town That People Thought Would Never Change," *New Yorker*, July 26, 2004, http://www.newyorker.com/archive/2004/07/26/040726fa_fact1.

18. Erikson, *Identity*.

19. Cohen, *Democracy Remixed*.

20. Michael P. Krezmien, Peter E. Leone, and Georgianna M. Achilles, "Suspension, Race, and Disability: Analysis of Statewide Practices and Reporting," *Journal of Emotional and Behavioral Disorders* 14, no. 4 (2006): 217–226; Daniel J. Losen, *Discipline Policies, Successful Schools, and Racial Justice* (Denver: National Education Policy Center, 2011); John M. Wallace Jr. et al., "Racial, Ethnic and Gender Differences in School Discipline among U.S. High School Students: 1991–2005," *Negro Educational Review* 59, no. 1–2 (2008): 47–62.

21. Duarte B. Morais and Anthony C. Ogden, "Initial Development and Validation of the Global Citizenship Scale," *Journal of Studies in International Education* 15, no. 5 (2011): 445–466.

22. Howard Gardner, *Five Minds for the Future* (Boston: Harvard Business School Press, 2008), 17.

23. Nancy L. Thomas et al., *Strengthening Civic Learning and Democratic Engagement* (Washington, DC: United States Department of Education, 2010), 14.

24. Defense Language Institute, "General Catalogue," http://www.dliflc.edu/archive/documents/DLIFLCcatalog2006-07.pdf; Sam Dillon, "Foreign Language Fades in Class—Except Chinese," *New York Times,* January 21, 2010, http://www.nytimes.com/2010/01/21/education/21chinese.html.

25. Esther Wojcicki and Michael Levine, "Teaching for a Shared Future: American Educators Need to Think Globally," *Huffington Post,* September 6, 2010, http://www.huffingtonpost.com/esther-wojcicki/teaching-for-a-shared-fut_b_706504.html; Nel Noddings, ed., *Educating Citizens for Global Awareness* (New York: Teachers College Press, 2005).

26. James Banks et al., *Democracy and Diversity: Principles and Concepts for Educating Citizens in a Global Age* (Seattle: Center for Multicultural Education, 2005).

27. Martha C. Nussbaum, *For Love of Country?* ed. Joshua Cohen (Boston: Beacon Press, 2002).

28. Lev Vygotsky, *Thought and Language* (Cambridge, MA: MIT Press, 1962).

## Chapter 7

1. Nansook Park and Christopher Peterson, "Moral Competence and Character Strengths among Adolescents: The Development and Validation of the Values in Action Inventory of Strengths for Youth," *Journal of Adolescence* 29, no. 6 (2006): 891–909.

2. A principal components analysis indicated that a single construct was being measured by this scale, accounting for 64 percent of the variance (eigenvalue = 1.93) and showing acceptable internal consistency reliability (Cronbach's $\alpha$ = .72).

3. The estimates and statistics for the final fitted model of students' post-intervention courage scores are offered in the appendix.

4. Cohen's $d$ = .17.

5. James Youniss, Jeffrey A. McLellan, and Miranda Yates, "What We Know About Engendering Civic Identity," *The American Behavioral Scientist* 40, no. 5 (1997): 620–631; James Youniss and Miranda Yates, *Community Service and Social Responsibility in Youth* (Chicago: University of Chicago Press, 1997).

6. James Youniss and Miranda Yates, *Community Service*, 623.

7. Meira Levinson, *No Citizen Left Behind* (Cambridge, MA: Harvard University Press), 241.

8. Michael J. Nakkula and Eric Toshalis, *Understanding Youth: Adolescent Development for Educators* (Cambridge, MA: Harvard Education Press, 2006), 43, 237.

9. Constance Flanagan, Peter Levine, and Richard Settersten, *Civic Engagement and the Changing Transition to Adulthood* (Medford, MA: The Center for Information & Research on Civic Learning & Engagement, 2009); Joseph Kahne and Ellen Middaugh, *Democracy for Some: The Civic Opportunity Gap in High School* (Medford, MA: The Center for Information & Research on Civic Learning & Engagement, 2008).

10. Thomas Lickona and Matthew Davidson, *Smart & Good High Schools* (Washington, DC: Character Education Partnership, 2005), 44.

11. Marvin W. Berkowitz, "Moral and Character Education," in *APA Educational Psychology Handbook, Volume 2: Individual Differences and Cultural and Contextual Factors*, eds. Karen R. Harris et al. (Washington, DC: American Psychological Association, 2011).

12. Judith Torney-Purta, 2002; Scott Keeter et al., 2002.

13. Judith Torney-Purta, "The School's Role in Developing Civic Engagement: A Study of Adolescents in Twenty-Eight Countries," *Applied Developmental Science* 6, no. 4 (2002): 203.

14. Scott Keeter et al., *The Civic and Political Health of the Nation: A Generational Portrait* (Medford, MA: The Center for Information & Research on Civic Learning & Engagement, 2002).

15. Sidney Verba, Kay Lehman Schlozman, and Henry E. Brady, *Voice and Equality: Civic Voluntarism in American Politics* (Cambridge, MA: Harvard University Press, 1995).

16. Ibid.

17. Ibid., 304.

18. Larry P. Nucci, "Social Cognitive Domain Theory and Moral Education," in *The Handbook of Moral and Character Education*, eds. Larry P. Nucci and Darcia Narvaez (New York: Routledge, 2008), 40.

19. Levinson, *No Citizen Left Behind*, 187.

20. Berkowitz, "Moral and Character Education."

21. Lickona and Davidson, *Smart & Good High Schools*, 45.

22. Fritz K. Oser, Wolfgang Althof, and Ann Higgins-D'Alessandro, "The Just Community approach to moral education: system change or individual change?" *Journal of Moral Education* 37, no. 3 (2008): 395.

23. Jason J. Barr and Ann Higgins-D'Alessandro, "Adolescent Empathy and Prosocial Behavior in the Multidimensional Context of School Culture," *Journal of Genetic Psychology* 168, no. 3 (2007): 231–250; F. Clark Power, Ann Higgins, and Lawrence Kohlberg, "The Habit of the Common Life: Building Character through Democratic Community Schools," in *Moral Development and Character Education: A Dialogue*, ed. Larry P. Nucci (Berkeley, CA: McCutchan, 1989), 125–143.

24. Oser, Althof, and Higgins-D'Alessandro, "The Just Community approach."

25. Erik H. Erikson, *The Challenge of Youth* (New York: Doubleday, 1965); Erik H. Erikson, *Identity: Youth and Crisis* (New York: W. W. Norton, 1968).

26. Levinson, *No Citizen Left Behind*, 185.

27. Lickona and Davidson, *Smart & Good High Schools*, 110.

28. Daniel Hart et al., "High School Community Service as a Predictor of Adult Voting and Volunteering," *American Educational Research Journal* 44, no. 1 (2007): 197–219.

29. Ibid., 214.

30. Academy of the Pacific Rim, "Pacific Rim Enrichment Program (PREP)," http://www.pacrim.org/apps/pages/index.jsp?uREC_ID=121105&type=d.

31. Nakkula and Toshalis, *Understanding Youth*, 240.

32. Erikson, *Identity*.

33. David Leonhardt, "Top Colleges, Largely for the Elite," *New York Times,* May 24, 2011, http://www.nytimes.com/2011/05/25/business/economy/25leonhardt.html?pagewanted=all.

34. Virginia A. Hodgkinson and Murray S. Weitzman, *Giving and Volunteering in the United States* (Washington, DC: Independent Sector, 1987); Scott Seider, Samantha Rabinowicz, and Susan Gillmor, "The Impact of Philosophy and Theology Service-Learning Experiences upon the Public Service Motivation of Participating College Students," *Journal of Higher Education* 82, no. 5 (2011): 597–628; Dwight E. Giles Jr. and Janet Eyler, "The Impact of a College Community Service Laboratory on Students' Personal, Social, and Cognitive Outcomes," *Journal of Adolescence* 17, no. 4 (1994): 327–339; Hart et al., "High School Community Service"; Gregory B. Markus, Jeffrey P. F. Howard, and David C. King, "Integrating Community Service and Classroom Instruction Enhances Learning: Results From an Experiment," *Education Evaluation and Policy Analysis* 15, no. 4 (1993): 410–419; Youniss and Yates, *Community Service*.

35. Verba, Schlozman, and Brady, *Voice and Equality*.

36. Nakkula and Toshalis, *Understanding Youth*, 48.

37. Annette Lareau, *Unequal Childhoods: Class, Race, and Family Life* (Berkeley: University of California Press, 2003).

## Chapter 8

1. Allen Ruby and Emily Doolittle, *Efficacy of Schoolwide Programs to Promote Social and Character Development and Reduce Problem Behavior in Elementary School Children* (Washington, DC: National Center for Education Research, Institute of Education Sciences, U.S. Department of Education, 2010).

2. Institute of Education Sciences, "Social and Character Development Research Program Awards," http://www2.ed.gov/about/offices/list/ies/social.html.

3. Marvin W. Berkowitz and Melinda C. Bier, *What Works in Character Education: A Research-Driven Guide for Educators* (Washington, DC: Character Education Partnership, 2005), 10.

4. K. Anders Ericsson, Ralf th. Krampe, and Clemens Tesch-Röhmer, "The Role of Deliberate Practice in the Acquisition of Expert Performance," *Psychological Review,* 100, no. 3 (1993): 363–406.

5. Howard Gardner, Mihaly Csikszentmihalyi, and William Damon, *Good Work: Where Excellence and Ethics Meet* (New York: Basic Books, 2001); Wendy Fischman et al., *Making Good: How Young People Cope with Moral Dilemmas at Work* (Cambridge, MA: Harvard University Press, 2004).

6. Marvin W. Berkowitz, "Moral and Character Education," in *APA Educational Psychology Handbook, Volume 2: Individual Differences and Cultural and Contextual*

*Factors*, eds. Karen R. Harris et al. (Washington, DC: American Psychological Association, 2011).

7. Angela L. Duckworth and Martin E. P. Seligman, "Self-Discipline Outdoes IQ in Predicting Academic Performance of Adolescents," *Psychological Science* 16, no. 12 (2005): 943.

8. Rafael Heller, "Adolescent Literacy 101: Vocabulary," http://www.adlit.org/adlit_101/improving_literacy_instruction_in_your_school/vocabulary/.

9. Brandi Simonson et al., "Evidence-Based Practices in Classroom Management: Considerations for Research to Practice," *Education and Treatment of Children* 31, no. 3, 2008, 351–380; Robert J. Marzano with Jana S. Marzano and Debra J. Pickering, *Classroom Management That Works* (Alexandria, VA: Association for Supervision & Curriculum Development, 2003).

10. Ron Ritchhart, *Intellectual Character* (San Francisco: Jossey-Bass, 2002), xxii.

11. The fact that curiosity appears on Ritchhart's list of intellectual character strengths as well as KIPP Infinity's list of performance character strengths underscores that these dimensions of character are not entirely distinct from one another.

12. Notes and observations about Fenway High School's mission and curriculum are based on the author's experience working there as a literacy teacher, house coordinator, and principal intern from 2003 to 2007.

13. Lisa Delpit, *Multiplication Is for White People: Raising Expectations for Other People's Children* (New York: Free Press, 2012); Meira Levinson, *No Citizen Left Behind* (Cambridge, MA: Harvard University Press, 2012): 83.

14. Thomas Lickona, Eric Schaps, and Catherine Lewis, *Eleven Principles of Effective Character Education* (Washington, DC: Character Education Partnership), 6.

15. Paul Tough, "What if the Secret to Success Is Failure? *New York Times Magazine*, September 14, 2011, http://www.nytimes.com/2011/09/18/magazine/what-if-the-secret-to-success-is-failure.html?pagewanted=all.

16. Berkowitz, "Moral and Character Education," 252.

17. John P. Galassi, Suzanne A. Gulledge, and Nancy D. Cox, "Middle School Advisories: Retrospect and Prospect," *Review of Educational Research* 67, no. 3 (1997): 317.

18. Richard Weissbourd, *The Parents We Mean to Be* (Boston: Houghton Mifflin, 2010).

19. Emily Bazelon, "Bullies Beware: Massachusetts just passed the country's best anti-bullying law," Slate, April 30, 2010, http://www.slate.com/articles/life/bulle/2010/04/bullies_beware.html.

## Appendix

1. Scott Seider and Jason Taylor, "Broadening College Students' Interest in Philosophical Education through Community Service Learning," *Teaching Philosophy* 34, no. 3 (2011): 197–217; Scott Seider, Samantha Rabinowicz, and Susan Gillmor, "The Impact of Philosophy and Theology Service-Learning Experiences on the Public Service Motivation of Participating College Students," *Journal of Higher Education* 82, no. 5 (2011): 597–628.

2. S. Marc Pancer et al., "Community and political involvement in adolescence: What distinguishes the activists from the uninvolved?" *Journal of Community Psychology* 35, no. 6 (2007): 741–759; Jeanne Funk et al., "The Development of the Children's Empathic Attitudes Questionnaire Using Classical and Rasch Analyses," *Journal of Applied Developmental Psychology* 29, no. 3 (2008): 187–196; Nansook Park and Christopher Peterson, "Moral Competence and Character Strengths among Adolescents: The Development and Validation of the Values in Action Inventory of Strengths for Youth," *Journal of Adolescence* 29, no. 6 (2006): 891–909; Jason M. Stephens, Michael F. Young, and Thomas Calabrese, "Does Moral Judgment Go Offline When Students Are Online? A Comparative Analysis of Undergraduates' Beliefs and Behaviors Related to Conventional and Digital Cheating," *Ethics & Behavior* 17, no. 3 (2007): 233–254; Tonia Bock, "Undergraduate Ethical Development in a University-Required Ethics Course" (paper presented at the meeting of the *Association for Moral Education*, Notre Dame, Indiana, November 15, 2008); Constance Flanagan et al., "School and Community Climates and Civic Commitments: Patterns for Ethnic Minority and Majority Students," *Journal of Educational Psychology* 99, no. 2 (2007): 421–431.

3. Howard S. Becker, "The Epistemology of Qualitative Research," in *Ethnography and Human Development: Context and Meaning in Social Inquiry*, eds. Richard Jesser, Anne Colby, and Richard A. Shweder (Chicago: University of Chicago Press, 1996), 53–71; Barney G. Glaser and Anselm L. Strauss, *The Discovery of Grounded Theory: Strategies for Qualitative Research* (Chicago: Aldine, 1967).

4. Aristotle, *The Nicomachean Ethics*, trans. David Ross, eds. J. L. Ackrill and J. O. Urmson (Oxford: Oxford University Press, 1998), 30.

# Acknowledgments

First and foremost, I am deeply grateful to the students, parents, faculty, and administrators at Boston Prep, Roxbury Prep, and Pacific Rim for inviting me into their respective school communities for the 2010–2011 academic year. Faculty members graciously allowed me to observe classes, advisory lessons, and community meetings. Students at all three schools gave up their lunch periods to participate in interviews, and parents spent valuable evening time speaking to me over the phone about their children's experiences at school. I am indebted to them all.

I am particularly grateful to the heads of school and principals at Boston Prep, Roxbury Prep, and Pacific Rim: Will Austin, Jenne Colasacco Grant, Michaela Crowley, René Dickhaut, Amanda Gardner, Elsie Huang, Scott McCue, Susan Thompson, and Amy Zaffuto. They not only invited me into their schools but also patiently answered my questions and helped me to track down various documents and sources of data. At each of the three schools, a faculty member was gracious enough to serve as the point person for the research study. These faculty members helped me to arrange classroom visits, administer the pre- and post-intervention surveys, and conduct interviews with faculty, students, and parents. In short, the study could not have happened without the tremendous support of Dave Berkley, Sarah Mielbye, and Michelle Stanfield-Adams.

This study could also not have taken place without the generous funding and support of the Spencer Foundation. I am particularly grateful to Lauren Jones Young, Susan Dauber, and Colin Ong-Dean as well as to Michael McPherson, Diana Hess, Maricelle Garcia, and Doris Fischer.

The transformation of this research study into *Character Compass* was aided tremendously by Caroline Chauncey at Harvard Education Press.

She was an enthusiastic supporter of this project from the start and offered a number of invaluable suggestions that have greatly improved the book's overall framing and coherence. I am also grateful for the support of Christopher Leonesio, Laura Madden, Rose Ann Miller, and Sumita Mukherji.

I owe a tremendous debt of gratitude to my doctoral and undergraduate research assistants, Sarah Novick and Jessica Gomez. Sarah began her doctoral work at Boston University just as this project was getting under way and immediate proved herself to be a tremendous young researcher. For the entire academic year, Sarah made weekly visits to Boston Prep to observe the high school ethics classes and to conduct interviews with Boston Prep high school students. As a result, there are significant sections of chapters 2 and 3 that simply could not have been written without Sarah's careful eye and skillful questioning. Sarah also played a crucial role in the development of this study's qualitative codebook and served as one of the coders for all of the qualitative interviews and field notes.

Jessica Gomez came onto the project as a full-time undergraduate research assistant over the summer of 2011. Jessica was responsible for the data entry of almost one thousand student surveys, transcribing nearly fifty qualitative interviews, and then working with Sarah and me to code all of the interviews and field notes. Jessica was responsible for hundreds of hours of crucial but painstaking work, and she approached these responsibilities with a meticulousness for which I will always be grateful. Jessica's work on the project was made possible by a grant from Boston University's Undergraduate Research Opportunities Program (UROP). Working with the tremendous undergraduates sponsored by UROP has been one of the highlights of my time at Boston University, and I am grateful to UROP director Dr. Tom Gilmore.

A number of Boston University undergraduates also contributed hours of data entry and transcription for this project. For this work, I am grateful to Julia Catalini, Leanne Curley, Kimberly McCurnin, Courtney Overgard, Rachel Paul, and Taylor Platt.

My father, Ross Seider, put his deep knowledge of Access and Excel to work on my behalf in order to transform each school's achievement and behavioral data into a coherent and workable form for statistical analyses.

All researchers should be blessed with a family member so dexterous with pivot tables and vlookups! I am equally grateful to my mother, Bonnie Seider, for her support and encouragement throughout the writing process.

The opportunity to carry out this project was possible only because of my tremendous privilege to serve as a member of the faculty of Boston University's School of Education. I am grateful to all of my School of Education colleagues and students for making every workday both meaningful and engaging.

Finally, between this project's start and conclusion, I had the tremendous fortune to marry my wife, Amanda. Life has been so much sweeter since our union, and I also lucked into a first-rate editor. Amanda was the first reader of the completed manuscript, and the book is significantly improved for her feedback and careful eye. Equally important, Amanda works hard every day to help children in Massachusetts receive the education they deserve, and her enduring belief that *Character Compass* can contribute to this work has been invigorating and inspiring.

# About the Author

Scott Seider is an assistant professor of education at Boston University, where his research focuses on the civic and character development of adolescents and emerging adults. He is a former secondary teacher in the Westwood (Massachusetts) and Boston Public Schools. Dr. Seider is the author of *Shelter: Where Harvard Meets the Homeless* (Continuum, 2010), which won the American Educational Research Association's Moral Development and Education Outstanding Book Award, and coeditor of *The Engaged Campus: Certificates, Minors, and Majors as the New Community Engagement* (Palgrave Macmillan, 2012). He also writes the "Civic Engagement on Campus" column for the *Journal of College and Character*.

# Index